D1555433

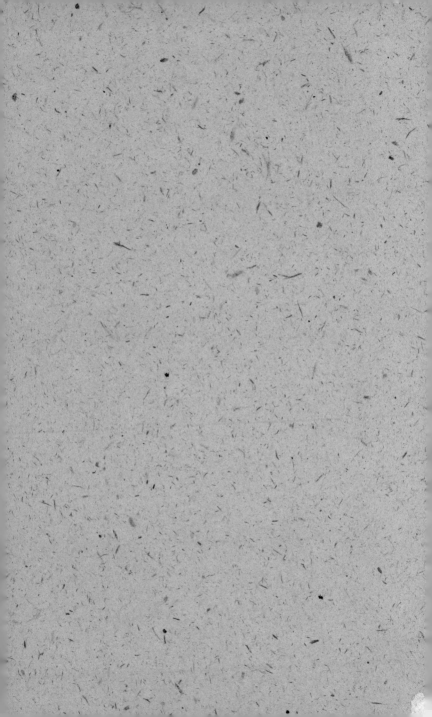

The
Grammatical
Lawyer

American Law Institute American Bar Association Committee on Continuing Professional Education

The Grammatical Lawyer

Morton S. Freeman
of the Philadelphia Bar

AMERICAN LAW INSTITUTE-AMERICAN BAR ASSOCIATION
COMMITTEE ON CONTINUING PROFESSIONAL EDUCATION
4025 CHESTNUT STREET • PHILADELPHIA • PENNSYLVANIA 19104

Library of Congress Catalog Number: 79-50329

Printed in the United States of America

To the women in my life—
  my mother; my wife, Mildred;
    my daughters, Janet and Roberta

Contents

Foreword

"The Grammatical Lawyer" first appeared in the June 1976 issue of ALI-ABA's *The Practical Lawyer*. It was introduced as "a new regular feature that will deal with matters of style, syntax, punctuation, and spelling that should interest attorneys." True to this promise, the inaugural column examined "Convince or Persuade?"; "Watch That"; "Is It Canceled or Cancelled?"; "Twice Possessive"; "Things About Numbers"; and "On Being Honorable."

"The Grammatical Lawyer" was warmly received. Each issue brought letters of commendation from members of the Bar. Its affection for the English language and appreciation of the variations in style that an understanding of word usage will accommodate accounted in part for the acclaim it received from the readers of *The Practical Lawyer*. More important, perhaps, in explaining its instant success was its arrival at a time of dissatisfaction in the profession with the level of competence in the use of the English language. This is not an indictment unique to lawyers. Such uneasiness seems to pervade the nation, if today's insatiable market for publications on English usage and style is an accurate index of the pandemic urge for self-improvement in this area.

It was thus to be expected that "The Grammatical Lawyer," when it came of age, would make its own way in the world. It now goes forth in this volume after a second look by its author. Each of the entries has been reevaluated, revised where indicated, and indexed. In addition, the book contains many articles that have not been previously published.

This is not a book of "legalese" for lawyers only. It is a book about all of the English language and, as such, its appeal and utility should extend well beyond the legal profession.

Morton S. Freeman, a Philadelphia lawyer, is The Grammatical Lawyer. As its author, he gave it flesh and substance, and made it a living presence in the profession. This he could accomplish because he is in fact a grammatical lawyer, once a rarity, but happily not as much today, thanks to him.

PAUL A. WOLKIN
Executive Director,
The American Law Institute-
American Bar Association Committee
on Continuing Professional Education

Preface

This book did not start out to be a book. It began as a series of jottings dealing with questionable and erroneous word usage, faulty punctuation, omitted hyphens, misspellings, misuse of numbers, and kindred matters observed in writings over a period of several years.

These misapplications of style and usage, together with corrected versions and explanatory notes, were incorporated into memorandums to be used by members of the ALI-ABA Office of Publications as guidelines for copy editors. The memorandums, somewhat dressed up, subsequently became articles entitled "The Grammatical Lawyer," a column published in *The Practical Lawyer.* This book contains all the published articles as well as some appearing for the first time.

The primary concern in all the articles was to provide guidance in attaining an acceptable standard of formal English. Formal English, the mode found in scholarly works and expository writings, is the style employed in all ALI-ABA books. It is a more demanding style, and one that is less idiomatic and hence frequently less free-flowing than that found in informal writings, in correspondence, or in newspapers. It is, however, the appropriate style for most law books.

Many of the articles center on word usage, an unstable field because judgments often change as usage once rejected becomes accepted by educated people. No consensus presently exists among English authorities, respected writers, or even dictionaries on many matters concerning either the choice or the arrangement of words.

Frequently, in fact, there is open disagreement. Members of panels on word usage and related matters are sometimes so divided that one might think they all spoke different languages. Certainly everyone will not approve every recommendation made in this book either.

It should be pointed out that since the articles initially had no index, there may be some minor overlapping of content. Also, some articles contain a postscript setting forth additional material related but not integral to the body of the article.

I am grateful to my friends and associates for their encouragement and assistance. I thank Paul A. Wolkin, whose idea it was to publish the memorandums as articles. I thank Meyer Kramer for his thoughtful advice and his incisive criticism of the galleys. I thank Louis Pilla, my mainstay, who not only copyedited the manuscript but made invaluable suggestions all along the way. And to my secretary, W. Harvey Keith, a particularly big thanks for having cheerfully typed what must have seemed to be an endless manuscript.

MORTON S. FREEMAN

How Forcible Are Right Words!

JOB—6:25

CONVINCED BEYOND A DOUBT

Convince and *persuade* have similar connotations—affecting someone's thinking to accomplish a purpose. But because of the peculiarity of idiom, they differ in application.

Consider, first, the verb *convince*. Idiomatically, *convince* may not be followed by an infinitive. It is incorrect to say, for example, "I convinced him *to* plead guilty." The sentence should be reworded to read either "I convinced him *that* he should plead guilty" or "*of* the wisdom of pleading guilty." A *that* or an *of* phrase may follow *convince,* but not an infinitive.

With *persuade,* on the other hand, any one of those three constructions—*that, of,* or *to*—is acceptable. For instance, there is no error in "I persuaded him *to* plead guilty." For whatever reason, *persuade* does not bear the restraint placed on *convince;* a person may freely *persuade someone to* but not *convince someone to.*

Although the meanings of these words are not precisely the same—*convince* means "to satisfy by argument or evidence"; *persuade,* "to influence a person to an action or a belief"—for all practical purposes they may be interchanged if the proper phrasing is kept in mind. In general, there is no real difference between "I convinced him that he should go" and "I persuaded him to go."

When precision in meaning is required, however, it ought to be remembered that *convince* is a static verb and *persuade* an active one. That is, a person who is convinced may not necessarily do anything about it unless he is then persuaded. One might convince a person that it is wise to consult a lawyer, yet be unable to persuade him to call for an appointment.

1

IS NO APOSTROPHE A CATASTROPHE?

The pluralizing of letters, figures, and symbols is a matter on which stylebooks differ. Some recommend the mere addition of an *s:* "The *4*s look like *7*s; the *n*s, like *m*s." Others prefer that an apostrophe precede the *s:* "The *4*'s look like *7*'s; the *n*'s, like *m*'s." These same distinctions apply to dates—the *1970*s or the *1970*'s.

Consistency, a prime element of style, requires that only one mode be used. Since the form *s* and *'s* are equally acceptable, either may be employed; but both should not appear in the same writing.

One detail, on which almost everyone agrees, is that although the letter, figure, or symbol should be italicized (underlined in typescript), the pluralizing *s* should be in regular type (or not underlined): *6*s, *6*'s; *B*s, *B*'s; *&*s, *&*'s.

The most widely followed style for forming the plurals of abbreviations is to add only an *s* to those abbreviations that have no internal periods—YMCAs, OKs, IQs—and to add an apostrophe and an *s* to those with internal periods —Ph.D.'s, J.D.'s.

NONE SHOULD KNOW BETTER

None, since it is a contraction of *no one,* should require a singular verb. Though that is the truth, it is not the whole truth.

By convention, *none* takes either a singular or a plural verb, depending on the thrust of the thought to be conveyed. If individual elements are being emphasized—in which case *none* stands for *not a single one*—certainly

2

a singular verb is needed. For instance, a statement such as "None of them is perfect" indicates that the items were evaluated separately, and "None of these witnesses is the right one" signifies that each witness was regarded individually. But if the elements are more logically considered as a group, then *none* has the sense of *not any,* and a plural verb is in order. To illustrate: In "No arrests have been made and none are expected," the emphasis is clearly on a plural. The sentence can aptly be restated: "No arrests have been made and *not any* are expected."

Recommendation: When uncertain whether to use a singular or a plural verb, and if a decision must be made promptly, it is safer to choose the singular.

AS YOU LIKE IT

So much has been written about the use of *like* versus *as* that probably no more should be heaped on that grammatical pile. Unfortunately, the continued misuse of these two words suggests that much of what has been written has been either misread or misunderstood.

Like is a preposition that compares nouns, pronouns, and noun phrases. A typical example is "He addressed the jury *like an expert.*"

As, on the other hand, is a conjunction used to introduce subordinate clauses, which, like all clauses, contain a verb. Stated in another way, if a verb is used, a clause results and *as* should introduce it: "He addressed the jury *as an expert would*" (*have addressed the jury* being understood). The verb is a signal to use *as* and not *like.*

And that is as it should be.

3

COMPRISE CAN SURPRISE

Comprise means "to contain or embrace." A unit comprises, or "is made up of," the elements of which it is composed. The elements, on the other hand, constitute, or "make up," the unit: "The estate *comprises* a manor house, two guest houses, and a stable." "The book *comprises* five chapters and a bibliography."

Unfortunately, considering how often it is improperly employed, *comprise* seems to thrive on misuse. For example, "Many counties comprise the state of Ohio" needs correcting, for it is the state of Ohio that comprises many counties. "He listed the elements that comprise the crime" is not right either. The crime comprises the elements.

Whenever doubtful about the correct use of *comprise*, the safest move is to replace it with "consists of" or "be composed of," which is what *comprise* means: "The estate consists of. . . ." "The book is composed of. . . ." Even avoiding *comprise* entirely would be no loss. It is such a starchy word that something simpler, the word *has*, for example, would be a welcome relief: "The state of Ohio *has* (instead of *comprises*) many counties." But because the whole comprises the parts, the passive voice "is comprised of" may not be used.

One caveat: Include is not a precise synonym for *comprise* despite such a listing by some dictionaries. What follows *comprise* is a complete list; what follows *include* is, or should be, only a partial one. For instance, "The book includes five chapters, a bibliography, and an index of subjects" means that the book has more than the sections mentioned. If *comprise* were the verb, the sentence would mean that the book contained only those segments, and nothing more. With *include*, more is to come; with *comprise*, all has been said.

4

DWELLING ON SPELLING

Some people consult a dictionary for spelling only when confronted by an unusual or a seldom-used word. And yet the spelling of many ordinary words, which some writers take for granted, ought to be verified to determine whether it is an accepted American spelling or merely a British relic.

Center and *theater*, for example, are American spellings; *centre* and *theatre*, British variants. *Honour* and *favour*, except in formal invitations, are more acceptably spelled *honor* and *favor*. In fact, except for *glamour*, this entire class of words has dropped the *u*.

Then there is the American *gray* and the British *grey*, *practicing* vs. *practising*, *connection* vs. *connexion*, *willful* vs. *wilful*, *ax* vs. *axe*, *goodby* vs. *goodbye*, *plow* vs. *plough*, and *offense* vs. *offence*.

The most persistent use of British spelling, however, seems to be the doubling of the final *l* when an *ing* or *ed* suffix is appended—*labelled* for *labeled*, *travelling* for *traveling*. The American rule, when adding these suffixes to a two-syllable word, is to double the final consonant if it is preceded by a single vowel, but only, and this is most important, if the second syllable is stressed. Hence *control, controlled, controlling,* the accent falling on the second syllable, but, with the accent falling on the first syllable, *cancel, canceled, canceling.*

INTERROGATORY

"He levied a charge of slander against him" is a sentence from a leading newspaper. Is *levied* being used correctly?

I think not. The word apparently meant was *leveled*. The only thing levied hereabouts is taxes.

PROBLEMS GROW FROM SUCH AS THESE

Such as is a phrase that introduces examples and illustrative material. To use it properly, a few important rules should be observed.

First, since *such as* introduces only selected items, following them with "and the like," "and so forth," or any other all-inclusive expression is improper. For example, in the sentence "Major professional sports are played in large cities, such as New York, Chicago, Atlanta, and so forth," *and so forth* should be deleted and *and* inserted between the last two cities.

Second, *such as* must be followed only by a noun and not by a prepositional phrase. To illustrate: "Major professional sports are played in large cities, such as in New York, Chicago, and Atlanta" should read ". . . such as (no *in*) New York, Chicago, and Atlanta."

In both examples, *such as* is preceded by a comma because the material it introduces, though informative, can be omitted without affecting the sense of the sentence (in the second example, the gist is that "major professional sports are played in large cities"). If what follows *such as* is necessary to the meaning of a sentence, then no comma should set it off. For instance, in "Major sports such as baseball, football, and basketball are well attended in large cities," a comma neither precedes *such as* nor follows *basketball* because that information constitutes the heart of the sentence. It is not that all sports draw big crowds, only that the kind named are well attended.

To be remembered: Such as is the correct combination, not *such . . . who, such . . . which, such . . . where, such . . . when.* In "The course is only for such lawyers who contemplate a specialty," and "The Urban League objects to such conditions which exist in the inner city," the *who* in the first example and the *which* in the second should be replaced by *as*.

AN ABBREVIATED VERSION

Abbreviations, except for those that are always required, such as Mr., Dr., A.M., and Ph.D., should be avoided in formal writing.

Some style manuals advance two reasons for eschewing abbreviations. First, taste; abbreviations, except in footnotes, tend to lower the tone of any writing. Second, clarity; not all abbreviations are understood by everyone. Those stylebooks further recommend spelling out, in English, the words that replace the abbreviations. To illustrate: "that is" should be used rather than *i.e.* or *id est;* "for example" rather than *e.g.* or *exempli gratia;* and "namely" rather than *viz* or *videlicet.* "A burglary includes many lesser offenses, for example (not *e.g.*), larceny and criminal trespass."

Because *et cetera* causes more problems than do most other expressions, it calls for special attention. In the first place, *et cetera* is spelled out only when the phrase itself is being referred to, as in this sentence. If, in a textual statement, an all-inclusive expression is needed, such English equivalents as *and so forth, and so on,* or *and the like* should be employed rather than *et cetera.* In footnotes and parentheticals, however, *et cetera* may properly be used, but only in its accepted form, the abbreviated *etc.*

Postscriptum: Etc. should not be preceded by *and,* as in "The bindings come in red, blue, white, yellow, and etc.," because *etc.* already has an *and;* that's what the *et* means.

7

ALL RIGHT, ALREADY

Words beginning with *al* and expressions including *all* have one thing in common: confusion. Take, for example, "The book contains 500 pages all together." What is meant, of course, is that the book has 500 pages in all, or in sum—*altogether; all together* is incorrect here. The two-word *all together* means "in a group," as in "To help us count the books faster, Miss Garrity put them *all together*."

Of course, this kind of error can occur only in writing; in conversation, *all together* and *altogether* sound alike, as do *all ready*, meaning "everything is prepared," and *already*, meaning "by this time."

The way to handle these *al-all* words and expressions when unsure about their spellings is to mentally omit the *al* or the *all*. If the meaning of the sentence is affected, an *al* word—*altogether, already*—is needed. If the sense of the sentence remains unchanged, then an *all* expression—*all together, all ready*—is proper. For example, "the prisoner had *already* made good his escape by the time the alarm sounded" is correct as it stands, but "The prisoner had *ready* made good . . ." is meaningless. On the other hand, "We entered the courtroom *all together*" is logical even without *all:* "We entered the courtroom together."

Since *all* merely adds emphasis, it can be omitted without affecting meaning—and be economical besides. Consider "The witnesses are *all together* and are *all ready* to testify" and "The witnesses are *together* and are *ready* to testify."

The phrase *all right* creates no spelling problem because it is properly spelled only as in this sentence. Although

8

alright is frequently seen—it is one of the most misspelled words in the English language—it does not belong in serious writing.

ASTIGMATIC ADVERBS

An adverb "squints" when it is placed so that it modifies either of two words, one preceding it and the other following. The way to treat a "squint" is to reposition the adverb, if possible, or else to recast the sentence entirely.

Example: "Filing briefs late generally influences the court's attitude." In that sentence, *generally* may modify either the adverb *late*, "Filing briefs *late generally* influences the court's attitude," or the verb *influences*, "Filing briefs late *generally influences* the court's attitude." Consider "The defendant's talking repeatedly annoyed the judge." Was the judge annoyed because the defendant *talked repeatedly?* Or was he *annoyed repeatedly* because the defendant was talking? One more: "A man who can do this well deserves your praise." Did the man *do* his job *well?* Or did he *well deserve* your praise? Inserting an adverb between *well* and *deserve*, like *certainly* or *surely*, will clarify the sentence: "A man who can do this well surely deserves your praise."

Since "squints" tend to obscure meaning, they should, of course, be most carefully avoided. But they slip past many a good writer. Grammarians still ponder Shakespeare's "There's a divinity that shapes our ends rough hew them how we will," which may be interpreted as either *shapes our ends rough* or *rough hew them how we will.*

9

TO EACH HIS OWN

Each, of course, is singular in number. When it is the subject of a sentence, the verb and any succeeding pronoun must be singular as well. Accordingly, the sentence "Each of those lawyers *belong* to different ABA Sections and hence *serve* in *their* own way" ought to be restated, "Each of those lawyers *belongs* to different ABA Sections and hence *serves* in *his* own way."

When *each* is not the subject of the sentence, a following noun should be singular or plural depending upon the position of *each* in relation to the verb. If *each* precedes the verb, the noun should be plural, as in "They *each were* considered for *positions* of honor." If it follows the verb, the noun should be singular: "They *were each* considered for a *position* of honor."

The following mnemonic device may help determine whether *each* should be treated as a singular or plural: If *each* precedes the verb, it is *PP*—precede, plural; if it is subsequent, it is *SS*—subsequent, singular.

INTERROGATORY

Is the sentence "It is necessary to try and keep the names straight" grammatically acceptable?

Not in formal writing. The infinitive *to try* should not be followed by the conjunction *and*. It needs another infinitive. *Try and* is colloquial and, if used at all, should be confined to informal writing. Other similar expressions are "Be careful and don't go . . .," which should be rephrased "Be careful not to go near the fire," or whatever. "Let's plan and go early" also needs an infinitive: "Let's plan to go early."

10

A CONTRAST IN COMPARISONS

The common practice of interchanging *compare to* and *compare with* in general English fails to justify such loose usage in formal writing or, indeed, in any other writing. Idiom requires that these phrases be used in different contexts.

Compare to is used when two things are only likened; that is, the comparison is merely of similarities, since the things being compared are basically dissimilar: "The judge's voice may be compared *to* the roar of the breakers; they both boom." "Counsel compared the new Act *to* a jigsaw puzzle." "The client compared her husband *to* a mule." All these comparisons, it may be noted, are figurative.

Compare with, on the other hand, is the form to use when things are being examined for both their likenesses and their differences. Here, however, the things being compared are of the same species: "The writing style of Justice Cardozo may be compared *with* that of Justice Brandeis." "Professor Tolson compared the British law *with* the American statute." "Howard's book on taxation is frequently compared *with* Regan's."

And then there is *contrast.* It is used only to point out differences: "The American system of jurisprudence contrasts sharply with the Russian system."

A caution: When *compare with* is used, an actual comparison should be made. To say, for example, "He employs six lawyers now, compared with five last year" makes no true comparison. Correctly stated, the sentence would read: "He employs six lawyers now, *whereas* last year he employed five."

IT IS SO PROVIDED

As connectives introducing a stipulation or demand, *provided* and *providing*, both meaning "on the condition that," are equally acceptable to some writers. For example, "Counsel may continue the hearing *provided* (or *providing*) he pays the arbitrators' fees." Others recognize only *provided*, inasmuch as it is a commonly accepted conjunction. *Providing*, they contend, serves more appropriately as a participle, as in "An organization *providing* full legal services is needed in the community." No such controversy surrounds *provided*.

The full phrase *provided that* is generally used on a formal level, as indeed it should be. Purists, however, insist that *provided* must always be accompanied by *that*, whatever the tone of writing. Regardless of their point of view, a widely accepted rule is to refrain from using *that* unless its omission causes confusion: "They agreed to a continuance *provided* counsel would file briefs within five days." No *that*, no confusion.

Footnote: Neither *provided* nor *providing* should be used when *if* would serve. A mere possibility or a simple condition should be introduced by *if:* "Court will convene *if* (not *provided*) the judge arrives." *Provided* and *providing* are appropriate in more highly structured sentences.

INFER RED

It may well be that the two most commonly confused words in the English language are *imply* and *infer*. The culprit is *infer; imply* ordinarily is blameless. A typical example is "Do you mean to infer that I am wrong?" *Imply*, of course, is called for, not *infer*.

To imply means "to suggest or say indirectly"; *to infer* means "to surmise or to draw a conclusion." A speaker who hints, *implies;* a listener who recognizes the hint, *infers.* In other words, the implier initiates; the inferrer receives.

The distinction between *imply* and *infer* is easily made if one remembers that just as *im* precedes *in,* one must *im*ply before another can *in*fer. "He implied in the first chapter that the law was unconstitutional. From the material presented, we must infer that this conclusion was merited." The author implied, the reader inferred.

TO LIE, TO LAY?

One reason why *lie* and *lay* are so often confused is that *lay* is both the present tense of *to lay,* meaning "to put or place," and the past tense of *to lie,* meaning, in this context, "to recline." "I *lay* my briefcase down" (present tense). "The culprit *lay* still on the floor" (past tense).

These verbs can be distinguished by remembering that whereas *to lay* is transitive and always takes an object (I lay the books down), *to lie* is intransitive and takes no object (I lie down to rest). If, in other words, a noun following the verb is essential to the meaning of the sentence, a form of *to lay* is required.

Confusing the present participle and the past tense of *to lay* with the same verb forms of *to lie* is common. Consider this sentence: "Not only was he laying on the floor when the police found him, but he laid there feigning sleep." Here, the two verb forms of *to lay* are mistakenly used for the corresponding forms of *to lie.* The sentence should read: "Not only was he lying on the floor when the police found him, but he lay there feigning sleep."

13

THE NUMBERS RACKET

A wag might say, "A number of things can be said about numbers." He would be right. One thing is that even though the word *number* is singular, the expression *a number*, when used as the subject of a sentence, takes a plural verb: "A large number of books *are* on the shelves." When, however, the subject is changed to *the number*, indicating a more particular number, a singular verb is required: "The large number of books on the shelves *is* (not *are*) most impressive."

A number that begins a sentence should be spelled out: "Fifty (not 50) lawyers were present." And since convention requires that a year be written in figures except in formal announcements, a year may not properly begin a sentence. For example, "1929 witnessed the collapse of Wall Street" needs changing to either "The year 1929 witnessed . . ." or "In 1929, Wall Street collapsed."

INTERROGATORIES

Is the expression *large size*, as in *a large-size room*, preferred to *large sized*?

Respected writers use both forms. On a formal level, the choice is *large-sized* room, a hyphen tying the modifiers together. *Sized* is preferred because it is an adjective, whereas *size* is a noun. Which raises another point—one should not say "this size room," but "this size of room."

A sentence read, "Griffin and Hine each have received $1,000." Why does the sentence sound awkward?

Because *each* is misplaced. *Each* implies a singular sense and should therefore not precede but follow a plural verb: "Griffin and Hine have received $1,000 each."

14

DUE TO CIRCUMSTANCES

Whether to consider *due* a preposition or an adjective only is a matter on which usage authorities disagree. Those who recognize *due* solely as an adjective have established principles on their side; those in the prepositional camp can bolster their position by pointing to wide usage.

Here are the facts. Traditionally, *due,* an adjective, has been used to modify a noun or pronoun, as in "The decision to continue the case was due to an overloaded calendar." In that sentence, *due* modifies *decision*—and no one opposes it. However, many respected writers use *due to* as a preposition as well, and it is at that point that a conflict arises. A typical example is "Due to an overloaded calendar, it was decided to continue the case."

The question is whether *due to* should be accepted as a preposition on a formal level. The answer is preferably not, although it really is a writer's choice. The need for prepositional *due to* is dubious, since many other suitable phrases are available, as this example points out: *"Because of* (or *Owing to* or *On account of*—not *Due to*) an overloaded calendar, it was decided to continue the case." Then again, abiding by grammatical principles is never offensive, even to the so-called avant-garde.

The following sentences are examples of *due to* used adjectivally: "The witness's absence due to circumstances beyond the lawyer's control was a fatal blow." "The collapse of the case was due to the plaintiff's unexplained absence." If *due* is being used as an adjective, *caused by* or *attributed to* can replace it without affecting the sense of the sentence, since those phrases mean *due to.* In the second example, *due to* follows a form of the verb "to be," a safe position, because there it always serves

15

as an adjective—a predicate adjective: "The postpone-ment was due to a power failure."

The trend to consider *due to* a preposition is so wide-spread that spurning such use, let alone criticizing it, seems pedantic and blustery. Prepositional *due to* is fast entering everyone's grammatical kit. But until the move-ment has been completed, it is wise, in serious writing, to hold it in abeyance.

Overdue: "Due to the fact that" is a wordy way of say-ing *since* or *because*.

DO GALLERYS NEED YOUR SUPPORT?

—No, but *galleries* do.

Forming the plurals of nouns that end in *y* is a procedure governed by established rules. Nouns with a final *y* preceded by a vowel (attorney, galley, joy) simply need an *s* (attorneys, galleys, joys). But those whose conclud-ing letter is preceded by a consonant (duty, hostelry, jury) require changing the *y* to *i* and adding *es* (duties, hostelries, juries).

Forming the correct plurals of nouns that end in *o*, how-ever, depends upon accurate memory or a willingness to consult a dictionary. If the *o* is preceded by a vowel, the plural is formed merely by adding *s* (radios, folios, ratios). But if a consonant precedes the final *o*, no simple rule exists to govern the formation of the plural. The writer is left to his own devices and must discover for himself whether *s* or *es* should be used: *echoes, banjos; volcanoes, dynamos; heroes, zeros; mottoes, halos; frescoes, concertos; cargoes, mementos.*

PARENTHESES CAN THROW CURVES

Parentheses are used to enclose explanatory or sup-plementary information not directly related to a sentence thought. It should be possible to omit the information so enclosed without changing either the meaning of the sentence or its structure. "The program for our annual meeting (it begins on May 16) should be ready soon."

When parentheses are used inside a sentence, the first word within the parentheses, except for a proper noun, is not capitalized even though it begins a complete sen-tence (an example of this point is the sentence you are now reading). No mark of punctuation is placed before an opening parenthesis; if punctuation is required there (and this frequently happens), it should be placed after the closing parenthesis, as in this sentence. Similarly, no mark of punctuation, except a question mark or an exclamation point, should follow the last word within the parentheses: "The annual meeting (I am glad you made it) was most stimulating; the next one (will you be there?) promises to be equally good."

When an independent sentence is enclosed in parentheses, it must be punctuated appropriately, with a final mark of punctuation placed inside the closing parenthesis, as in the example that follows. (This is the last example of the correct use of parentheses.)

What prepositions should be used in stating a person's resi-dence?

One lives *in* a city, *on* a street, *at* a number. John Thomas, for example, may live in Peoria, on Broad Street, at 46.

HOWEVER IT'S SAID

To most writers, only the sentence position and punctuation of *however* are matters of concern. They all agree that *however*, meaning "yet" or "nevertheless," indicates a contrast.

The position most effective for *however* is early in a sentence, but not at its very beginning. Since *however* contrasts what precedes with what follows, when it opens a sentence it in effect produces a comparison with the immediately preceding sentence. In many instances, though, the writer had not intended this contrast. Some authorities go so far as to recommend that a sentence should never begin with *however* because it is seldom used correctly in that position. At the end of a sentence, *however* is such a weak modifier that its use may be completely unwarranted. *However* is ordinarily most effective when placed somewhere in between, but sooner rather than later.

Consider this example: "We must be sure, however, that the promotion is distributed widely." There, *however* properly appears early in the sentence, stressing "We must be sure." *However* could be moved even nearer to the front, and the emphasis would change accordingly. In "We, however, must be sure . . ." the stress now falls on *We*, indicating that it was our responsibility and no one else's. The placement is based simply on what the writer has in mind.

When *however* connects two independent clauses, as in "The book has many chapters; however, the one on ERISA is the longest," it is punctuated as in the example: preceded by a semicolon and followed by a comma.

Finally, and fortunately, as an adverb meaning "in whatever manner," *however* is problem-free; it may appear unpunctuated almost anywhere in the sentence: "However he studied, he could not learn." "He could not learn however he studied."

SEPARATED COORDINATES

Coordinate adjectives, two or more adjectives that independently modify the same noun, are normally followed by commas. For example, in (1) "He is a shrewd, bustling lawyer"; in (2) "Daniel Tabachnick is a decisive, sharp-minded person"; and in (3) "We value timely, comprehensive, and well-written books," the adjectives are of equal value. They are therefore followed by commas.

Coordinate adjectives can readily be distinguished from their noncoordinate counterparts by the flexibility with which they may be (a) rearranged, (b) separated by *and*, or (c) used as predicate adjectives without causing either awkwardness or an appreciable change in meaning. The following sentences, based on the foregoing examples, illustrate the three methods of testing for coordinate adjectives: (1) "He is a bustling, shrewd lawyer" —adjectives rearranged; (2) "Daniel Tabachnick is a decisive and sharp-minded person"—*and* inserted; (3) "The books we value are timely, comprehensive, and well-written"—predicate adjectives.

Noncoordinate adjectives, on the other hand, carry unequal weight and hence cannot satisfactorily pass those tests; consequently, they are unpunctuated. For example, in "He is an alert young lawyer," *young lawyer* is a unit, which, in turn, is modified by *alert*. Similarly, in "The judge prefers a gray flannel suit," *flannel suit* is an adjective-noun combination modified by gray.

IT'S DATED

In formal, nonmilitary writing, a date is written in the following order: month, day, year: *April 1, 1979*. If the day is not included, no comma separates the month and year: *April 1979*. But if the full date is given, the year, according to most stylists, becomes parenthetical; thus unless it ends a sentence, a comma is required both fore and aft: "The bill was signed by the President on April 1, 1979, while he was vacationing at Camp David."

The number following a month should be a cardinal number: *April 1*. The number preceding a month should be an ordinal: *the first of April*. It is therefore proper to say that Memorial Day is celebrated on either *May 30* (not *May 30th*) or *the thirtieth of May*. Although opinion is divided, ordinal numbers are preferably spelled out (*first*, not *1st*).

INTERROGATORIES

If a last-minute catastrophe cancels an event, is a new date set on the spot properly called an *alternative* date?

Commonly it is so called, but properly it should not be. *Alternative* implies the existence of a choice, but none was offered here. It was a last-minute decision. The date replacing the canceled one should more aptly be called a new, a fresh, a revised, or a substituted date.

Is this sentence grammatically correct: "I shall appreciate it if you will send me the latest catalog"?

It is not. Since *it* has no antecedent, the sentence should be reworded: "I shall appreciate your sending me. . . ."

20

ANY TIME ANYWHERE

Words and expressions involving *any* present their own peculiar problem: whether to adjoin the word that follows *any* or to let it stand alone. In other words, should these *any* compounds be written open or closed?

Anyone, for example, is a one-word pronoun, as in "Anyone may join." But when it means "any single person or thing," it is a two-word phrase, stressing *one:* "Any one of those men may join" or "He would vote for any one of them."

Anybody, meaning "anyone," is always spelled as a single word except when it refers to a corpse: "Despite the search, the sheriff could not find any body."

Although opinion is divided on how to spell *anymore,* a colloquialism occasionally found in respectable writing, it is preferably written as one word when used to mean "any longer": "We do not try cases anymore." In all other contexts, two words should be used: "Although we wanted two more books, we would not ask for any more." But whether written as one word or two, idiom requires that *any more* (or *anymore*), as in the foregoing examples, be used only in a negative sense: "not try cases anymore"; "not ask for any more."

Anyway, when meaning "in any event" or "anyhow," is written as one word: "Despite the witness's death, the case will be tried anyway." For all other meanings, the expression should be written as two words: "Any way you do it will be satisfactory." "The defendant was not really questioned in any way." To determine which spelling to use, see whether the word *whatever* can sensibly replace *any.* If so, *any way* is the proper choice: "Any (or *Whatever*) way you do it will be satisfactory."

Miscellany: Any place is an informal expression for *anywhere.* "The bailiff could not be found *anyplace*" should, on a formal level, be changed to *anywhere.* But *anywheres* is completely unacceptable on any level. It belongs "nowheres."

Any time must be spelled open, since the one-word spelling *anytime* is not a recognized English word.

All the foregoing rules governing the use of *any,* excepting those governing *any time,* also apply to compounds beginning with *some.*

SINGULAR PLURALS

In the English language, idiom and grammar often act like strangers. For example, some plural words, illogically and solely because of idiom, take singular modifiers.

Perhaps the most frequently seen of this eccentric group is the plural noun *few* modified by the singular *a*—"A few arrived early." Another oddity is a type of phrase beginning with *many.* Like *few, many* indicates a number greater than one; nevertheless, it is frequently used with the singular *a,* as in "Many a lawyer was confused by the Tax Reform Act." What is more, and to complicate matters further, *many a* may be reversed if an adjective is interpolated. Although the phrase "A many lawyers" is unacceptable, "A great many lawyers" is not.

Some idioms expressing distance and time also defy grammatical principles of number. For instance, "*a five-foot* pole" and "*a five-minute* drive" consist of a singular (*a*), a plural (*five*), and a singular again (*foot, minute*). However, when these measures are restated in unhyphenated forms, the inconsistencies disappear as the plurals emerge: "His pole measured five *feet.*" "The drive lasted five *minutes.*"

SUPERLATIVES ARE THE BEST

The superlative form of an adjective or an adverb indicates the highest or lowest degree of a quality or quantity among three or more persons, objects, or ideas. It is formed by adding the suffix *-est* to the positive form of a word or by placing *most* or *least* before it (*brightest, most learned, least wanted*).

Whether to use the *-est* ending or the preceding *most* or *least* ordinarily depends on the number of syllables in the core word. The superlative of a one-syllable word is usually constructed with *-est* (*largest, fastest*); that of a three-or-more-syllable word always with a preceding *most* or *least* (*most suspicious, least knowledgeable*); but that of a two-syllable word with either *-est* or *most* or *least*, whichever sounds more appropriate (*handsomest, most handsome, tenderest, most tender*).

Adjectives and adverbs that name absolute qualities, however, cannot logically be compared, since their attributes cannot be affected. They are superlative degrees in themselves. Among such words are *perfect, equal, absolute, round, straight, dead, empty, full, essential, everlasting, matchless, mortal, universal,* and *supreme.* To illustrate the effect of an absolute, consider the adjective *full.* A can is full, for example, if it is filled with a liquid to its very brim. It is then as full as it can ever be. Another can of the same size cannot be made any *fuller,* nor, if there are still other cans, can any one of them become the *fullest* can of all. Or again, something *unique,* since it is one of a kind, cannot be any *more unique* than it already is.

Some absolutes, however, are subject to a special kind of comparison. With the aid of a qualifying term, degrees of approximation can be indicated, as in *nearly equal, more nearly circular, almost absolute,* and *a little more square.* Thus qualified, absolutes may properly be used, even in formal writing.

Addendum: Although these qualifying expressions are permissible, the comparative form *more* may not qualify by itself, despite the Constitution's "a more perfect Union."

A MATTER OF INTEREST

Although some dictionaries regard *disinterested* and *uninterested* as synonyms, probably because common usage has blunted their meanings, if these words are not differentiated, the English language, and all who use it, will be the losers.

Disinterested means "lacking both self-interest and bias." A judge, for example, is a disinterested participant in a trial if he is not prejudiced toward the litigants and presides impartially. His disinterestedness, although expected, is nevertheless a desirable and proper attitude.

Uninterested means "apathetic or not interested." An uninterested judge feels no concern for the matter before him; he is actually indifferent to it. His is an unworthy attitude, considering the responsibilities he bears.

And then there is just plain, simple *interest.* A person interested in something may yet have no interest in it. The word *interest,* in this last sense, refers, of course, to a proprietary interest. An interest in the success of a bar association project, for example, is unrelated to any attribute of ownership.

24

WATCH THAT

Whether to use *that* or *which* to introduce relative clauses sometimes poses a troublesome question: "Ours is a corporation (*which* or *that*) owns two subsidiaries." It is a generally accepted rule that clauses introduced by *which* are nonrestrictive; those begun by *that*, restrictive.

A nonrestrictive clause merely provides incidental or nonessential information about a previous word; even if the clause is entirely omitted, the basic meaning of the sentence will remain intact. Consider "The *Civil Trial Manual*, which is regularly supplemented, is much in demand." Without the *which* clause, which is merely descriptive, the sentence will nevertheless survive: "The *Civil Trial Manual* is much in demand." That sentence not only makes sense but holds the primary thought the writer wishes to convey.

A restrictive clause, on the other hand, since it defines and limits its antecedent, is essential to meaning; removing it materially impairs the sentence. In "A book that lacks an index is not particularly useful," the clause *that lacks an index* is the crux of the thought; without it—"A book is not particularly useful"—the sentence obviously makes little sense.

Since restrictive *that* clauses are essential, they are not set off by commas; nonrestrictive *which* clauses are.

INTERROGATORY

Two plural forms for *money*—*moneys* and *monies*—are both used. Is one form preferred to the other?

Moneys is recommended, whether referring to the medium of exchange of various countries or of a particular form of money within a country.

25

SELF PROBLEMS

Reflect for a moment on *yourself*. This word, like other *self*-ending pronouns—*myself, himself, ourselves*—serves as both an intensive pronoun, emphasizing the doer— "The Judge himself said it"—and a reflexive, turning the action of the verb back on the doer—"With the first words out of his mouth, the witness perjured himself."

The function of an intensive is clear—simply to emphasize. Its placement in a sentence is not important as long as it unmistakably refers to the noun to be stressed: "The secretary herself gave the report" or "The secretary gave the report herself." Sometimes, however, a sentence is so constructed that the arbitrary placement of an intensive makes it difficult to tell which noun is to be emphasized. For instance, "The many tax issues should consume a major part of the seminars themselves" would be clearer if rephrased "The many tax issues themselves should consume. . . ." It is better to place an intensive near its noun or pronoun, preferably next to it. A good rule: The closer the position, the clearer the meaning.

The chief problem with reflexive pronouns is their occasional faulty use as the second member of a compound subject or object. Take as an example "The President and myself are pleased with the progress being made in the SALT talks." Good English requires that *I* be used instead of *myself*, since the subject of a sentence must be in the nominative case. If an object of a verb is involved, as in "The photographer snapped the prisoners and ourselves entering the courthouse," then the objective case is needed: *us* for *ourselves*.

Particular care must be exercised when a reflexive pronoun is preceded by a preposition because many idiomatic expressions are formed by combining prepositions with other words or phrases. For example, it is correct to say "I wrote it by myself," since *by myself* is used as a single idiomatic unit meaning "alone or apart from others." But it is incorrect to say "It was written *by myself*," since *by* is a simple preposition here and requires the objective case—in this instance *me*.

IT'S FORBIDDEN TO FORGET

Forbid, to be used correctly, should not be followed by *from*. Idiom requires that an infinitive or a gerund be used instead.

To illustrate: "The Supreme Court ruled that states may not forbid pharmacists from advertising prescription drug prices" needs an infinitive, ". . . may not forbid pharmacists *to advertise* . . . ," or a gerund, "may not forbid pharmacists' *advertising*." Most writers favor the infinitive and customarily use it. The gerund, because it is cumbersome, lacks force. Certainly "The guard forbade the prisoner to leave" sounds more commanding than "The guard forbade the prisoner's leaving."

Memory aid: Remember the formula 4 bid 2. It will steer a sentence away from a *from*.

INTERROGATORY

A bothersome expression is "Trusting that this suggestion will satisfy your client. . . ." Please comment.

First, *trusting* is misused for *hoping*. Second, even if *hoping* were used, the phrase would lack force. It is better to say *We hope that* or *We think that* or *We believe that*. In fact, to be more concise, you might even omit the *that*.

TITLES—PERSONALLY TREATED

Leading style manuals recommend that titles be capitalized when they precede personal names—Professor Herbert Maimon, President E. B. Lamb—but lowercased when they follow names—"Mr. Herbert Maimon, a professor of law, will be addressing us"; "Mr. E. B. Lamb is now the president."

A troublesome question, however—and one that has no uniform answer—is how to treat a title when it is substituted for a specific name. Should a second reference to Professor Maimon, for example, read "The *Professor* (or *professor*) then began to lecture"? Most stylebooks agree that except for preeminent titles, such as those of heads of state, a title replacing a personal name should be lowercased—thus *professor* in the foregoing example.

Despite the trend away from capitalizing titles, their treatment should rightfully be a writer's preference, unfettered by rigid rules. For one thing, the writer's relationship to his field is likely to have a decided, and understandable, bearing on the way he handles titles. Certainly the writings of lawyers abound in capitalized titles, especially when members of the judiciary are concerned. A typical example is "We know that Judge Murphy intends to revise his book. We also know that the Judge is preparing a supplement." No disapproval here.

JUST BETWEEN US

The prepositions *between* and *among* have distinct uses. *Between* (originally *by twain*) is used when only two items are being considered—"The choice is between nolo contendere and a plea of guilty"—and *among,* when there are more than two—"The files were divided among the five lawyers."

The rule governing the use of *between,* however, is subject to one notable exception: *between* is correctly used even when more than two elements are involved if the elements are closely associated and, though considered individually, are related to one another. To illustrate: "The Constitution regulates trade between the states." "Agreements were reached between the five nations."

When *between* refers to two objects, only the word *and* properly connects them. Any substitute for *and*—*to, or,* or a dash—is unacceptable. For example, in "The office handled between 60 to 90 indigent clients," *and* should replace *to;* in "The difference between a 7 per cent mortgage or a 9 per cent mortgage is substantial," *or* needs changing to *and;* and in "His term of office was between 1962-1970," the date should be rewritten "1962 *and* 1970." To repeat, the correct combination is *between . . . and.*

Because *each* and *every* refer to single items, the phrases *between each* and *between every* are generally regarded as incorrect, despite their use by Shakespeare, Scott, Dickens, and other reputable writers. It is logical to assume that two items are required for something to come between. Therefore, instead of writing, for instance, "A lawyer should spend a few moments in contemplation *between every trial* (or *between each trial*), it is better to say "between trials" or "after every trial."

A word of caution: The expression *between you and I* is so often used, even by officials in high stations, that it merits special attention. Since *between* takes the objective case, the *I* in "between you and I" should be changed to *me*—"between you and me."

IT CUTS A PRETTY FIGURE

Determining how to treat numbers, whether to express them in figures or spell them out, has spawned almost as many schools of thought as there are possible variations in style. Some stylists think that, except in certain specified situations, numbers from one through ninety-nine should be spelled out; others draw the line at twenty; and still others at ten or even nine. No matter which way numbers are handled, a respected authority seems to support that theory.

The lack of consensus is probably justified, in part, by the different kinds of writing being considered. Manuals concerned with formal writing almost unanimously recommend the spelling out of numbers from zero to 100. They maintain that numbers so treated lend dignity to the text, making it appear less commercial.

Modern business practice, on the other hand, normally avoids the writing out of numbers. Since business correspondence and advertising are designed to catch the eye and tell the story quickly, figures serve best.

Many stylebooks, including those of newspapers, stand somewhere in between. They prefer that numbers from one to ten be written out and that figures be used thereafter. Their reasoning is that spelling out two-digit numbers wastes valuable space and that, furthermore, these numbers are more easily remembered as figures.

On one related matter of usage all stylists seem to agree —numbers in the same category should be treated alike. How to treat them, however, depends on the style of the writing: "Of the 20 witnesses present, 3 testified" or "Of the twenty witnesses present, three testified." In any case, if one of the numbers exceeds ninety-nine, figures must be used throughout for the sake of consistency: "Of the 107 witnesses present, 3 testified."

If two sets of numbers appear in a sentence, one should be written in figures and the other in words: "Two mortgages exceeded a 15-year term; nineteen, a 25-year term; and thirty-three, a 30-year term."

One thing more: It is logical to use only figures for numbers in a series: "The tickets were issued in lots of 5, 10, 15, 20, and 25."

WHICH "CON" YOU TRUST?

Judging by the frequent misuse of *continuous* and *continual,* the distinction in meaning between them must be confusing. And yet that distinction simply depends upon whether or not the action referred to has been interrupted.

Continuous means "without cessation," which, of course, precludes any interruption. The term, to state it in another way, properly describes a continuity that is unbroken, that lasts without pauses or breaks: "The roar of the waterfall is continuous." "The machinery has been in continuous operation for fifty hours."

Continual, on the other hand, means "frequently or closely repeated." This term implies a broken succession, a recurrence at intervals: "The continual ring of a telephone can be annoying." "Continual lateness will affect a student's grades."

A close-to-home example of both words is "When turned on, the water runs continuously; but when turned off, the darned faucet drips continually."

ON BEING HONORABLE

Common courtesy titles, such as *Mr., Mrs., Ms.,* and *Messrs.,* are properly abbreviated when they precede a surname, whether or not a person's given name or initials are included: "Messrs. Herman Kerner and A. G. Parlante have arrived. Mr. Wells and Ms. Edith Browne are expected soon."

When the title of respect *Honorable* is used, the opposite is true, at least in formal writing. Convention requires that *Honorable* be spelled out and followed by the person's given name or initials—and, in addition, be escorted by a preceding *the*: "The monograph was prepared by the Honorable Edwin Smyth." But in a second reference, the title of that person's public position may be substituted for his given name or initials: "With this thought, we conclude the biography of the Honorable Judge Smyth." Although *Honorable* is always capitalized, *the* is lowercased when the title appears in a text or the body of a letter.

In informal usage, the abbreviation *Hon.* is permissible, but a given name or initial must intervene between the shortened title and the surname. Contrary to the rule in formal usage, *the* should not precede *Hon.* "We were addressed by Hon. W. H. Keith."

These rules are also applicable to the term *Reverend*.

INTERROGATORY

I rarely use *ever* with *seldom* (*seldom ever*) and seldom see *ever* with *rarely* (*rarely ever*). **Are these combinations justified?**

Never. Neither *rarely* nor *seldom* should be accompanied by *ever*—ever.

DASH IT ALL—

Many uses of the dash are self-evident and thus need no explaining. For example, a dash serves to indicate a break in thought: "If you read *Postmortem Estate Planning*—and I'm sure you will—you'll learn about disclaimers."

There are two specific uses of the dash, however, from which some writers consistently abstain, perhaps because they feel more comfortable with words or other marks of punctuation. And yet in each instance the dash might be the better choice.

The first case is the use of the dash rather than terms such as *namely, in other words,* or *that is:* "The lawyer had only one interest (*that is*)—litigation." "Tourists must have their passports, visas, and health forms (*in other words*)—all the necessary documents for travel." In these cases the dash not only is more effective, since it stresses what follows, but spares words as well.

The second useful, though frequently avoided, function of a dash is to set off a compound description from the rest of the sentence: "Mr. Borland's article—lucid, compelling, imaginative—is outstanding." Commas, which are ordinarily used, make such a sentence read *staccato:* "Mr. Borland's article, lucid, compelling, imaginative, is outstanding."

The dash can also clarify an apposition that might otherwise be misleading. For instance, the sentence "Three lawyers, Mr. Emas, Mr. Hess, and Mr. Patrick, were engaged in a lively discussion" could be misconstrued as referring to six persons. With a dash, the meaning immediately becomes clear: "Three lawyers—Mr. Emas, Mr. Hess, and Mr. Patrick—were engaged in a lively discussion."

BYE, BYE, BIMONTHLY

Bimonthly is a word that can cause confusion, and does. The reason: it has two irreconcilable meanings—"occurring every two months" and "occurring twice a month."

Since clarity is central to good writing, it is better not to use *bimonthly* when referring to those periods, but rather to spell out what is meant: either *every two months* or *twice a month*. In that way, all doubts will be avoided and the ambiguous *bimonthly* put to rest: "Checks will be issued twice a month; the bulletin every two months." Furthermore, for the sake of variety, "twice a month" may be expressed by *semimonthly* and "every two months" by *every other month*.

Biannual, fortunately, has only one definition—"twice a year." It is synonymous with *semiannual*, the only distinction being, slight as it is, that *semiannual* implies an interval of approximately six months. With *biannual* there is no such implication.

And *biennial*, meaning "every two years," is completely trouble-free; it doesn't even have a synonym.

WHILE I HAVE TIME

In formal writing, *while*, as a conjunction, is safely used only in its temporal sense, "during or at the same time," as in "While the court is in session, no unnecessary noise will be tolerated."

In informal writing, however, *while* is often used to mean "although," "and," or "but." These liberal definitions are acceptable, as long as they make clear that time is not meant: "While he disliked the executrix, he did admire her integrity." No confusion there. In the following examples, however, *while* is ambiguous. (1)

"While counsel was an expert in his field, he opposed any form of specialization"; (2) "Judge Alter served as president in 1945, while his son served in 1970"; (3) "Defense counsel always rose to cross-examine, while plaintiff's counsel never did." To conform the examples to formal usage, *while* should be replaced by *although* in the first instance; *and,* in the second; and *but* or *whereas* in the third.

Even in general English, writers would do best to avoid *while* if its meaning might be misconstrued. For instance, in "While Dennis was working at night in the law library, he saw Janet often," either time or concession could be inferred. If time was intended, the sentence should read: "When Dennis was working. . ."; if concession, "Although Dennis was working. . . ."

INSIDE, OUTSIDE, WRONG SIDE

The prepositions *inside* and *outside* should not be immediately followed by the word *of.* Its use there is superfluous and awkward.

To illustrate: Both in "The judge was last seen standing outside of the courtroom" and in "You may find the supplements just inside of the red manual," the *of* contributes nothing useful. Those sentences are smoother with *outside the courtroom* and *inside the red manual.*

When referring to time or distance, *inside of* is used to mean "in less than," as in "The survey will end inside of a month." This expression enjoys some authoritative support, but *within* is a better choice: "The survey will end within a month."

A final point: Outside of is a colloquialism when it means *except for:* "Except for (not *outside of*) the Appendix, the manuscript is complete."

AND BOTH ARE PROPER

When *both* is used as either an adjective—"He bought both books"—or a pronoun—"He bought both"—it presents no problems. If it serves as a correlative conjunction with *and,* however—"He bought *both* books *and* supplies"—clarity and orderliness demand parallelism, which is obtained by following *both* and *and* with the same kind of grammatical phrasing. If a noun, prepositional pharse, or clause follows *both,* then a noun, prepositional phrase, or clause, as the case may be, should follow *and.* "He was blind both to color and form," for example, should read "He was blind *to both* color and form" or "*both to* color and *to* form." "The new courthouse will serve both the needs of the legal profession and of the business community" should be rephrased either "the needs *of both* the legal profession and the business community" or "*both* the *needs* of the legal profession and *those* of the business community." The kind of parallel structure used is optional.

And is the only conjunction properly paired with *both.* In "The judge invited both the lawyers as well as their wives to his chambers," *and* should replace *as well as.* Moreover, since *both* never refers to more than two persons or things, a sentence such as "Counsel immediately spotted both the judge as well as the bailiff and his aide" needs to be corrected. Deleting *both* is the easy remedy.

INTERROGATORY

Is the expression *as good or better than* correct?

The expression, correctly stated, should read *as good as or better than,* in which good has an *as* before and behind. A better way yet to handle the phrase is to spell it out completely: "Her rendition was as good as his, if not better."

DOUBLE BURDEN

A verb acting in a dual role may often seem to function properly when it really does not. Particular care should be taken to ensure that a verb does not simultaneously serve two discrete masters—that it is not employed in two different capacities at the same time.

Consider this example: "The book is clearly written and therefore helpful to young lawyers." The *is* in that sentence serves both as an auxiliary verb to the past participle *written* and as a linking verb to *book* and *helpful*. In that double role, the verb is burdened by a load that should be carried by two verbs. Corrected, the sentence would read: "The book is clearly written and *is* therefore helpful to young lawyers."

Applicable rule: A verb should not be omitted if the omission imposes on another verb a duty it cannot perform.

WHEN PERSONS BECOME PEOPLE

A group of *people* consists of many *persons;* that is, *persons,* when assembled, are *people.* A few individuals, say three or four, are always *persons:* "Three or four persons entered." But if their number increases, *persons* become *people:* "One thousand people entered the stadium."

People, furthermore, is commonly used with rounded numbers, large or small: "About 50 (or about 100) people were present." But when uncounted groups become exact, *people* revert to *persons:* "Forty-nine persons were present."

37

People is also used to refer to a large, indefinite number of individuals: "He was elected by the people." But when it is assumed that the group involved was somewhat small, *persons* is preferred: "The crime was committed by persons unknown."

THE ARBITRARY "WHITCH"

A restrictive clause—one that provides information necessary for a full understanding of a sentence—should be introduced by *that* and not by *which*. When two restrictive clauses are near each other, however, and one is an adjective clause describing an antecedent, *which* should arbitrarily introduce the adjective clause to avoid the unpleasant repetition of *that*. Such a wordy convention is more easily understood if illustrated.

In the following sentences, both *that*'s are ordinarily required; the restructured examples contain the substituted arbitrary *which* (introducing the adjective clause). "He was so explicit *that* there was nothing *that* could have been misconstrued" (nothing *which* could have been misconstrued). "The mayor announced *that* Judge Webster would receive the community award *that* is presented annually" (award *which* is presented annually). "The judge's expression was the kind *that* said *that* counsel should refrain from interrupting" (kind *which* said).

One caution: Usually clauses introduced by *which* are either parenthetical or nonrestrictive. Such clauses are preceded by a comma and, unless they end a sentence, followed by one, as in "Clad's brief, which consisted of two pages, covered the subject thoroughly." No comma, however, and this should be noted, precedes an arbitrary *which*.

38

WHILE AWAY FOR AWHILE

The problem with *while* and *awhile* lies not in what they mean, but in which word to use in a given sentence. Normally both words serve the same thought equally well; the choice depends on the construction the writer thinks is most suitable.

While is a noun meaning "a space of time." It generally is used in a three-word phrase beginning with a preposition, as in "Study *for a while*" or "You will see the judge *after a while*." One exception, though, is the idiom *a while ago*, which is not preceded by a preposition: "The office was closed *a while ago*."

The one-word *awhile*, on the other hand, meaning "for a short time," is an adverb and should be used only to modify verbs, as in "Study *awhile*" or "Since court will convene soon, wait *awhile*."

If *a while* is preceded by a preposition, that three-word phrase then assumes the same meaning as the single word *awhile*. There is no noticeable difference, for example, between "Let's read *for a while*" and "Let's read *awhile*."

INTERROGATORY

Is the sentence "The proposal, circulated by the ABA and which will be put into final form soon, covers four pages" grammatically objectionable?

The expression *and which* (or, for that matter, *and who*) should be preceded by another *which* (or *who*) clause. To be correctly stated, the example should read: "The proposal, which the ABA circulated and which will be put. . . ."

IT'S VERY LIKELY TRUE

Very, when used as an intensive, serves no real purpose and should rarely, if ever, appear in writing. To illustrate: "Hers was a *very* long trial" is just as informative without *very*.

In some constructions, however, *very* is essential—for instance, to escort *likely* when that word is used as an adverb meaning "probably." Idiom requires that, when so used, *likely* must be preceded by a qualifying word such as *very* or *most* or *quite*. Therefore, in "The hearing will very likely be held tomorrow," *very* properly modifies *likely*.

Sometimes it is *very* that needs company. According to a formal rule, *very* should never directly modify a past participle—another adverb must come between them. A sentence such as "The newspaper seems *very concerned* with the trial" requires changing to *very much concerned* or *very greatly concerned*.

When a participle has lost its verbal effect, however, and is considered an adjective instead, this rule no longer holds. In such cases, *very* may be used alone: "The defendant appears very tired." "The brief is very complicated." Determining whether a participle has lost its verbal effect and should therefore be treated like an adjective, however, is an almost insurmountable problem. And the guidelines are far from precise. The rule generally followed is that if the word signifies a quality or condition, as do *determined* or *dignified*, it should be regarded as an adjective. But if action is indicated, as in *excited* or *disturbed*, then the participle should be considered a verb.

When in doubt, prudent writers omit *very*. They lose nothing except a useless word.

"A" IS FOR APPLE

Ordinarily deciding whether a word should be qualified by *a* or *an* presents little difficulty. It is just a matter of sound.

Words beginning with the sound of a consonant are commonly modified by *a*, regardless of whether the first letter is a consonant, as in *a* brief and *a* file, or a vowel sounding like a consonant, as in *a* eulogy (*y* sound) and *a* once-over (*w* sound). To repeat, it is the sound that counts.

Words beginning with vowel sounds, on the other hand, are always preceded by *an—an* appeal, *an* exemption. Again, the initial sound determines which article to use, and not the initial letter itself.

Words beginning with an aspirated *h* present the only problem. Should they be modified by *a* or *an?* Examples: *a* or *an* hallucination, *a* or *an* hysterical person, *a* or *an* habitual frown. Interestingly enough, either article is acceptable in these constructions, although contemporary usage strongly favors *a*.

In phrases such as "an historic document" and "an hilarious story," *an* is becoming less common and, possibly for that reason, sounds rather stilted. *An* is best reserved for words that start with an unaspirated or silent *h*— an hour, an heir, an honest opinion—despite the official volume *The White House: An Historic Guide.*

Afterthought: Letters of the alphabet are preceded by the article that agrees with their pronunciation: an *m*, an *r*, a *t*, a *u*. The same rule applies to abbreviations and symbols: *an FBI* case, *an H.R.* bill, *an NLRB* rule, but *a NATO* project, *a UFO* sighting.

A CAPITAL FAMILY

Nouns designating family members (*father, mother, uncle,* and so on) are capitalized when used alone—"I saw Mother yesterday"—or when regarded as an essential part of the family member's name—"Aunt Roslyn arrived with Uncle Seymour." In these cases such designations function as proper nouns.

When a word indicating a family relationship is not regarded as part of a name and is preceded by a possessive pronoun, it is lowercased: "I saw my mother yesterday." "My nephew Michael became a lawyer."

As to those family titles customarily accompanying a name—Uncle Thomas, Aunt Arleta, Grandma Courte—opinion is divided on whether to capitalize or to lowercase when a possessive pronoun is involved. Some respected writers, on the theory that a possessive pronoun reduces the term to a common noun, feel the lowercase is proper: "They went to the law office of their uncle Thomas." Others say that the two elements of those names are indivisible—"His Aunt Arleta is your secretary"—and that not even a possessive pronoun can sever them. These writers capitalize, as do most of us.

INTERROGATORY

Many stylebooks condemn the phrase "under separate cover." Practically, though, the expression seems necessary. Is this not true?

No. A specific reference to the way delivery is to be made is more informative: in another envelope, by special delivery, by air mail, by messenger.

JUST A SHADE DIFFERENT

In each of the following sentences, a firmly rooted idiom has been misused: "This is a different set of circumstances than the one we had previously experienced." "The presentation is different, considering the evidence, to all those heard today."

Proper idiomatic usage requires that *different* be followed only by *from,* and not by any other preposition. In the examples, therefore, *from* should replace both *than* and *to. Different than* is gradually acquiring acceptance in the literary community because of its smoothness—"It was different than the Judge realized" flows more easily than "It was different from what the Judge realized"—and because of its conciseness—"They use different filing systems today than in 1959" is briefer, and more practical, than "They use different filing systems today from those which they had in 1959." Some *different from* constructions even sound distorted. Compare "The ALI Council is drafting it from a different viewpoint than we are" with "The ALI Council is drafting it from a different viewpoint from that from which we are." Nevertheless, it is wise to observe convention, at least in formal writing, and to remember that different things differ *from* each other.

There is one exception—*different than* is properly used when differences are being compared. For example, no impropriety exists in "All the presentations differ from one another, but Mr. Hart's is more *different than* the others." In that sentence, *than* is governed by *more* rather than by *different.*

"SO AS" IT SHOULD BE

Convention has long approved the use of *as . . . as* in positive statements—"The law is only as effective as its

43

support"—and *so . . . as* in negative ones—"The new rules are not so clear as they might be." In general writing, however, widespread usage has elevated to respectability the use of *as . . . as* in both positive and negative comparisons.

In formal writing, on the other hand, the traditional distinction is still frequently observed. *So . . . as* remains preferred for negative statements, even those containing words that merely imply a negative, such as *hardly* and *scarcely:* "The defendant's brief is *hardly so* well prepared *as* the plaintiff's."

In questions, too, these expressions should be distinguished for the sake of clarity. For example, "Is Judge Thornton so old as the solicitor?" implies that the questioner already knows the solicitor's age and wants to make a comparison, but "Is Judge Thornton as old as the solicitor?" simply asks whether their ages are similar.

MAKING MUCH OUT OF A LOT

Consider the phrase *a lot of,* as in "There is a lot of precedent for that ruling."

The noun *lot,* meaning "a considerably large number of persons or things," is found on all levels of usage. In spite of this acceptance, in formal writing *lot* should be employed in one of its conventional senses, such as "a measured portion of land," and not substituted for *much, many,* or *a great deal of.* The first paragraph, therefore, should read: "There is *much* (or *a great deal of*) precedent for that ruling."

Furthermore, when *many* is actually intended, as in "He has many clients," replacing it with *lots of* or *a lot of* is a poor choice for two reasons: the phrase is both colloquial and wordy. But if *a lot* is used, at least it should be spelled that way, not *alot.*

44

A SOME TIME THING

Some time, a two-word phrase consisting of an adjective and a noun, means either "an amount of time"—as in "Spend some time daily in CLE"—or, when used as the object of a preposition, "at a particular time"—as in "At some time soon, the trial will begin."

Sometime, on the other hand, is a one-word adverb meaning "an indefinite or a future time," as in "Write to me sometime" or "Drop by to see me sometime."

Sometime and *some time* are easily distinguished by simply omitting the expression from the sentence and observing the effect upon the meaning. If there is no noticeable change, no loss in meaning, as in "The manuscript is due (*sometime*) in the near future," *sometime* is the correct word. But if the meaning is affected, if the sense of the sentence requires the omitted expression, then the two-word *some time* must be used; for example, "Next week the judge will put *some time* aside to review the matter."

The same distinctions regarding *sometime* and *some time* apply to *someday* and *some day:* "We hope counsel will choose *some day* agreeable to everyone." "They expect to try the case *someday.*"

INTERROGATORY

Would you please comment on the sentence "Some of those arrested included government agents"?

Since *include* has a meaning of "some," *some* and *included* do not belong in the same sentence. Either delete *some of,* so that the sentence will read "Those arrested included government agents," or substitute *were* for *included:* "Some of those arrested were government agents."

100 PROOF

Although most dictionaries list *prove* as having two past participles, *proved* and *proven, proved* is the form generally preferred: "He has proved his point." "The defendant has been proved guilty."

Proven was originally a Scottish word used in legal parlance. It has been fighting an uphill battle for general recognition, but its progress is slow. Diehards who object to its intrusion into the English language brand *proven* an impropriety, and never use it. Some reputable writers, on the other hand, accept it as an attributive adjective before a noun: a proven success, a proven point. Still others, a smaller group, sanction *proven* in any position if it will enhance the cadence of the sentence: "It has proven to be a happy event."

Since *proven* has received limited acceptance only, it is wise, at least in formal writing, to use it solely as a direct modifier of nouns and to use *proved* when a verb is called for. Oddly enough, lawyers seem to prefer the word *proven,* which may prove a point.

WHO USES "WHOM"?

Whether to use *who* or *whom* to begin a question is sometimes clouded by the presence of an "interrupter," an expression such as *do you think, do you suppose, do you believe.*

Consider the following example: "Who (Whom) do you think will win the election?" The proximity of the interrogative pronoun (who, whom) to the nominative *you* in the interrupter (do you think) leads some people to the objective case *whom.* They do not lack company, for this kind of misconstruction is so common that some authorities now consider it acceptable English. Though the use of *whom,* except after a preposition (with whom) is fast disappearing, on a formal level, nonetheless, the grammatical distinctions between *who* and *whom* are still generally observed. Therefore, "Whom do you think will win the election?" in formal usage, at least, is incorrect, even though it sounds right.

The simplest way to decide between *who* and *whom* is to imagine the sentence without the interrupter. For instance, without *do you think* the example would read "Who will win the election?" It is unlikely that anyone would say or write "Whom will win the election?"

However, no one expects to hear telephone operators relinquish their familiar "Whom shall I say is calling?" That phraseology has Long Distance behind it.

IT'S A COMMA THING

When a word belongs equally to two or more preceding phrases, a comma should be placed before that word. This rule is more easily understood when illustrated.

Consider these sentences: "The statute of limitations was his primary, really his only defense." "The Court just learned about, and certainly had not previously known of the number of bail skips." Both sentences require a second comma to tie the first phrase to the concluding word. With this comma the sentences read: "The statute of limitations was his primary, really his only, defense." "The court just learned about, and certainly had not previously known of, the number of bail skips." The added punctuation rids the sentences of any ambiguity, tying *primary* and *only* to *defense*, in the first sentence, and *learned about* and *known of* to *the number* in the second.

WHEN THE PAST IS PRESENT

Ordinarily the past tense lives up to its name. It expresses actions that occurred in the past, as in this simple sentence: "Walter filed the writ yesterday."

With complex sentences, however—those having both an independent and a dependent clause—a question that sometimes arises is what tense belongs in a dependent clause when it follows a past-tense verb in an independent clause. The rule is that the verb should normally be in the past tense, not the present: "The prisoner said his name was Percy Walton and that he *lived* (not *lives*) in Milltown." The fact that the prisoner still lives there is beside the point. Consider some others: "The defendant wondered aloud whether the law *was* (not *is*) just." "The Court Administrator explained what the new rules *meant* (not *mean*)."

When a permanently true fact, however, one as true in the past as in the present, is expressed in a dependent clause, this rule is not commonly applied. Here, even though the verb in the independent clause is in the past tense, the verb in the dependent clause is in the present: "He *reminded* the pupils that water *freezes* (not *froze*) at 32° F." "The early navigators *proved* that the earth *is* (not *was*) round." But since the "permanent-truth rule" applies to dependent clauses only, a sentence with just one verb, even though it expresses a timeless truth, will not qualify: "Runnymede *was* (not *is*) the birthplace of the Magna Carta." "George Washington *was* (not *is*) the father of our country."

According to a second convention, in indirect discourse—those quotations that summarize a speaker's words—a present tense in the direct quotation is converted to a past tense in the indirect statement. To say it in another way, when someone is being quoted indirectly, a past tense form is required.

Direct quotation: Mr. Torrey said, "We are mailing our catalog today."

Indirect quotation: Mr. Torrey said that we *were* mailing (not we *are* mailing) our catalog today.

Punctuation extra: Indirect discourse, as in *The Dean said that it should be sent along,* is not enclosed in quotation marks. Therefore, avoid this hodgepodge: *The Dean said that "It should be sent along."*

ADVERBS THAT JINGLE, JANGLE

Two adverbs ending in *ly* should not be written close together unless they modify the same verb, as in "The thought was accurately and adequately expressed." As a matter of style, repetitive lilting sounds are best avoided. For example, in "It is done quickly, generally," a separation would have been better—"Generally, it is done quickly." But the sentence would sound better still if only one adverb ending in *ly* were used: "In general, it is done quickly."

Careful writers write for the ear rather than the eye.

Is it proper to use the word *overly*?

It is an acceptable word, used by many careful writers. But ordinarily the prefix *over* is the better choice. Phrases such as *overly enthusiastic* and *overly supplied* sound starchy. *Overenthusiastic* and *oversupplied,* by comparison, are simpler and more economical.

49

A PERCENTAGE BEATS NOTHING

In "He is right a percentage of the time, but not all the time," *percentage* is used colloquially to mean "a part"—"He is right *a part* (or *some*) of the time." In "There is no percentage in writing briefs all day," *percentage* again is used colloquially, this time to mean "profit or advantage." On a formal level, however, *percentage* means "a portion of the whole" and is acceptably used only if accompanied by a qualifying adjective, such as *large* or *small*—"A *large* (or *small*) percentage of those expected arrived."

Although *percentage* and *per cent* now have similar meanings, only *per cent* is customarily used after numerals. Writers disagree, however, on how to express percentages. Some spell out the number and follow it by *percent*, "fifty percent"; others prefer a figure and a symbol, 50%. Still others differ only in that they spell *percent* as two words—"fifty *per cent*." But most writers use numerals followed by the two-word *per cent*, rejecting both the symbol, %, and the one-word *percent*: "The rate of interest is now 8 per cent." This last is the style generally used in formal writing.

If an *of* phrase follows *per cent* or *percentage*, the number of the verb should agree with the number of the object of the preposition. To illustrate: "Ten per cent of the judiciary *is* here" (an *of* phrase with the singular *judiciary* as the object of the preposition); "Ten per cent of the lawyers *are* here" (the object of the *of* phrase, *lawyers*, is plural).

Addendum: Per cent, an abbreviation of the Latin *per centum*, has been anglicized and no longer requires a period. Fractions should be written as follows: 8.5 per cent; 5.25 percent; one half of 1 per cent.

IF YOU ONLY KNEW

Modifiers are words, phrases, or clauses that restrict or qualify a word or group of words. Their function is to make meanings clearer, more precise, and more descriptive than they otherwise would be. Normally modifiers should be placed as close as possible to whatever words they modify—directly before them, if possible. If improperly placed, they can obscure or even alter the meaning of a sentence.

In the following examples the meaning changes as the word *only* assumes a different position in each succeeding sentence. The need to place modifiers carefully is thus underscored.

1. He thought that he would study *only* Latin.
   [He would study no other language.]
2. He thought that he would *only* study Latin.
   [He would study Latin, not teach it.]
3. He thought that he *only* would study Latin.
   [He would study Latin, but not master it.]
4. He thought that *only* he would study Latin.
   [No one else would study Latin.]
5. He thought *only* that he would study Latin.
   [He thought about nothing else.]
6. He *only* thought that he would study Latin.
   [He thought about it, but did nothing.]
7. *Only* he thought that he would study Latin.
   [He was the only one who thought so.]

Some of the examples, of course, may be interpreted differently. The point, however, is that unless modifiers are properly placed, sentences might suggest a variety of meanings.

PLACE THE BLAME ON MAME

"When he blamed it on me, I was so aggravated I gasped." Many grammarians might justifiably criticize the use of *aggravated* and *blamed* in that sentence.

Aggravate pertains to conditions. One may aggravate—worsen—an existing condition, but not aggravate a person. *Blame* is properly placed on a person but not on a condition.

In everyday parlance, *aggravate* is used to mean "to annoy" or "to irritate," as in "Counsel's tardiness aggravated the judge." But in any writing in which greater precision is exercised, the traditional sense of *aggravate*, "to worsen" or "to intensify," should be observed: "Neglect aggravated the plaintiff's wounds."

Blame takes the accompanying preposition *for:* "Counsel blamed Mr. Blanton *for* the accident." In informal usage, *on* is frequently found: "Counsel blamed the accident *on* Mr. Blanton."

Caution: The expression *blame on* has the approval of some respected writers. Hence it is not to be criticized—but it need not be used either.

Is there any rule that governs the use of *in* and *into* in idioms?

None that I know of. There is no rational explanation, for instance, why *put* may take either *in* or *into*, but *place* only *in:* "We put the pencil *in* (or *into*) its holder," but "We placed the pencil *in* (not *into*) its holder."

IT'S ABOUT TIME!

Perhaps the most frequently used abbreviations are A.M. and P.M. They are, of course, simple indicators of time and should cause no problems: "He arrived at 9 A.M. and left at 1:15 P.M."

A few alarms, however, may be sounded. For one thing, when these abbreviations are used, the hour should not be spelled out (not *nine* A.M.) and the word *o'clock* should be omitted (not 9 A.M. *o'clock*). On the other hand, if A.M. and P.M. are themselves omitted, the hour should be both spelled out and followed by *o'clock:* "Court will convene at nine o'clock" (not 9 *o'clock*).

The expression "10 A.M. yesterday morning" is redundant. Since A.M. and *morning* mean the same thing, one of them does not belong. The time should be stated as "10 A.M. yesterday" or "ten o'clock yesterday morning."

Noon is best given as 12 noon, not 12 M (meridies); midnight as 12 midnight or just midnight, not the confusing 12 P.M.

If only the hour is stated without reference to minutes, no colon or zeros are necessary—10 A.M. rather than 10:00 A.M. In print, A.M. and P.M. are usually set in small capitals, as in this sentence; but in typescript, where the choice is between capital and lowercase letters, the lowercase *a.m.* and *p.m.* are preferred. Regardless of the style selected, no space should appear between the letters.

CAN WORDS BE SEEDED?

Only one verb in the English language ends in "sede" —*supersede;* three end in "ceed"—*exceed, succeed,* and *proceed;* and all the others in "cede"—*secede, precede, concede,* and so forth. The word in this grouping most frequently misspelled is *supersede.* Its internal sibilant, it should be noted, is *s*, not *c*.

FRACTURED FRACTIONS

A *unit modifier* is generally defined as two words brought together by a hyphen to form a one-thought modifier. Common examples are a *two-part* book, a *long-term* loan, and a *ten-day* trip. If, however, the modifying words and their nouns are readily understood without hyphens, no hyphenation is required—*real estate* tax, *common law* principle.

Fractions, when expressed in words, are governed by the same rule of hyphenation applicable to all other unit modifiers. That is, when used as adjectives, they are hyphened—a *one-third* part, a *two-thirds* majority. But when used as nouns—*one third* of the book, *two thirds* of the jurors—they are written open.

The key to all this lies in simply remembering not to hyphenate when a fraction is followed by an *of* phrase: "A two-thirds vote wins, but two thirds *of the vote* is hard to come by."

What is the rule for forming the plural of *cupful*, *spoonful*, and other such words?

These words form their plural by adding *s* at the end: three *cupfuls* of coffee (one cup filled three times). If three cups were filled, cups would be pluralized and *full* written separately: three cups full of coffee (three separate cups). All such words are handled similarly.

LET'S REASON IT OUT

The sentence "The reason the case was continued was because a juryman fell ill" says the same thing twice. Since *because* means "for the reason that," in effect the sentence says, "The reason the case was continued was for the reason that a juryman fell ill." A sentence cannot justifiably accommodate both *reason* and *because;* one word must go.

There are two ways to handle such a construction. The first is to begin the sentence with *the reason was* and follow it either with a noun clause introduced by *that,* as in "The reason was *that* the dean refused to see him," or with a noun alone: "The reason was the dean's *refusal* to see him." The *that* clause is ordinarily used.

The second way is to omit *the reason was* and simply use *because*. Sentences such as "The reason we feel bad is because he's gone" survive as well without the introductory phrase. In fact, without it—"We feel bad because he's gone"—the sentence gains in brevity and in force.

Another similar expression, *the reason why,* though just as redundant as *the reason is because,* is nevertheless considered acceptable idiom. Whether to use the phrase at all, however, is another matter. In some instances, *why* is unnecessary; in others, *the reason.* For example, in "The reason why the controller likes his job is the salary he gets," *why* is superfluous: "The reason the controller likes his job. . . ." The message in "I know the reason why he left" is just as clear without *the reason:* "I know why he left."

An entirely different construction with *reason why* uses *reason* as a verb. Lord Tennyson immortalized that use in his "Charge of the Light Brigade": "Theirs not *to reason why,/*Theirs but to do and die."

55

TWICE POSSESSIVE

The double possessive consists of an *of* phrase followed by a possessive noun or pronoun (a guest *of* Mr. Smith's). Technically called a double genitive, the construction is used to distinguish a particular possession from among an undifferentiated group of related possessions, all belonging to one owner. A common example might be "That remark of the moderator's caused . . . ," in which a specific remark is being singled out for discussion.

To determine whether a reference requires a double possessive, *among* should be substituted for *of* and the phrase completed. If the sentence reads sensibly, a double possessive form is required. For example, "Stuart is a friend of my brother's" implies that my brother has other friends—it may be reworded "Stuart is a friend among my brother's friends." But "Stuart is a friend of my brother" does not carry any such implications. Or again, the double possessive is called for in "Lauren Rose is a regular pupil of Miss Harriet's" (rather than "of Miss Harriet") because Lauren Rose is just one of a number of pupils who Miss Harriet teaches.

If what is possessed is not restricted to a specific number, the *among* test will fail. In the following examples, since *among* cannot sensibly replace *of*, a double possessive form is out of order: The *remarks* of the *moderator* (not *moderator's*) caused . . . The *works* of *Sir Walter Scott* (not *Scott's*) were . . . The *investments* of his *uncle* (not *uncle's*) seemed. . . .

In some instances a sentence that needs an *'s* changes meaning when the *'s* is omitted. For example, "Here is a picture of the President's" means a picture belonging to the President, but "Here is a picture of the President" refers to a likeness of the President. And what if the sentence were to read "Here is the President's picture"? Out of context the sense is entirely up to the reader.

LEAVE IT AND LET IT BE

Does it matter whether you *leave him alone* or *let him alone* as long as you go away? Not really. The phrases are equally acceptable, even in formal writing, and the message they convey, certainly in everyday parlance, is the same.

Generally speaking, *leave* means "to go away from"; *let,* "to permit or to allow." But when they are accompanied by *alone,* the key word, the two become interchangeable. Although this synonymity has not always existed, the passage of time has so molded common usage that *leave alone* has come to mean "permit to remain in solitude." Dictionaries now attribute to *leave alone* the same sense conveyed by *let alone.*

Yet, despite the consensus, some careful writers, on the premise that accepted usage is not necessarily compatible with good usage, differentiate those phrases. They use *let me alone* for "don't bother me" and *leave me alone* to mean "get going."

In other idioms, especially when the intended meaning is "to permit," only *let* is standard—"Let it be," not "Leave it be."

An article on correlative conjunctions—*either . . . or, neither . . . nor*—spoke of a balancing of two elements. Should these conjunctions be used with only two elements?

No, although in most instances only two elements are involved. Remember, "Neither snow, nor rain, nor heat, nor gloom of night stays. . . ." Good grammar.

TITLE SEARCH

When an article—*a, an, the*—is the first word in a title of a publication, it should be omitted if it follows a possessive noun or pronoun. The reason: In that context the article sounds awkward and distorts the syntax.

Consider "To be published soon is Goldberg's *A Lawyer's Guide to Commercial Arbitration*" or "His *The Basic Problems of Evidence* will be distributed soon." In these examples, the omission of the article, changing the titles so that the sentences read "Goldberg's *Lawyer's Guide to Commercial Arbitration*" and "His *Basic Problems of Evidence*," improves cadence; and the titles naturally adjust to fit the syntax.

A full title may of course be cited; but when it is, the sentence should be cast so that a possessive does not adjoin the article. The first example, for instance, could read: "To be published soon is Goldberg's new book, *A Lawyer's Guide to Commercial Arbitration*."

A companion concern is the use of a preposition between the name of an author and the title of his book. Ordinarily the title should not be placed after a preposition, but should instead be in apposition to a noun. Consider "Colson's book on *Capital Gains and Losses* discusses the computation of tax." The sentence should read either: "Colson's book, *Capital Gains and Losses*, discusses . . ." —without the preposition *on* and with the appositional title encased in commas—or appear with the title lower-cased and thus treated as the subject: "Colson's book on capital gains and losses discusses. . . ."

This rule applies as well to chapter headings. For instance, the sentence "The chapter on 'Hearsay' contains a full analysis" might be reworded: "Chapter Seven,

'Hearsay,' contains . . ." or "The chapter on hearsay contains. . . ."

In sum: Watch out (1) for an introductory article in the title of a book preceded by a possessive and (2) for a preposition between an author's name and the title of a book or between a chapter and its heading. Omit the article in the one and the preposition in the other.

THE FIRST AND THE LAST

Although *firstly* properly begins a numerical sequence, and some respected writers do use it, nonetheless it is better to use *first*. *Firstly* sounds pretentious, and says no more than *first*.

Writers who begin with *firstly* naturally continue with *secondly, thirdly,* and so forth. And theirs is probably the style most commonly followed. The simplest, most concise numerical order, however, is *first, second, third,* and so on. This kind of series, furthermore, avoids an awkward *sixteenthly,* for example, if the numbers run that high.

By the way: (1) The wordy expression *first of all* serves no purpose; *first* says it all. (2) In current English, when *first* is written next to a cardinal number, *first* precedes: "The first 15 applicants are here." Although a number smaller than four, according to some stylists, may either precede or follow *first*—"The three first applicants will be hired"—the better practice is to place *first* before the number: "The first three applicants. . . ." (3) As with *first, last* usually precedes a cardinal number: "The last two provisions have been misinterpreted." This, in spite of Coleridge's "the fifty or sixty last years of her life."

OF THEE I SPEAK

The use of the preposition *of* after *all* or *both*—*all of* the books, *both of* the books—is optional, but in formal writing *of* is preferably omitted. Consider these illustrations: "All of the court's rules have been changed" and "Both of the codes will soon be published." In the examples, *of* is unnecessary and can be deleted without affecting the meaning. In fact, the omission reduces wordage and to that extent improves the sentences: "All the court's rules have been changed." "Both the codes will soon be published." Some writers, nevertheless, when they feel that an *of* enhances sentence rhythm, exercise the option and use it.

When a pronoun is involved, however, an *of* after *all* or *both* is no longer optional; it is required: "*All* (or *Both*) *of* them will arrive shortly."

Of course: Of has a way of slipping into phrases where it does not belong, for example, "He stepped *off of* the plane" and "The boat docked *alongside of* the pier." And also note that "getting a loan *off of* (instead of *from*) the treasurer" is an illiteracy.

A MATTER OF PRINCIPLE

The problem with homonyms, words that sound alike but are spelled differently, is that sometimes their spellings are confused. One such pair is *principal* and *principle*.

One way to keep them separate is to remember that when *principal* means "main or chief" it is an adjective and that the *a* in adjective is repeated in *principal*. For example, in "Thompson is the principal witness," *principal* is an adjective; ergo *a* in *principal*. When used as a noun, *principal* usually means "a leader or governing head": "Mr. Simpson is the principal of the Barnaby High School." In the financial world, *principal* designates (1) the main body, or capital, of an estate, (2) an invested capital that bears interest, or (3) a sum owed as a debt.

Principle, meaning "a governing rule or truth" or "a standard of conduct," is always a noun: "The *principle* of *respondeat superior* is well entrenched." A helpful memory aid is to think of *rule* and to associate the final *e* of *rule* with the final *e* of *principle*.

SUFFICIENT UNTO THE DAY

Idiom requires that the adverb *sufficiently* be followed either by the infinitive *to*, as in "Counsel was sufficiently engaging to charm the jury," or by the preposition *for*, as in "He was sufficiently prepared for any contingency," but not by *as, that,* or *so that.*

For example, in "Some young lawyers are sufficiently naive as to believe whatever a client says," the *as* should be deleted—*sufficiently naive to believe.* In "The members considered him sufficiently well versed that they named him counselor," a proper revision would be *considered him sufficiently well versed to name him counselor.* "The stamina of young lawyers is sufficiently enduring so that they can work long hours" might be reworded *sufficiently enduring for them to work long hours.* The idiomatic strictures governing *sufficiently* are narrow, but in formal writing they should be observed.

Afterthought: Before using the adjective *sufficient,* it is wise to see whether *enough,* a shorter and less pretentious word, may suitably serve. If it does, it might well be the better choice.

61

A CREDIBILITY GAP

Although a sentence such as "It is an *incredulous* (instead of *incredible*) situation" is sometimes heard, it is incorrect. *Incredible* and *incredulous*, despite their common root, the Latin *credere*, "to believe," have different meanings and are therefore not interchangeable.

Credulous means "willing to believe." It refers only to people and implies an overtrustful, simple-minded belief —a willingness to believe too easily: "A person so credulous will not make a good counselor."

Credible, a word more commonly used, means "believable." Like *credulous*, it refers to people, but it applies also to testimony, documents, and statements: "The jury found the testimony credible." "The credibility of the statement was not an issue."

Creditable, which means "worthy of belief or praise," has developed a meaning of "suitable or acceptable." In this sense it sometimes serves as a neutral word, one like *interesting* or *adequate*—neither complimentary nor disparaging: "His summation of the case was creditable." When praise is intended, *creditable* is normally accompanied by an inflating adverb: "His summation of the case was *highly* creditable."

What rules govern the use of *ago?*

I am not aware of any rule, but I offer an alert. Because both *since* and *ago* refer to the past, they should not accompany each other. A qualifying clause after *ago* should start with *that*, and not *since:* "It was over three years ago, according to my memory, *that* (not *since*) we tried such a case."

ADOPTING THE ADAPTABLE

The reason behind the misuse of *adopt* and *adapt* may be misspelling—their spellings differ by only one vowel. Confusion is compounded when they appear in the same context, as in "The board, after adopting the rules, adapted the program to them."

Adapt means "to make suitable or to adjust to meet requirements": "The juveniles failed to adapt themselves to their confinement." *Adopt* means "to take as one's own or to accept formally," as in "The executor adopted his idea." An easy way to distinguish the two words is to remember that *adapt* includes *apt,* meaning "fit or suited to the purpose," which is what one who adapts does— makes fit or suitable.

Adopt is always followed by a direct object: "We adopted the formula." "The Committee unanimously adopted the rules." *Adapt,* on the other hand, although it sometimes takes a direct object—"The firm adapted the space to its current needs"—is usually employed intransitively and followed by *to, for,* or *from:* "Understanding counsel adapts himself *to* the needs of his clients"; "The spare office will be adapted *for* storage"; "The theory of the case was adapted *from* sections of the Restatement."

THINK NEGATIVELY

It goes without saying that the correlative conjunction *neither* should be followed by *nor,* not *or:* "He is *neither* tall *nor* short." But what stumps some people, at least momentarily, is whether to use *nor* or *or* after other negative words. Take, for example, "Several of the families had no food *or/nor* money with which to buy it." Which word does correct usage require, *or* or *nor?* Or are both proper in this context?

Generally if the effect of the first negative word, *no* in this instance, runs into, or is felt by, the second part of the sentence, then *or* should be used. In such a case, no change takes place in the sentence structure, and the same negative applies to each part. Hence in the example, *or* would be called for, since the sentence in effect reads "*no* food and *no* money with which to buy it." Other examples: "They need *never* dance *or* sing *or* otherwise play together" could be restated as "*never* dance, *never* sing, *never* play," and "The speaker said *nothing* that was particularly stimulating *or* that was particularly informative," meaning "*nothing* that was particularly stimulating, *nothing* that was particularly informative."

If, on the other hand, the negative is fenced in, that is, its effect does not carry over to the second part of the sentence, then *nor* is required: "We have written *nothing* about his background, *nor* do we ever mention it" or "He received *no* remuneration for his efforts, *nor* was he commended. *Or* would not serve in either example because the negatives, *nothing* and *no*, do not apply to the next part of the sentences—"*nothing* do we ever mention it" and "*no* was he commended" make no sense. The effect of the initial negative clearly has not carried through.

All this does not mean, however, that the "rules" are not at times intentionally overlooked to achieve emphasis. Certainly the *nor* in "We will not beg *nor* steal" adds a sense of assertion and a stress that would be lacking if *or* were used. In these situations, using *nor* to emphasize the second negative is accepted practice.

A POSSESSIVE FAMILY

Although "This is a painting of Renoir's" is grammatically correct, "This is the Renoir's house" is not. The apostrophe is misplaced in the second example. A singular proper noun, when preceded by *the,* becomes a proper adjective and therefore takes no apostrophe—*the Renoir house.* A plural proper noun is made possessive by simply adding an apostrophe—*the Renoirs' house.*

The plurals of both proper and common nouns are formed in the same way—by adding *es* to nouns that end in *s* and just *s* to those that do not: loss, losses; gain, gains; Giles, Gileses; Renoir, Renoirs. Likewise, their possessive cases are formed in the same way—that is, by adding *'s* either to a singular noun (Ginny*'s* brief) or to a plural noun not ending in *s* (men*'s* lounge) and by adding just an apostrophe to a plural noun ending in *s* (ladies*'* day).

A common error, as pointed out in the first paragraph, is putting a family name in the possessive singular when a plural is required. Such mistakes are particularly prevalent with names like Bush, Thomas, or Lopez, names ending in a sibilant. These errors are avoided if the names are first pluralized and then made possessive: *Bushes', Thomases',* and *Lopezes'.*

A GUARANTEE MAKES IT SAFE

The puzzlement about which of the two spellings *guarantee* and *guaranty* is appropriate is easily solved. *Guarantee* may be used in any context and may safely serve as both a verb and a noun: "We guarantee our product, and we put our guarantee in writing."

Although *guaranty*, too, has served in both capacities—as a verb and as a noun—established business usage has virtually eliminated any verbal function. The contract that *guarantees* the quality of service of a product is, in the world of commerce, the *guaranty*. But apart from this specialized business use, *guaranty* and *guarantee*, as previously pointed out, are interchangeable as nouns. Which term to use, therefore, is simply a matter of personal preference: "The *guaranty* (or *guarantee*) will expire in two months."

FLIM-FLAMMABLE

Flammable might be considered something of a neologism—a new word or expression. Unknown in the eighteenth century, it is today probably the word most frequently used to mean "capable of being set on fire."

The word was originated by fire underwriters who were concerned that *inflammable*, the usual sign of warning on petroleum trucks, might be thought to mean "nonburnable." Since the prefix *in*, meaning "not," converts many words into a negative form—*insecure, inexcusable, indefinite*, for example—*inflammable* could be dangerously confusing. *Flammable* was coined to remove all doubt.

Flammable is now accepted even in formal English as a synonym of *inflammable*. Nonetheless, only *inflammable* may be appropriately used in one particular context—when considering a person's behavior. In "He has an inflammable temperament," *flammable* would be unsuitable.

The antonym of both *flammable* and *inflammable* is *nonflammable*.

DOES JR. HAVE SENIORITY?

Personal names should be completely spelled out in formal writing. The name Richard Allen, for example, should not be abbreviated Rich. Allen; Benjamin West, Benj. West; or Samuel Clemens, Sam'l Clemens, even if the person himself habitually signs his name that way.

If *Junior* or *Senior* is part of a person's name, custom requires that *Jr.* or *Sr.* accompany the name when it is used in full—that is, when a surname follows either the given name or the person's initials: "Answers to Interrogatories were received on Monday from Mr. Edwin M. Irish, Jr., and Mrs. H. R. Hawthorne, Sr." When the last name, however, is used without a given name or initials, the *Jr.* or *Sr.* is omitted: "But the Answers of both Mr. Irish and Mrs. Hawthorne were incomplete."

Although opinion on the subject is divided, a comma should preferably be placed both before *Jr.* and *Sr.* and, unless ending a sentence, immediately after them: "Thomas R. Howell, Jr., is the new dean." According to most stylebooks, if two family members who are not father and son share the identical name, the designation *II* or *2d* should be used in place of *Jr.* to indicate the second bearer. If a Roman numeral is used, no comma follows the name: "Thomas R. Howell II is the new dean." But with ordinal numbers (2nd or 2d, 3rd or 3d), whether to use commas is a matter of personal preference: "Thomas R. Howell, 2d, is the new dean."

INTERROGATORY

You use the word *Appendixes*. What happened to *Appendices?*

It was stored in a file marked Archaic. Instead of Latin plurals, current usage prefers English plurals in words like *appendixes, indexes, memorandums,* and *formulas.*

A PREPOSITIONAL PROPOSITION

An earnest believer in the facetious statement "A preposition is an improper word to end a sentence with" removes from his grammatical resources a rich mine of idiomatic expressions. The chestnut is not untrue; it is simply not the whole truth.

No one disputes the formal rule that in normal word order a preposition should be placed before the word it governs. And no one denies that a sentence should not end with an awkward or a superfluous preposition, as in "Where is he at?" or "Where shall I deliver it to?" But good reason exists to quarrel with the viewpoint that a sentence may never end with a preposition.

As a matter of writing style, prepositions, especially on a formal level, are normally interred within a sentence to make certain they do not rise up at the end. But in some instances an idiom must be used or else precise meaning, and flavor, suffers; and many idioms do end in prepositions. Take, for example, "After her eviction, the widow had no one to turn to," or "This is the whip he beat her with," or "What should we talk about?" In each example, the sentence unfolds according to a natural word order that places the preposition at the end, where, incidentally, it contributes a certain vigor. If good taste and common sense are not violated, sentences so constructed should not be criticized.

Some prepositions, when relocated, dully grind a sentence to a halt. Consider "Handed the jury list, counsel immediately looked it over," in which a clear message ends on a normal upbeat, versus "Handed the jury list, counsel immediately looked over it." In addition to the several possible imprecise meanings, the sentence ends awkwardly and limply.

Yet many challenge this thinking and insist that any sentence ending in a preposition is *ipso facto* unacceptable. They would invert the previous examples: "After her eviction, the widow had no one to whom to turn," "This is the whip with which he beat her," and "About what should we talk?" All grammatically proper, but stilted and unnatural.

Authorities, generally, believe that ending a sentence with a preposition, if idiom or rhythm demands it, is proper. Winston Churchill, chided for doing just that, reportedly answered: "I agree. It is a practice up with which I cannot put." When it came to precise diction, the Prime Minister was a man you could depend on.

COME TO YOUR CONSENSUS

Everyone agrees that there is a consensus if everyone agrees. But everyone does not agree on how the word *consensus* should be used or even how it should be spelled.

Consensus is misused if preceded by *general*—"The general consensus was to boycott"—or if followed by *of opinion*—"The board sought a consensus of opinion." Since *consensus* denotes "a general agreement or collective opinion," neither the preceding *general* nor the following *of opinion* is necessary. In fact, either addition makes for redundancy.

The misspelling, usually "concensus," may reflect a belief that the word has something to do with a census. Actually, *consensus* is related to *sense*, with the prefix *con-* ("together") enlarging the meaning to a shared feeling or a common sense.

NOW THAT'S ITALICS!

Italic type, so named because it was invented by Italians, is reserved for setting off distinctive words or phrases. The guidelines that determine what is or is not distinctive have become standardized over the years.

The most common use of italics is to indicate the titles of books, newspapers, magazines, and plays, as well as the names of ships, trains, and airplanes. They are also used to indicate foreign words and phrases not yet accepted into the English language—"He was given *carte blanche*"; also letters of the alphabet—"There are two *t*'s"; and words used as words rather than for meaning—"in *regrettable*." Employing italics solely for emphasis, however, is generally frowned upon.

An author's name preceding a book title should not be italicized—"The best book on the subject is by Earl Colson, *Capital Gains and Losses*"—nor should a *the* that begins a title when the syntax requires a *the* anyway—"He reads the *New York Times*," not "He reads *The New York Times*."

In manuscript or typescript, italics are indicated by underlining.

INTERROGATORY

An article condemned the use of unnecessary words. But what is unnecessary? Certainly repetition, since it adds emphasis, is not useless.

No argument with emphasis or with using repetition to achieve it. Extraneous verbiage, however, like an overgrown garden, needs weeding: Sierra Nevada Desert, 9 p.m. tonight, Mt. Fujiama, recur again, Jewish rabbi, two twins, pizza pie. All are filled with superfluity.

BARELY UNDERSTOOD

Hardly, scarcely, and *barely,* although not true negatives, possess such a negative quality that they require the same treatment as true negatives. If used with another negative, the illogical "double negative" error results.

Run-of-the-mill double negatives that include *hardly, scarcely,* or *barely*—"The expert witness said he could not *hardly* read the handwriting" or "The client had *scarcely* no money left"—pose no problems. They are patently unacceptable and hence can be easily avoided by careful writers.

Other pitfalls are perhaps less obvious. Take, for example, "The defendants do not have a single witness or hardly any evidence." *Hardly,* because of its inherently negative meaning, must negate its own affirmative verb. Without one, the preceding *not* carries through so that in effect *not* and *hardly* are combined. Restated, the sentence would read, "The defendants do not have a single witness *and have hardly* any evidence." Consider another: "Without hardly a shred of evidence, counsel proved his case." The coupling of *without* and *hardly,* two words with a negative force, is objectionable. To correct the example, either *with* should replace *without* —"*With hardly* a shred of evidence"—or *without* should remain and *hardly* be deleted—"*Without* a shred of evidence."

An even more common error is the use of *than* after these three adverbs instead of *when.* "Hardly had the crucial moment passed *than* another set in" is idiomatically incorrect, as is "The jury had barely announced its verdict *than* a witness fainted." In both these instances, *when* is required. Perhaps the misuse of *than* for *when* is erroneously patterned after *no sooner,* a phrase correctly followed by *than* because *sooner* is a comparative

71

form. Example: "The bailiff had *no sooner* sat down *than* the defendant leaped at him." But if *hardly* were used, the sentence would need changing to read, "The bailiff had *hardly* sat down *when* the defendant leaped at him."

THE MARK OF POSSESSION

When joint owners conduct a business under both their names, only the last name needs an apostrophe: Lord and Taylor's department store; Johnson & Johnson's bandages. When ownership is separately held by two or more persons or organizations, each name receives its own apostrophe: Wright's and Sansom's positions; mortgagors' and mortgagees' signatures; the title company's and their customers' records.

A compound noun is made possessive by adding an apostrophe to its last element: the brother-in-law's objection; the editor in chief's blue pencil; someone else's idea. The same rule applies to plural compounds; the apostrophe is placed at the end: the brothers-in-law's objection. Caution must be used, however, to ensure that the first element is pluralized before an apostrophe is added to the last: the two brothers-in-law's objections, not the two brother-in-laws' objections, mistakenly pluralizing *law*.

When a noun that would become possessive in the customary way is followed by a nonessential appositive, possession is shown by the appositive and not by the noun: "It was Judge Jackson, the senior *judge's*, decision." Even such designations as *Jr.*, *Sr.*, *2d.*, and *II* follow this rule: John D. Rockefeller, *Jr.'s*, wealth. But in all these cases, an *of* phrase usually serves better than an apostrophe: the decision of Judge Jackson, the senior judge; the wealth of John D. Rockefeller, Jr.

A SUBSTITUTE CAN BE REPLACED

Replace and *substitute* are not synonyms. *Replace* means "to take the place of"; *substitute* means "to put in place of." If a red book is removed and a blue book put in its place, the blue book is substituted for the red, and the red is replaced by the blue. But since the distinction between these words is nebulous and of little practical effect, they ordinarily may be freely interchanged if the preposition each takes goes along with it.

Idiomatically, *replace* is followed by *by* and *substitute* by *for*. Therefore, in "The Board of Governors was substituted last year by a seven-member *ad hoc* Grievance Committee," *substituted* should be changed to *replaced* or the sentence reversed: "A seven-member *ad hoc* Grievance Committee was substituted last year *for* the Board of Governors." One more: "The substitution of Weyl's settlement agreement by Kraus's was unwise" needs changing to "The substitution of Weyl's settlement agreement *for* Kraus's was unwise." To repeat: The key to the proper use of *substitute* and *replace* lies in the prepositions they take—substitute *for;* replace *by.*

INTERROGATORY

Which is the preferred spelling: *adviser* or *advisor?*

Both spellings are acceptable and used by respected writers, although the *-er* form is predominant. Those who tend toward this form should be consistent when a similar choice exists with other nouns. However, most nouns do not offer an alternative. *Assessor, depositor, counselor, interrogator,* and *devisor,* for example, have no other accepted spelling. And note that only *advisory* is proper, even though the noun may be spelled *adviser.*

IS IT WISE TO PLURALIZE?

Should Shakespeare have said "Cowards die many times before their *death*" or "before their *deaths*"? Is it right to say "The teacher knew all the students by their first *name*" or "by their first *names*"? Or is it simply a matter of personal preference?

A basic rule governing plurals generally is that the number in a sentence should be kept the same throughout. For instance, in "Collect *the books*, rebind *each one*, and then store *them* by color," the middle clause should be changed to "*rebind them*," making all three objects plural: collect *books*, rebind *them*, store *them*.

But when a plural possessive—*their, our, your*—modifies a noun, it is not always clear whether the noun should be singular or plural. In some cases a writer must be led solely by his own judgment. For example, it is correct to say either "Many people expressed their *opinion* on the subject" or "their *opinions* on the subject," or "We will analyze the statements according to their *meaning*" or "their *meanings*."

The English language, in this matter of nouns modified by plural possessives, is in a state of flux; no firm rule applies in every case. Writers must often be their own guides, and they should not be faulted whatever their decision.

It is possible, however, to formulate a general rule: When the noun following a plural possessive is concrete, a plural noun is required; when it is abstract—that is, when it represents a shared feeling or emotion—a singular noun is better; and when it hovers a little over each side, it becomes a writer's choice. To illustrate: "The two senators from Ohio changed their *seats*" (concrete, plural); "The two senators from Ohio changed their *ideology*" (abstract, singular); "The two senators from Ohio changed their *mind* (or *minds*)" (in between, take your pick).

A BALANCED LOAN

Two ordinary financial terms are *loan* and *balance*. In banking and bookkeeping contexts, these words have specific meanings—a *balance* is the amount still due on a *loan*.

In general English, however, the sense of both words has been liberally expanded. For one thing, *loan*, traditionally a noun, is now freely used as a verb: "The bank loaned him $2,000." Even some grammarians have come to recognize *loan* as a verb, possibly on the theory that swimming downstream with widespread usage is easier than paddling the opposite way with purists. This acceptance aside, many careful writers still reject *loan* and use *lend* instead—"The bank decided not to *lend* him (instead of *loan* him) $2,000." In so doing, they restrict *loan* to its function as a noun—"He made a *loan* of $2,000."

Similarly, in general usage the definition of *balance* has widened to incorporate the meanings "rest" and "remainder." These subversions, however, unlike that of *loan*, have received little support; in fact, they are considered colloquialisms, best avoided in formal writing. In "We spent the balance of the evening in the library" and in "The balance of the trial will take about five days," for example, *rest* or *remainder* should replace *balance*.

Preferably, *balance* should be confined to its commercial meaning; it rests more comfortably with credits and debits.

IT HAD NO EFFECT

Affect and *effect* are sometimes mistakenly interchanged, probably because they look and sound so much alike. And yet their differences should be easily recognized.

Affect, meaning "to exercise an influence on," is customarily used as a verb—"His plea did not seem to affect the jurors." *Effect*, meaning "a result," is normally a noun —"His plea had no noticeable effect on the jurors." To distinguish them, bear in mind that just as *a* (for *affect*) comes before *e* (for *effect*), something must affect before there is an effect: "Counsel's efforts to affect the judge's thinking had no effect on him."

Postscript: The verb *to effect* means "to bring about." It is more frequently used in the passive voice than in the active, and primarily in formal English: "Changes in the regulations *were effected* (brought about) last year." The plural noun *effects*, meaning "goods or property," is rarely used. It is found mainly in legal writing: "The *effects* of the deceased will be sold at the auction." The noun *affect* is a technical psychological term.

INTERROGATORY

Are the terms *complected* and *complexioned* interchangeable, or is one preferred to the other?

The accepted word meaning "facial complexion" is *complexioned*. *Complected*, although commonly used, is inappropriate. It certainly does not belong in formal writing—and preferably should not be used at all. Say, for example, "He is light complexioned," not *complected*.

DON'T ALIBI YOUR MISTAKES

When laymen misuse terms that are the common property of a profession, it is, though not entirely excusable, at least understandable. But when professionals misuse the same terms, it is not only inexcusable but incomprehensible. Lawyers should be particularly careful, since words are their stock in trade, to avoid loose, imprecise language.

Take *alibi*, for example. An *alibi* is "a plea or fact of having been elsewhere when an offense was committed," as in "The defendant's alibi was that he was in Chicago at the time of the robbery." All too often, however, *alibi* is substituted for the noun *excuse*—"Counsel offered no alibi (excuse) for his lateness"—or for the verb *justify*— "Counsel need not alibi (justify) what she did." Since *alibi* serves no more meaningfully than the word it replaces, its use is pointless and thus inappropriate.

During the Watergate Affair, the term *impeach* was often bandied about in the meaning of *convict*. It was not unusual to read or hear something like "If Nixon is impeached, he will not be entitled to a pension." *To impeach* merely means "to charge." It is not a synonym of *remove* or *convict*.

And then there is *collide*. A sentence such as "The two cars collided together on a busy street" is poorly stated and technically inaccurate. *To collide* implies a coming together; the *together* after *collide*, therefore, is redundant. Furthermore, a *collision* involves two objects that are in motion; hence a moving car cannot collide with a parked vehicle or a tree or anything stationary. Informally, of course, a moving vehicle can, and does, collide with anything, even the side of a barn.

77

Hanging has been outlawed almost everywhere, but when it is necessary to refer to that heinous act, it is incorrect to say "The prisoner was hung." *Hung* is the past tense of *hang*, as in "I hung the picture last night," but *hanged* is proper when the reference is to a person. Perhaps a deed so cruel merits its own special tense.

PARALLELS NEVER MEET

Correlative, or parallel, conjunctions—*either . . . or; neither . . . nor; both . . . and; not only . . . but also* —should be balanced; that is, the same grammatical phrasing should follow each conjunction. When this is not done, changing the position of the conjunctions will usually correct the imbalance.

Consider the following defective sentences, each of which precedes alternative corrections. "The book should *neither* be revised *nor* reprinted": "The book should be *neither* revised *nor* reprinted" or "should *neither* be revised *nor* be reprinted." "The court *not only* approved broadcasting *but also* audiotaping": "The court approved *not only* broadcasting *but also* audiotaping" or "*not only* approved broadcasting *but also* approved audiotaping." One more: "*Either* the claim should be litigated *or* abandoned": "The claim should be *either* litigated *or* abandoned" or "*Either* the claim should be litigated *or* the claim should be abandoned." In the corrected versions, the same construction—noun, verb, or whatever— follows both conjunctions.

Caution: Sentences employing correlatives should be scrutinized for imbalance. If necessary, they should be adjusted to ensure that both sides weigh the same and that neither tips the scale.

VIGOROUS VERBS

The force of a sentence may be measured, to a good extent, by the vigor of its verb. Verbs ignite the sparks that give life and movement to a sentence. And the power they generate far exceeds that of the most carefully selected noun or adjective.

Therefore, when there is a choice, a verb should be used instead of a verb-noun combination or a verb-adjective derivative. For example, "He delivered a lecture on discovery procedures" is more simply stated, "He lectured on. . . ." Rather than "Counsel has an inclination toward putting off until tomorrow what should be done today," a direct, economical statement is "Counsel is inclined to put off. . . ." One more: "The staff lawyers held a conference for the purpose of discussing the latest regulations" reads better, "The staff lawyers conferred to discuss. . . ." Not only can a verb revitalize a flaccid sentence, but it can also streamline an awkward one, lopping off redundancies and deadwood.

Specific concrete verbs are more informative and colorful than those that are generalized. Instead of bland terms like *say* or *remark*, for example, try *shout, cry, rave, bellow, scream, rant, thunder,* or maybe even *whisper.* In place of "Counsel *walked* down the hall," use *strode, strutted, hurried, ran, dashed, raced,* or merely *strolled,* if appropriate. Rather than "The witness *looked* at the jury," consider *stared, gazed, surveyed, examined, regarded, viewed, glanced,* or some other arresting verb. Maybe *smirked.*

Concentrate on verbs. The more they tell, the better. Nothing else can so enliven a sentence or fire the imagination.

ARE YOU SURE YOU'RE INSURED?

The words *ensure* and *insure* are interchangeable when used in the sense of "to make certain." Examples: "Constant study will *ensure* (or *insure*) good grades" or, conversely, "A close watch will *insure* (or *ensure*) a current inventory." In this sense the preferred spelling is *ensure*. But when the meaning is "to indemnify against loss"—"Please insure the package"—it is not a matter of preference; the only acceptable spelling is *insure*.

In England, and to a lesser extent in Canada, some life insurance companies use *assurance* instead of *insurance* in their names: Canada Life Assurance Co. They reason that since death is a certainty, the policyholder is assured of eventual payment. Casualty companies, of course, do not make that claim.

Assure is the appropriate word if the intent is to impart a sense of trust in what is being said or done: "We assure you that there will be no overcharge."

A summarizing example might be "Although an *insured* investment may *ensure* a good yield, it still may not *assure* the investor of steady, long-term growth."

When should the word *ever* be hyphened?

Hyphen *ever* when it modifies a modifier of a noun, as in "We're experiencing an ever-growing problem." Usually *ever* precedes an *-ing* word: ever-developing situations, ever-rising tides, ever-increasing size. When *ever* and its companion follow a verb, they take no hyphen: "The problems we are experiencing seem ever growing." Some *ever* words are always hyphened, regardless of their position: ever-faithful, ever-present, ever-ready; and a few are always written solid: everblooming, evergreen, everlasting, evermore.

STAY WITH THE RIGHT KIND

To say that *kind* has been treated unkindly may sound silly, but it is so commonly misused that this judgment is warranted. Everyone knows what *kind* means; it is a simple, everyday word—"I like this kind"—yet in matters of number and agreement it is frequently mistreated. If *kind* were given the attention it deserves, multiple benefits could ensue, for similar problems arise with *variety, species, class, sort, type, size, breed, brand,* and *quality.*

The addition of a superfluous *a* or *an* to *kind of* (kind of a, kind of an) is a very common error. *Kind* indicates a class, whereas *a* or *an* points to a single thing. In the following examples, therefore, the *a* should be deleted: "He's the kind of a client we all dislike" (kind of client); "What kind of a witness do you think he'll make?" (kind of witness).

Since *kind* is a singular form, it should not be modified by *these* or *those,* but by *this* or *that,* despite King Lear's "These kind of knaves I know." Only when mentioning several kinds, a variety, is a plural form proper (*these* or *those* kinds). And even that "acceptable" plural construction is subject to criticism on a high, formal level, for in such writing only the singular *kind* is considered good usage. Instead of saying, for instance, "These kinds of services are inappropriate," a suitable recast would be "services of this kind," which employs plural elements while retaining the singular *this kind.*

A related question is whether *kinds* must be followed by a plural noun. Either a singular or a plural form may be correct, depending upon the meaning to be conveyed. For instance, "Five kinds of *paper* are used in these books," but "Five kinds of *books* are made from this paper."

A *kind thought:* Despite the widespread use of *kind of* in the sense of *somewhat* or *rather,* this usage is best avoided: "The judge is *rather* (or *somewhat* but not *kind of*) short-tempered."

HAVE HYPHEN, WILL TRAVEL

Centuries of use have fixed the spelling of most English words, but others used in combination to express a single thought are in a state of transition. Today's trend is to amalgamate associated words into one-word compounds, usually in two steps. First, the two separately spelled words are hyphened, and then, at some later time, forged into a consolidated unit.

Take the word *baseball,* for example. Originally two words—*base ball*—it became *base-ball* and then the one-word *baseball.* The term *air plane* has similarly traveled from *air-plane* to *airplane,* while other *air* words have remained grounded. Air force, air express, air raid, and air time, for instance, have not flown at all. Each *air* word, therefore, must be considered individually. Although *boyfriend* has closed the gap, *girl friend,* at least in some dictionaries, is still spelled open. *Today* and *tomorrow* used to be hyphened. And although a one-word *postman* may deliver hyphened *postal-cards,* he still works out of a two-word *post office.*

A long list of compound words—spelled first as two words, then hyphened, and now conjoined—could be compiled. But the spellings would not necessarily conform to those in every dictionary, since no consensus exists on how words in transition are to be treated. A writer, therefore, must in self-defense rely on a dictionary in which he has confidence.

RECIPROCAL AGREEMENTS

Reciprocal in many contexts is synonymous with mutual —a mutual agreement, for example, is the same as a reciprocal agreement. In that instance the relationship affects both parties simultaneously. But if people act at different times, their deeds are not mutual but reciprocal. Ellwood, for example, although he prepared a brief for Stuart, could not ask him to perform a mutual service later. That service would have to be reciprocal. A kindness extended by someone in the winter, if repaid in the spring, is reciprocal, not mutual.

A further distinction is that *mutual* refers to the way two people feel—what they sense or what they represent to each other. That which is mutual, therefore, concerns sentiments or emotions; it does not apply to tangibles. Reciprocal acts may deal with material things. An exchange of gifts is a reciprocal action.

In sum: When *mutual* will serve, *reciprocal* may replace it, although normally *mutual* is the preferred word. When *reciprocal* is used, however, *mutual* may be substituted only when no time sequence and no tangibles are involved.

INTERROGATORY

You once pointed out that the plural of *agenda* is *agendas*. What about *medias?*

There is no such word. Since *media* is the plural form, it cannot be pluralized further. And it must always take a plural verb. In "The news media has a strong investigative arm," for example, the verb should be *have*.

AS TO "AS TO"

As to, when used to begin a sentence, can effectively emphasize a following word or thought: "As to Judge Wayne, you can always count on a quick retort." "As to your liability, it is a matter to be considered later." Except as a sentence opener, however, many careful writers avoid *as to* because the expression, when embedded in a sentence, is awkward, wordy, and sometimes even improper.

As to is incorrectly used, for instance, when it escorts *whether,* as in "The magistrate expressed doubt as to whether a prima facie case had been presented." That sentence should read, ". . . expressed doubt whether a prima facie case. . . ." To repeat, *as to* should never immediately precede *whether*.

Similarly, the need for *as to* before *what, how,* or *why* should be closely examined. In "The question as to why he went will be resolved soon," *as to* is unnecessary. "The question why . . ." is sufficient.

When a construction requires a grammatical connective, usually a single word will serve better than *as to*. Among the many adequate substitutes for *as to* are *concerning, regarding,* and, better yet, simpler prepositions such as *about* or *of*. For example, "Counsel was in doubt *as to* his guilt" and "The court established rules *as to* conduct" might be changed to "Counsel was in doubt *about* his guilt" and "The court established rules *of* conduct."

If *as to* cannot be suitably replaced, it must, of course, be used. But if it can be avoided, the sentence will improve.

A SO-CALLED THING

Expressions that follow *so-called,* unless they are misnomers or slang, should not be enclosed in quotation marks. The sentences "The so-called Dead Man's Rule was ignored" and "The court admitted the so-called spurious claims without objection," for instance, are set out as they should be. *So-called* is sufficient by itself to set off *Dead Man's Rule* and *spurious claims;* they need no quotation marks. In fact, quotation marks would be considered redundant.

The same reasoning applies to expressions that follow *termed, called,* and *known*—no quotation marks enclose them either. They are properly written as follows: termed a qualified plan, called a demurrer, known as the Tax Reform Act.

Quotation marks are required, however, when *so-called* is not used but implied. Had *so-called* been omitted in the first two examples, *Dead Man's Rule* and *spurious claims* would have been enclosed; for example, "The court admitted the 'spurious claims' without objection."

Expressions following *entitled, named, endorsed, marked,* and *signed* are treated differently. They are encased by quotation marks because they are considered very definite terms. Examples: entitled "Vesting," named "Jonathan Volpe," marked "49-B," signed (or endorsed) "Lois T. Stapleton." One exception: Quotation marks should not be used when italics are required—"He referred to the book entitled *Basic Accounting for Lawyers.*"

Nota bene: The term *so-called,* as in the examples above, is hyphened when it precedes a noun, but not when it follows one: "His office, so called, was a vacant store."

MINUSCULE IS PRETTY SMALL

"Even a miniscule violation of the sacred is sacreligious."
It would be understandable if the two misspelled words
in that sentence went unnoticed, for those spellings are
frequently seen in print.

Perhaps the misspelled version of *minuscule*, that is,
miniscule, is fashioned after words like *minibus* and *mini-
camera*, in which the *mini* stands for "miniature." *Minuscule*, however, is based on *minus*, and therein lies the
way to remember it.

Sacrilege, the noun form of *sacrilegious*, means "a violation of something consecrated to a deity." Although
religious is commonly assumed to be its root word, this is
not so. Religion may supply the roots, but it contributes
nothing to the spelling.

SENSUOUSLY SENSITIVE

Ignoring the distinction between *sensuous* and *sensual*,
merely because their meanings have been blurred by
widespread interchange, is unjustified. Although in common usage both words refer to gratification of the
senses, on a more precise level that is not so.

What is *sensuous* refers to something that "appeals to
the senses," to the intellect; *sensual* implies "indulgence
of the senses," satisfaction of the baser desires. *Sensuous*
means refined, sensitive, in good taste; it pertains to
those senses associated with aesthetic purposes, the
appreciation of color, form, sound. *Sensual* means carnal,
gross, worldly, often referring to the sexual and to the
gratification of physical appetites.

It is believed that *sensuous* was coined by John Milton when comparing logic and rhetoric with great poetry. He referred to poetry as "simple, sensuous, and passionate." Since then, the word has been a part of the English language.

MUCH ADO ABOUT NEITHER

The chief concern, when using correlative conjunctions, is to employ the right combination. Consider this example: "The clerk is not either efficient nor loyal." That sentence should be reworded "The clerk is not *either* efficient *or* loyal" or "The clerk is *neither* efficient *nor* loyal."

A more complex problem arises when a correlative conjunction joins a mixed subject, one noun a singular and the other a plural. What number should the accompanying verb be? The answer: The verb should agree in number with the nearer subject. For instance, "Neither the judge nor the witnesses *have* entered the courtroom," but "Neither the witnesses nor the judge *has* entered the courtroom."

The verb, because it is applicable to only one of two subjects, may create an uncomfortable, imbalanced feeling. This uneasiness can be avoided by recasting the sentence "The judge *has* not entered the courtroom, and neither *have* the witnesses," thus giving each subject its own verb. "Neither the judge nor I *am* leaving" also sounds strained, and for the same reason. Simply rephrasing the sentence to "Neither of us *is leaving*"— noting, of course, the *is leaving*—remedies the awkwardness.

"Neither of us *are leaving*" is *verboten*.

A PARTY OF ONE

Except when required in legal contexts, *people* should be referred to as *persons*, not as *individuals* or *parties*. In general usage, *party* means "a body of people": Socialist Party, hunting party, dinner party. When used to indicate a *person*, it is considered slang or, at best, commercialese. For example, in "The party you recommended visited us today," *person* should replace *party*. The commonplace question "Is he the party who called?" should be rephrased *person who called* or, better yet, *man* or *woman* who called, if the sex is known. Telephone operators, of course, may disregard all this; their use of *party* is so entrenched as to be fully accepted.

Referring to a person as an *individual*—"I know the individual monopolizing the conversation"—implies an unpleasant character. Unless disparagement is intended, the term is best avoided. It is proper, however, to employ *individual* when contrasting or distinguishing one person from a collective body, such as an agency or a corporation. In these instances, the emphasis is on the singleness of the person: "This statute applies to *individuals*, not to *corporations*."

INTERROGATORY

I know there is something peculiar about "If we cooperate together, we'll get the legislation through," but I can't quite pinpoint it.

The redundant *cooperate together* most likely is bothering you. Although people may work together, band together, or even agree together, they may not *cooperate together*, since the *co* in *cooperate* means "together." The example should read: "If we cooperate, we'll. . . ."

PARAMETERS ARE NOT PERIMETERS

Many careful writers do not intentionally ignore good word usage. But some are inadvertently lured into poor word usage by the impressive sound of technical terms.

Parameter is one such word that seduces many writers. They use it, mainly in the plural, to mean boundary, perimeter, or limit. But *parameter* is not related to those words; it is a mathematical term denoting "a quantity that varies with the conditions under which it occurs."

Many specific words in the English language express the meanings that *parameter* tries to displace. There is no good reason, therefore, to dip into a technical glossary. Take as examples, "The instructions set out the parameters of our authority" and "The United States Supreme Court has gone beyond the parameters set by our State Supreme Court." In the first example, *limit* or *extent* would serve well; and in the second, *boundaries*. All are precise and more readily understood words.

Another word currently in vogue is *burgeoning*. *To burgeon* does not mean "to proliferate," "to mushroom," or "to expand rapidly," definitions loosely attributed to it. It means "to bud" or "to sprout." Consequently, *burgeoning* is properly applied to something just beginning, as in "The burgeoning effects of the 1976 Tax Reform Act need immediate attention." But it is incorrectly applied to something that has reached a developed state, as in "The burgeoning need for legal representation by the poor is an insolvable problem" or "The burgeoning population of urban prisons has become critical." A more appropriate choice of words might be "The *growing* (or *rapidly expanding*) population of urban prisons. . . ."

Remember: No one is ever criticized for preferring the simple word to the fancy.

THAN WHO?

It is not unusual to hear someone stumble over a sentence like "Ogden enjoys reading more than her," and then add hastily, "I mean more than she." Query: Which is correct, *her* or *she?* The answer: Both.

Actually, the correctness of the statements depends upon the context of the conversation. As set out here, what was really meant cannot be determined. If the speaker wanted to say that Ogden did not enjoy her as much as he liked reading, then *her* is proper—in effect, Ogden enjoys reading more than he enjoys her. If, however, what was meant was that Ogden enjoyed reading more than she did, then *she* is correct—Ogden enjoys reading more than she enjoys reading.

The confusion can be resolved by remembering that a pronoun following *than* takes the subjective or objective case, depending upon whether that pronoun is the subject or object of the verb. Examples using the subjective case pronoun are "You will arrive earlier than *I* will arrive," in which the verb is restated, and "Mr. Clarke is older than *I* (am)," in which the verb is implied. The constructions are equally suitable. In "The Commissioner respects Glancey more than (he respects) *me*," the objective case *me* indicates the intended comparison. But another meaning is found in "The Commissioner respects Glancey more than *I* (do)," in which, to compare the degree of respect I and the Commissioner have for Glancey, the subjective case is used.

Recommendation: To avoid the pedantic sound of a sentence ending with a subjective case personal pronoun, supply the missing verb: "The Swedes are taller than they are" rather than "taller than they."

LA COMMA

Although most stylebooks recommend that a comma be used before a conjunction in a series of three or more members—*red, white, and blue*—some writers prefer to omit it. And yet its omission can cause confusion, even misunderstanding, whereas its presence never does. Take, for example, "He turned over all his holdings, houses and lands." In that sentence, *houses* and *lands* might be construed as explaining the word *holdings.* But with a comma preceding *and*, three distinct elements become immediately evident: *holdings, houses, lands.* Consider another: "The books on the shelf are red, blue, brown, black and yellow." How many differently colored books are on the shelf? If the answer is five, a comma after *black* would dispel any doubt: *red, blue, brown, black*, and *yellow.*

Generally editors of periodicals and newspapers, perhaps to save space, disagree with this thinking; they omit serial commas even at the expense of possible confusion. And confusion frequently occurs. For example, this sentence appeared in a daily newspaper: "The new courtroom consists of an anteroom, a large jury room equipped with air conditioning and a commodious judge's chamber." The statement, read quickly, could be interpreted to mean that the jury room is equipped with air conditioning and a commodious judge's chamber.

Since serial commas aid clarity, the better practice is to use them regularly. They will not harm a sentence—may even help it.

A MAJORITY BEATS THEM ALL

If a candidate in an election received more votes than were received by any of his opponents, did he win a *majority* of the votes or a *plurality?* Or, since he was "tops" either way, did it really make any difference? It might have. In some elections, "tops" is not good enough; the winner needs to gain for himself more votes than are won by all his competitors combined—a *majority.*

A *plurality* is the greatest number of votes, but less than half, garnered by one of three or more candidates. If Elaine Thompson receives 40 votes, Walter Peterson 30, and Herbert Wistner 20, Elaine's plurality is 10—the difference between her vote and that of the second highest vote-getter.

A *majority,* on the other hand, is a number greater than half the total vote, which means any number over 50 per cent. Simply stated, if 100 votes are cast, the candidate receiving 51 or more votes holds a majority.

Voting aside, the word *majority* should not be regarded as a synonym of *most* or *major.* The sentence "He spent a majority of his time in the library," for example, properly stated should read "most of his time" or "a major part of his time." *Majority* connotes a number, but time, an abstract concept, is not countable. It is correct to say, however, "He spent a majority of his hours in the library," since hours are countable units. To reiterate, *majority* relates to the greater of two parts that make a whole.

INTERROGATORY

What do you think of the phrases *a half a loaf* and *a half of a loaf?*

Neither one is accepted idiom; both are wordy besides. It is better to use *half a loaf* or, better yet, especially on a formal level, *a half loaf.*

YOUR FINALIZED WORD?

Words that have not been accepted into the English langauge, especially verbs, should not be used. Thinking that such words can make a writer or speaker seem impressive is false.

One such word is *finalize,* a term that grates on readers and listeners alike. Yet its use persists despite criticism by writers and editors and almost anyone else concerned with the elements of style. John F. Kennedy used *finalize* twice in his inaugural address, and his was a speech carefully edited by Harvard University professors.

Creating new words for which there is no genuine need should be discouraged. Certainly the meaning of *finalize* is readily conveyed by *complete, conclude, finish, resolve, make final, put in final form, wind up, wrap up, terminate,* and *end.* Probably there are others, many as economical as *finalize.*

Some unabridged dictionaries list *finalize* and similar coinages—such as *to author* for "to write" and *to orchestrate* for "to arrange or to organize"—but their acknowledgment of words that have insinuated themselves into general use is no recommendation.

WHO INDITES THE INDICTMENT?

There are two words pronounced precisely alike, one a common legal term, the other found in literary works written before the nineteenth century. The words are *indict* and *indite.*

The attention of lawyers is called particularly to the latter term, not that its use is recommended—it is not—but to avoid thinking that *indict* is meant when *indite* is intended. Such a mistake could be embarrassing.

Indict, of course, means "to charge with a crime" or "to accuse." *Indite* means "to write" or "to compose." Since *indite* is seldom, if ever, found in current usage, how it is customarily employed has little relevance. Except for authors who seek out odd or archaic words just to impress their readers, the likelihood is that *indite* will not be found in today's writings.

THE BRIDE DID NOT SAY NEE

The term *nee* is hardly found anymore. It is primarily reserved for wedding announcements in newspapers: "Mrs. Edwards, nee Cambridge, studied at Goucher." *Nee,* a French word meaning "born," is used to refer to a married woman's maiden name.

Since the designation *nee* refers to a surname alone, it would be incorrect to say: "Thelma Edwards, nee Thelma Cambridge." A baby at the moment of birth inherits a surname only and receives a first, or given, name later. Even acquiring a name through marriage does not affect the *nee* designation.

The use of *nee* has been extended to areas quite foreign to its traditional sense. These include, according to Webster, groups, inanimate objects, and almost anything else that has had successive names: the Milwaukee Braves, nee the Boston Braves; sonata for flute, oboe, and basso continuo, nee sonata for violin and harpsichord.

Webster aside, it is best to use *nee* in accordance with its traditional meaning. The admonition is particularly applicable in formal writing.

Aftermath: Precisely spelled, *nee* needs an acute accent— *née*—placed over the first *e*. And there is another spelling, too—*né*—a rarely used masculine form. *Nay* is the pronunciation of both words.

BECAUSE CLAUSE

Sentences beginning with a negative clause—"Bolton did not attend the seminar"—followed by a clause beginning with *because*—"because his name was inadvertently omitted as a panel member"—raise a serious question of punctuation. The entire meaning of the sentence rests on whether a comma follows the negative clause. Perhaps the best advice is simply to read the sentence both with and without the comma, and then to compare the meanings.

The preceding, unpunctuated example—"Bolton did not attend the seminar because his name was inadvertently omitted" is a case in point. The sentence could be construed in two ways: (1) Bolton refused to attend because his name had been omitted (maybe it embarrassed him); (2) Bolton did not attend, but not for the reason mentioned (maybe his wife fell ill).

If the first sense was meant, a comma before *because* would unmistakably express that meaning: "Bolton did not attend the seminar, because his name was inadvertently omitted." The *because* clause now distinctly sets out the reason for Bolton's absence. If the second sense was wanted, the sentence would need rewording. For example: "Bolton did not attend the seminar, but not because his name had been inadvertently omitted."

Fortunately, no ambiguity attaches to an affirmative *because* clause. Consider "Nordstrom attended the seminar because he wanted to learn." The clause sets forth the reason for his attendance simply and clearly —showing how confusing a little *not* can be. If one were added to the Nordstrom example—"Nordstrom did *not* attend because he wanted to learn"—we would be back with Bolton again.

DEFINITELY SO

Definitive and *definite* do not mean the same thing; it is inaccurate to speak of something as *definitive* when *definite* is meant. *Definite* means "precise" or "defined" —definite appointments, definite offers, definite opinions.

That which is *definitive* is conclusive. It is unalterably final. Once a definitive step is taken, for instance, no further action follows. From a definitive statement, there is no appeal.

In terms of tangible things—books, for example—a definitive work is comprehensive. Such a volume treats a subject as fully and as extensively as can be done at that time.

Roundup: Definitive works often contain definite statements, but definite statements, unless all-inclusive, are not definitive.

DON'T CAPITALIZE YOUR ASSETS

It is impossible to give rules that will cover every conceivable problem in capitalization. But by considering the purpose to be served and the underlying principles, it is possible to attain a considerable degree of uniformity.

Style Manual
—UNITED STATES GOVERNMENT PRINTING OFFICE

Everyone agrees that proper topographical names are capitalized—Philadelphia, Mount Fuji, Cape Hatteras, Strait of Gibraltar. What sometimes causes concern is whether to capitalize the generic term, or common noun, following a proper name. Many stylebooks prescribe this simple formula: a common noun—*mountain, island, lake, river*—that is part of a name is capitalized. To exemplify, both elements in these names are capitalized: the Rocky Mountains, Rain Forest, Nile Delta, Walden Pond, English Channel, White Sulphur Springs, Cook County.

When using two or more proper names, however, whether to capitalize the accompanying generic term depends upon its placement. If the term follows the two names, it is lowercased: spanning the Monongahela and Ohio *rivers;* vacationing between the White and Green *mountains.* (But the U.S. Government Printing Office *Style Manual* capitalizes these common nouns as though they were part of the proper names; hence *Rivers* and *Mountains* in the examples.) But when a common noun precedes the proper names, the opposite is true—all the nouns are capitalized, generic and proper: traveled on *Lakes* Erie and Superior, climbed *Mounts* Whitney and Ranier.

If used descriptively or alone, a generic term is not part of a proper name and therefore is lowercased: the valley of the Delaware, the Delaware River valley, the valley.

Is there a difference in usage between *each other* and *one another?*

The difference between the phrases is not generally observed in informal English, but careful writers use *each other* when only two persons are involved and *one another* when there are more than two. Distinguishing between the phrases is good practice: "The prosecutor and the defendant spoke sharply to each other." "The twelve jurymen argued heatedly with one another."

97

A MOMENT WITH THE MEDIA

The words *media* and *memento* have really nothing in common except, perhaps, their frequent misuse in print, each in its own way. It may be fortuitous, but the errors sometimes are found in the same writing.

The problem with *media,* a plural Latin form of *medium,* is that some writers use it as they use *agenda,* with a singular verb. Unfortunately, consistency in this case is not a virtue. Although *agenda* as a singular noun has met with general approval, *media* has not. A sentence such as "The news media is a potent force in shaping public confidence" is therefore improperly put. The singular *is* should be changed to *are,* or the plural *media* to *medium.*

A sentence in a journal read, "A momento of the honor being bestowed on the media that has done so much for us. . . ." Besides the misuse of *has* for *have* in that sentence, the word *memento* is incorrectly spelled. To avoid this spelling error, the word *memory* might be associated with *memento;* both start with the same syllable and a memento should refresh one's memory.

DEFECTIVES ARE DEFICIENT

Defective and *deficient* both refer to a person or thing that lacks something considered necessary or important for proper functioning. But there, despite the equating of *defective* and *deficient* in some dictionaries, the similarity ends.

Defect implies an imperfection or flaw; *deficit* refers to a shortage or lack. Something that has defects, since it has discernible faults, does not measure up to standards; hence *defective.* Generally the defects are faults of quality. A *deficit*, being an insufficiency, gives rise to something *deficient*, that which is incomplete. This shortcoming involves quantity.

Of course, a defective person or object may be deficient, too. A person who is mentally deficient, one who lacks normal intelligence, can also be physically defective—flatfooted and nearsighted, for example.

The use of proper prepositions: Defect takes the preposition *in* when something tangible is involved—"The defect in that binder is a broken middle ring"—and takes *of* when it is intangible—"The defect of his personality is an enlarged ego."

One more thing: When a preposition is needed, *deficient* wants *in*.

THE DRUNK TOOK A DIVE

The verb *to dive* sports two past tenses: *dived* and *dove*. In baseball parlance the form always used is *dove:* "Mickey dove for the ball, and came up with air." On a formal level *dived* is more common, but *dove* is stealing a few bases even there.

The word *drunk* has nothing to do with *dive* except that it might be a good place to get drunk. But the adjective *drunk*, like the past tense of the verb *dive*, has two commonly used competing forms. Journalists may say, for example, either "The drunken driver was apprehended" or "The drunk driver was carted to the hoosegow." On a serious writing level, however, *drunk* is used predicatively, that is, after a form of the verb *to be*—"Thornwell was drunk last night"—and *drunken*, attributively, that is, before a noun—"Thornwell is still a drunken man."

THE ASSASSIN WHO NEVER KILLED

If a public official is killed by treacherous violence, expiring on a day different from the day of the actual attack, was he assassinated on the day of his death or on the day of the attack? No consensus exists among authorities, but the weight favors the day of the attack.

When Caesar was stabbed, he fell dead at the foot of Pompey's statue the same day. But William of Orange was twice "gunned down," losing his life on the second attempt. President James A. Garfield, shot on July 2, 1881, died from his wounds on September 19, 1881. The question is, When were these men assassinated?

Black's Law Dictionary defines assassination as a murder, which it unquestionably is. But an assassin is a person who, whether successful or not, tries to kill a public figure.

Some dictionaries, succumbing to popular understanding that an assassin must actually kill a public official, no longer define *assassin* as one who merely makes an attempt. This technical "inaccuracy" is now supported in newspaper reporting by the phrase *would-be-assassin* for an attempt that fails.

Obiter: The word *assassin,* derived from the Arabic *hashshashin,* refers to a Muslim sect, which, under the influence of the drug hashish, attacked Christians during the Crusades.

Since an assassin is someone who, because of political motivation, murders a public figure, John Wilkes Booth has two infamous designations. He was not just the murderer of Abraham Lincoln but his assassin as well.

POSSIBLE, YES; FEASIBLE, NO

What is feasible is possible, but the converse is not necessarily true. The reason: *possible*, a broader, more general term, embraces *feasible*. What is possible can potentially happen; what is feasible can certainly be done. Clearly, if something cannot occur in the first place, nothing can be done about it.

In some areas *possible* and *feasible* are interchangeable: "Delivery of the briefs by messenger is *feasible*" (or *possible*). But in other areas, they are not: "Since today is Saturday, it is *possible* (not *feasible*) that the judge will be out." *Feasible* implies that something is desirable and can be done easily: "The plan for integration is feasible and can be put quietly into effect." *Possible* connotes likelihood: "It is *possible* (not *feasible*) that the house will be sold by next week."

Feasible suggests practicability when it refers to what can be done and suitability when it describes what can be used to advantage.

Finis: Possible is not a synonym of *probable* or *plausible*. *Possible* is often followed by *that*; *feasible* never is.

Although legalisms, generally, are in disfavor, the expression *and/or* keeps popping up. Is there a suitable alternative?

The expression *and/or* points to three possibilities: (1) A, (2) B, or (3) A and B. The recommended way to handle this expression is to omit the word *and* and the slanted line, the virgule, and to add the words *or both*. For example, instead of "His choices are A and/or B," the sentence would read "His choices are A or B, or both."

AN "E" FOR SPECIAL

People who use *especial* and *special* interchangeably perhaps pay no attention to the difference in their spellings—or meanings. And yet that one-letter distinction is a bellwether to be heard.

Especial connotes "exceptional, extraordinary, outstanding": "The law is of especial significance to actuaries." "This matter is of no especial importance." *Special* means "particular or specific": "This insurance plan has special features." "They issued a special class of stock."

In everyday writing the longer word *especial* is losing out to its shorter brother *special*. Because of this trend, *special* is now frequently being used, whether or not entirely suitable. But the need to distinguish between them, for the sake of preciseness, nevertheless continues. This need is particularly true with their adverb forms because *specially* is often inappropriately substituted for *especially*.

Especially has several meanings—"chiefly, unusually, notably, principally"—that are not applicable to *specially*. For instance, in the following sentences, replacing *especially* with *specially* would be improper: "Many were at fault, but Hagerman should especially be blamed." "During this past month we had especially good attendance."

The adjective forms, *special* and *especial,* are a different matter because they are more companionable. *Special* and *especial* can be interchanged in some contexts. Consider these examples: "Craig Hall is an *especial* (or *special*) friend." "We publish books for the *especial* (or *special*) benefit of law students." No special differences arise there.

JURIST PRUDENCE

"What is a synonym for *jurist?*" is a fair question. An automatic, unthinking reply might be *judge.* That answer, since it is partly right, deserves a passing grade, but little more.

A judge is, or at least should be, a jurist; but a jurist is not necessarily a judge. The definition of *jurist,* "one versed in the law," embraces different kinds of legal students: lawyers, judges, scholars, teachers.

Lawyers, since they know better, should not follow the lead of some newspapers and label every judge a jurist—even though it would be nice to think so.

DON'T LITTER SENTENCES

A literal account of a fracas may be helpful in establishing the facts. But if such a report states that the participants *literally tore each other apart,* its validity might be questioned. Had they literally torn each other apart, pieces of flesh would have been strewn about. The word intended was *figuratively,* not *literally;* but in this example even *figuratively,* as is frequently the case with *literally,* serves no purpose.

Literally means "in fact" or "true to the letter." Though intended merely for emphasis, it is not a proper substitute for *figuratively.* On the contrary, *literally* and *figuratively* are antonyms; *figuratively* means "not literally" or "metaphorically."

Neither the definition nor the use of either word, however, troubles anyone. The difficulty usually stems from a desire to make a strong point stronger still by saying something was *literally* so when, in actuality, it was not.

Literally, though accurately used, adds nothing, for example, to "The Senator literally filibustered for eight hours." If the word *figuratively* contributes nothing to the meaning of a sentence, it, too, should be excised. The test is the word's value to the sentence; for instance, in "The bar's hackles (have you seen them?) were *literally* (really *figuratively*) standing on end," *figuratively*, though correct, would still be excess baggage.

Rx: Since *literally* and *figuratively* seldom add meaning, weigh carefully before using.

ETHICS BUILDS MORALS

Although the words *ethics* and *morals* have similar meanings, both referring to proper human conduct, they enjoy distinctive applications. *Ethics* suggests a science, a code, an established standard of behavior; *morals* can be considered the practice of ethics.

The science of ethics, more commonly referred to as a *code of ethics*, functions as a guide for conduct for large groups—professions, businesses, or society in general. A person who abides by the code is considered ethical—honorable, upright, incorruptible.

Morals refers to a personal code of propriety, a standard by which individuals live in society. It may, with some people, be founded in religion. Often it has a sexual connotation. Morals concerns one's feeling about the rightness or wrongness of matters involved in everyday living.

Mix-up: Since ethics is a science that studies moral values, that which is ethical must also be moral. But it is inappropriate to equate morals with ethics, even though what is moral has ethical overtones: a moral man, an ethical concept.

IS A KUDO AN INSIGNE?

Much has been written about the curious spelling of some English words. How these spellings evolved is only of etymological or historical value. Practically their development is of no importance today.

Consider the word *kudos,* for example, which means "acclaim" or "glory." The final *s* in *kudos* does not convert it into a plural; it is a singular, and the accompanying verb is singular accordingly: "Kudos *was* heaped upon counsel by both the legislature and the committee he represented." There simply is no such thing as a *kudo.*

The term *insignia,* on the other hand, a plural word, has a singular form, *insigne.* To a good extent, however, *insignia* has come to displace *insigne,* and it is now considered both a singular and a plural: "The Medal of Honor *is an insignia* of valor." "A cluttered desk and books strewn on the floor *are the insignia* of a busy lawyer."

From *insignia* has evolved an anglicized plural version: *insignias.* This latter form, frequently found even in careful usage, creates a second choice: "Merit badges are *insignias* (or *insignia*) of accomplishment." The singular *insigne,* the original Latin form, meanwhile has atrophied—a condition that does not outlaw it. For example, "A black robe is the insigne of the judiciary" is still a good sign.

BRING GREEN; TAKE A CHANCE

"Take it with you." "Bring it to me." Those two sentences exemplify the proper use of *take* and *bring.* The gist of the difference is simply one of direction—someone may bring home the bacon, but if he carries part of it to the office the next day, he takes it with him.

Bring refers to motion toward a person or place; *take*, to motion away from a person or place. *Bring* implies "*come* to my place with. . ."; *take* implies "*go* to your place with. . . ." Stated in another way, the direction of *bring* is toward the speaker; the direction of *take* is away from him.

As simple as these everyday verbs are, they are frequently confused. Webster, unfortunately, has helped muddy the waters with one of its definitions of *bring:* "to take or carry along with one." Those interested in precise meanings, however, need not agree with that definition.

WHEREABOUTS IS IT?

Is it *his whereabouts is* or *his whereabouts are?* The answer: *Whereabouts,* although plural in form, is a singular word and so needs a singular verb—"The whereabouts of the missing bank teller *has* not as yet been revealed."

A trend is growing to consider *whereabouts* a plural in the following kind of construction: "The whereabouts of the fugitives are unknown." There, obviously, more than one fugitive is referred to and a plural verb, so the argument goes, is required. "Not so," say many grammarians, who contend that only location matters and not the number of people involved. Since the fugitives' hideaway is unknown, they point out, one must assume that they are still together; hence only one *whereabouts.* And one of anything takes a singular.

KEEP IT ABOVEBOARD

Above has trod a somewhat uneven grammatical path. No one objects to its use as a preposition—"above the chart"—but when employed either as an adverb or as an adjective, it has not been well received.

Above is commonly used adverbially to mean "mentioned earlier," as in "the rule cited above" or "the above-described example." Even though those phrases are grammatically correct, some writers spurn them in favor of less stodgy, more free-wheeling constructions: "this point," "this fact," "these considerations," or, if need be, "the rule previously cited," "the preceding rule," "the rule previously mentioned." In the light of today's trend toward more natural wording, expressions that are less mechanical and less obtrusive merit consideration.

A practical, though unimportant, objection to the phrase "the rule cited above" is that in printed matter the rule sometimes appears on a previous page and is therefore not physically above the sentence being read.

Although some dictionaries recognize *above* as an adjective—"the above rule"—it should not be used as one in formal writing. Finally, *above* as a noun—"see the above"—has almost no authoritative support. And none can be expected.

Is *never* used properly in "Though there was argument on the motion, Judge Myles never required a brief"?

In that context the adverb *never*, meaning "not ever," is too strong. To express simple negation, use the adverb *not*. The example should be reworded: "Though there was argument on the motion, Judge Myles *did not require* a brief."

HEADQUARTERS IS CAPUT

The word *headquarters* may be regarded as either a singular or a plural noun. The number that the following verb takes is governed by the sense of the word that modifies *headquarters*. To explain: If Boston is the site of a firm's headquarters, the chances are a sentence would read, "The company's headquarters *is* in Boston." Since *company* is a singular word, its possessive form also connotes a singular, and a singular verb naturally follows. Yet *are* would not be incorrect; it is just a writer's choice.

If *their* were used instead of *company's—their* head-quarters—the verb in all likelihood would be changed to *are*. *Their* is a plural, and it bestows a plural sense on *headquarters:* "Their headquarters *are* in Boston." But here, too, no inflexible rule controls and again the writer has an option.

Advice from headquarters: Careful writers do not use *headquarter* as a verb. The sentence "The American Law Institute is headquartered in Philadelphia" should be reworded: "The American Law Institute has its head-quarters in Philadelphia."

WHY FORE MEANS LOOK OUT

If people agreed on the meaning of a word, what the word actually was would not matter for purposes of communication. On every Monday, for example, a chair could be called a door and on Tuesday vice versa, with no confusion. Some words, however, have two disparate meanings, a condition that can mislead or, at the least, bewilder a reader.

Take *forgo* (with the variant spelling *forego*) as an example. It means "to abstain from" or "to relinquish the enjoyment or advantage of": "The author agreed to forgo remuneration until publication day." *Forego*, a separate dictionary listing, means "to precede" or "to go before in time or place," as in *the foregoing paragraph.* That *forego* has no variant spelling. This mishmash means that although *forgo* may properly be spelled "forego," the converse does not apply—*forego* may not be spelled "forgo."

A similar problem arises with *forebear.* It, too, has a variant spelling, *forbear.* A *forebear* is a "forefather," an "ancestor"; "Like his *forebears* (or *forbears*), he was a trapper." But when *forbear* implies "resisting or refraining from," it may be spelled only that way: "The witness could not *forbear* expressing chagrin."

To come full circle, a synonym of this *forbear* is *forgo.*

IMPORTANT THOUGH IT BE

It may sound like a play on words, but *importantly* is sometimes mistakenly used for *important* because to some writers *importantly* sounds more important.

Consider this sentence: "The survey will drag on for years and, more *important* (or more *importantly*), will bankrupt us all." Some writers would prefer *more importantly*, perhaps because of its pretentious ring; but most would let the sentence stand. They would argue that the adverb *more importantly* means "in a more important way," whereas the intended meaning is *what is more important.* That being so, the adjective *important* is required because an adjective may follow *is*, a linking verb, but an adverb may not.

THERE'S NO DOUBT ABOUT IT

When expressing doubt, a sentence should leave no doubt what is meant. *Doubt,* both as a verb and as a noun, is used somewhat differently depending on the type of sentence in which it appears.

First, consider a negative statement: "The defendant has no doubt that he will be exonerated." When negation is expressed, *doubt* is regularly followed by *that.* This kind of statement does not indicate doubt, but actually denies it. Second, consider an interrogative: "Does the arbitrator doubt that we are truthful?" A question also takes *that.* Third, a positive statement: "The police doubt whether the fugitives are still within the state." This is an affirmation of genuine doubt. In such statements, *whether* always follows *doubt.*

Further thoughts: (1) If the third example is reworded, *that* replacing *whether*—"The police *doubt that* the fugitives are still within the state"—the belief originally expressed becomes disbelief. (2) *If,* when used for *whether,* is informal. *Whether* should introduce noun clauses, not *if.* (3) The foregoing rules govern the use of *doubtful* as well.

THE LAST TO KNOW

There are two similar words in the English language that in some contexts run very little risk of being misused, one for the other. The words: *last* and *latest.* The reason: they both mean "most recent."

Those words have been used interchangeably in that sense for generations. The synonymity of *last* and *latest* to mean "most recent" is now accepted on all levels of writing. Both the last and the latest opinion on a subject, for example, refer to the most recent one.

Despite this general acceptance, all usage authorities are not in accord. Precise wording, some say, limits *last* to mean "final" and only *latest* to mean "most recent."

Last does suggest an end, and *latest* does point to what is current. The latest report indicates an expectation of another. The last report, although also the latest, connotes a finality. If an author is asked for a copy of his last book, exactly what is meant? It would seem more tactful to request his latest. Asking for his last might frighten him.

The battle on these words rages on. The last of it has not yet been heard. At least that's the latest report.

GOOD HEALTH KEEPS PEOPLE HEALTHY

It may surprise those who have carefully differentiated between *healthy* and *healthful,* ascribing precise meanings to each, to learn that time has blurred their distinctions. Today some usage authorities regard *healthy* and *healthful* as interchangeable.

The primary meaning of healthful is "conducive to health." Strictly speaking, what promotes good health is healthful. Things such as food, climate, and recreation might be so categorized—yet they may also be described as *healthy.* One meaning of *healthy*, at least in some dictionaries, is "giving health," the same as for *healthful.*

Basically, *healthy* implies a state of good health, of well-being: "A healthy advocate is a vigorous advocate." But a statement like "Drinking orange juice is healthy" has become well established through common usage. *Healthy* is now widely recognized in both senses.

For the sake of clarity, it is wise to abide by traditional meanings: "Healthful climate and healthful food keep people healthy." Nothing's unhealthy about that.

ADJACENT IS NOT CONTIGUOUS

It is important that lawyers do not confuse the words *adjacent* and *contiguous*, especially since they are commonly employed in some legal documents. In general usage, these terms are considered synonyms and are therefore freely interchanged. On a formal level, however, their differences are worth preserving.

Adjacent means "close at hand" or "neighboring." *Contiguous* connotes a touching. A person's property may be adjacent to another's and still be a measurable distance away. Two lots separated by a road, for example, are adjacent but not contiguous; they do not actually abut or border each other. *Black's Law Dictionary* defines *adjacent* as "lying near or close to; sometimes contiguous; neighboring," and then cites this opinion: "*Adjacent* implies that the two objects are not widely separated, though they may not actually touch."

At one time, grammarians objected to *adjacent to* on the ground that since *ad* means *to,* the phrase was redundant. Idiom, however, has long established the expression. A purist desiring to avoid the phrase can, in some instances, shorten *lot adjacent to*—"His lot is adjacent to mine"—to *adjacent lot*—"We have adjacent lots." The need for this trimming, however, is difficult to discern.

SEMICOLONS DO HALF A JOB

The semicolon has a specific purpose—to separate elements of a sentence. Convention has so clearly established its use that inserting a semicolon in its proper place is all but automatic.

(1) A semicolon is used between two distinct parts of a compound sentence when the conjunction has been

omitted: "The charge has been made; the verdict is now up to the jury." In this kind of sentence a comma and a conjunction, or a period alone, could serve instead of a semicolon. The pause occasioned by a semicolon is longer than that caused by a comma; the pause following a period is even longer.

(2) When commas are used within a clause of a compound sentence, especially the first clause, a semicolon separating the clauses, even though joined by a conjunction, makes the sentence clear: "That is to say, when a bill is enacted into law, society must adjust to it; but the adjustment can be quick."

(3) A semicolon is required before a conjunctive adverb sandwiched between independent clauses: "It has been a long trial; however, a victorious one" (the second clause in the example is elliptical, with *it has been* understood). These transitional adverbs, preceded by a semicolon, normally are followed by commas, but a trend to omit them is gathering momentum. Their use, however, is still preferable except after one-syllable adverbs—*thus, hence, so*—and the two-syllable *also*.

(4) In enumerations or items in a series, the items should be separated by semicolons, especially when internal punctuation is needed: "The lecturers were John T. Allanhead, of Boston; Cynthia R. Magruder, of Atlanta; and Rachel E. Galfand, of Tulsa." "Lawyers would find it difficult to function without the services of Prentice-Hall, Inc.; The Bureau of National Affairs, Inc.; and Commerce Clearing House, Inc."

A solid idea: The word *semicolon* needs no separating hyphen. Also, semicolons are placed outside quotation marks.

IT'S RIGHT, REGARDLESS

One may correctly say "Despite your comment . . ." or "Regardless of your statement," but not "Irregardless of what you say. . . ." *Irregardless* is not a legitimate part of the English language.

Since *ir* and *less* both have a negative force, their use in the same term is redundant. Perhaps those who use *irregardless* are thinking of words such as *irregular*, *irrelevant*, and *irreparable*, in which the prefix *ir* means "not," or else are mistakenly mixing *irrespective* and *regardless* and coming up with the oddity *irregardless*.

According to an editorial in the *American Bar Association Journal*, *irregardless* is a favorite word among lawyers. Pointing out that it is grammatically unacceptable, the editorial condemned it as "a meaningless verbal bastard." Efforts to legitimize it have not yet succeeded.

INTERROGATORY

Is there a difference in meaning or acceptance between *interpretative* and *interpretive*?

None that I know of. It is the same word with two different spellings. The older and more widely used form, however, is *interpretative*. Other similar combinations raise similar questions. *Preventive*, for example, is preferred to *preventative;* in fact, it is wise to avoid the latter spelling entirely. Although shorter words are normally preferred to longer ones, their derivations must be considered. *Interpretative*, for example, is preferred because of its Latin derivation.

114

HOW BIG IS ENORMOUS? SO-O-O BIG

A few words about *enormity* and *enormousness* are warranted because one of them is occasionally misused in legal periodicals. That word is *enormity*.

Enormity should be employed only in the sense of "monstrous wickedness or outrageousness." It does not imply size or physical dimensions; and therefore it is best avoided when "hugeness" is meant. An example of its proper use is "The enormity (the heinousness) of the crime shook the entire community."

The word suggesting vastness or immensity is *enormousness*. It may refer either to intangibles—"The enormousness of his knowledge is beyond belief"—or to tangibles—"The blueprints indicated a large building, but no one imagined such enormousness."

In a sentence like "The enormity of organizing so many files was overwhelming," which appeared in a daily newspaper, detecting the misuse of *enormity*, in time, can avoid an "enormous" error.

BEST REGARDS

Consider has several meanings, each governed by its own idiomatic construction. It is most often used to mean "to believe to be" or "to judge." In that sense *consider* is not followed by *as*—"The bar considers Judge Trilling a qualified judge" (not "considers Judge Trilling *as a* qualified judge")—nor is it followed by a clause—"The tax expert considers the brief incomplete" (not "considers the brief *is incomplete*"). But when *consider* means "to study," "to examine," or "to discuss," *as* is then required: "Professor Morris considered Johnstone first as a teacher

115

and then as a judge." "If you consider her as a lawyer, you will find her successful; but if you consider her as a housewife, you will find a complete washout."

Regard has one meaning so similar to the first sense of *consider* that the two words are, in fact, frequently interchanged. However, there is a small but important difference in the way they are handled. *Regard* requires an *as* in a sentence like "Baker regards it as a privilege." *Consider* does not.

Appendix: The verbs *count* and *deem* are like *consider*. They would not take *as* in the "Baker" example. Also, *as* is not idiomatic with *appoint, name, elect,* and *brand.* "Leyden was named Chief Counsel" (not *as* Chief Counsel).

IT MATTERS KNOT

In nautical terms, a *knot* is a measure of speed. If a ship is traveling at 15 knots, it will cover 15 nautical miles in one hour. Its speed is almost, but not exactly, equivalent to an hourly land speed because a sea mile is longer than a land mile—6,080 feet versus 5,280 feet. A sea mile, therefore, equals 1.15 land miles.

A common error is to ascribe to *knots* a "per hour" speed: "The ship was traveling at 15 *knots per hour.*" A *knot* is just as much a unit of speed as is a *mile per hour.* Hence the *per hour* following *knot* is surplusage.

Unknot it: To consider a knot simply a measure of distance is a mistake. As pointed out, a ship that travels at 15 knots will cover a distance in one hour of 15 nautical miles, not knots.

ARE YOU INTO IT?

No sooner had the prisoner shouted, "Go jump in the lake," than the judge bellowed, "Throw him in the slammer." Everyone, no doubt, has heard a similar dialog in which *in* is equated with *into*, for this practice is so widespread that even some dictionaries now consider the prepositions synonyms. It is nonetheless better to differentiate between them.

Traditionally, *in* has indicated "location within"—"The judge is in his chambers"—and *into*, "motion to a point within" or "from outside to inside"—"He ran into the judge's chambers." The distinction between *in* and *into* is typified in the following examples: "The convict walked *in* the courtyard" (within the courtyard) and "The convict walked *into* the courtyard" (he entered it); "We drove *in* a blue sedan" and "We drove *into* a blue sedan" (a striking difference!). The primary caution is to use *into* with verbs of motion unless an idiom is involved. Also, *into*, in another sense, reflects a change of form: "The brief is divided into three sections."

Into should not be confused with the two separate words *in* and *to*. The *in* in the adverb-preposition combination modifies a verb, as in "The escaped convict turned himself in to a parole officer." If *in to* had been written as a single word—"The escaped convict turned himself into a parole officer"—the sentence would not only be inaccurate but ludicrous. This type of problem is sometimes best avoided by rewording—for example, substituting *surrendered* for *turned himself in.*

COME AROUND ABOUT NOON

About means "approximately," as in "There were *about* (instead of *around*) 200 lawyers present." *Around* refers to motion: "The gavel rolled *around* (not *about*) the chairman's desk." Clearly, *around* and *about* are not companionable and should not accompany each other. For example, in "Counsel will produce around about twenty character witnesses," *around* should be omitted.

The expression *at about* is redundant. A report may properly read "The meeting began at 10 A.M." (precise time) or "about 10 A.M." (approximate time), but not "*at about* 10 A.M." (confused time), even though this last is frequently heard.

Since *about* signals an approximation, it should not precede an exact figure. In "About 507 men were there," for instance, either *about* should be omitted or a round figure used.

The same general rule applies to spanning figures: "The report said the thief was about twenty-five to thirty years old." Here, too, *about* is superfluous and should be deleted or just one age mentioned. And since both *about* and *estimate* indicate an approximation, the two words do not belong in the same sentence. In "The amount of money stolen was *estimated* to be *about* $4,000," one guess is enough.

INTERROGATORY

When should Latin terms be hyphenated? How about letters to designate shapes or abbreviations?

Latin phrases, even when used as modifiers before a noun, should not be hyphened: bona fide offer; prima facie evidence; per diem employee; ex officio member. Letters used to form adjectives are always hyphened: S-curved; V-necked. When they accompany nouns, the rule wavers. Usually a hyphen is used: a G-man, an I-beam, the V-sign—but X ray is preferably written open.

FOLLOW THE LEADER

Customarily a list of items is introduced by the expression *as follows*. The singular form *follows* should always be used, whether the preceding noun is singular or plural. Both of the following sentences, for example, are correctly stated: "The description *is as follows*" and "The elements *are as follows*." Idiom simply disregards grammatical convention here; the number of the preceding noun is immaterial. Another line of reasoning, which arrives at the same result, is that *as follows* is an impersonal expression, *it* being the unexpressed subject. *As follows*, therefore, really means *as it follows*.

Some writers, to maintain a plural sense, evade idiom and use *as follow* when a plural noun precedes: "The verdicts rendered today are *as follow*." But this approach has received little approval. The idiom calling for the singular *follows* prevails even in the face of succeeding multiple items: ". . . *are as follows*: $100 to Moffett; $500 to Bock; and $900 to Frazier."

When *as* is omitted, grammatical principles then apply: "A description *follows*" or "The descriptions *follow*."

DISTINCTIVELY YOURS

Distinct and *distinctive* are related words, but that grants no license to use them interchangeably. *Distinct* means "plain," "clear-cut," and "easily perceived": "The expert testified that the thumbprint on the glass was distinct." *Distinctive* emphasizes the quality of being "different, characteristic, set apart from others": "The writing style of Justice Cardozo was distinctive." Even without his signature, an opinion would be recognized as having come from his pen.

119

Both *distinct* and *distinctive* can aptly describe the same person or thing, each in its own way—for example, "Winston Churchill's distinct enunciation was a political asset; his distinctive phraseology, an orator's delight."

A companion word is *distinguish*. Used as an adjective, it implies eminence or renown: "Judge Learned Hand was a distinguished jurist." However, the verb *to distinguish* has the sense of differentiating among several things, pointing out those features that identify objects or people: "It is easy to distinguish a defendant from his counsel. The lawyer is relaxed."

THE GRADUATE

When lawyers are asked to name the law school they attended, they may respond in one of several ways. If they use the verb *graduated,* they should accompany it with *from*. Strictly speaking, a school *graduates* a student and a student *is graduated from* a school: "Vassar still graduates more women than men"; "More men than women are graduated from Villanova."

Today both of the following examples are considered correct: "Mr. Littleton graduated from the Chicago Law School" and "Mr. Littleton was graduated from the Chicago Law School." The latter sentence, in the passive voice, sounds somewhat old-fashioned; the active form—*graduated from*—is in current favor.

A common but improper construction is "He graduated law school last year." That missing *from* impairs the sentence.

Misconceptions: Alumni may, but need not, be graduates of a school. An alumnus (male) or an alumna (female) simply attended a school, whether or not he or she received a diploma. A college dropout is as much an alumnus or an alumna as a summa cum laude graduate.

120

LIKE TO BE WISE?

Consider *likewise*—not the word itself, but its two components, *like* and *wise*, both of which are frequently used as suffixes. As with other constructions, these acceptable suffixes suffer only if overused or, quite naturally, if misused.

Because *-like* may properly be attached to almost any noun, it is seldom misused. The only concern is its spelling—whether or not to hyphenate. Everyday compounds with *-like*—statesmanlike, childlike, officelike, businesslike—need no hyphen unless the root word ends in *l:* girl-like, bell-like. But with temporary compounds—that is, those created for a particular writing—a hyphen, though not required, is preferred, especially if the root word has two or more syllables: monument-like; cataclysmic-like; statistics-like.

-Wise, meaning "in the manner of," as in clockwise, lengthwise, edgewise, is a useful, sensible suffix of long standing. Unfortunately, some writers have recently taken the license of using *-wise*, usually in an abstract sense, to mean "in reference to." They freely convert to adverbs any noun that suits their fancy, even those stigmatized as jargon: functionwise; marriagewise; marketwise.

-Wise compounds have a pseudotechnical ring to some speakers and writers, who may feel that these words convey a sense of broad effectiveness, as though the one expression encompassed entire concepts. Others, no doubt, think they are being economical in condensing three or four words into one *-wise* word. Not so. Consider "Pricewise, we have received no complaints." This could be said more agreeably and with even greater brevity: "Everyone likes our prices."

All temporary -*wise* compounds are not to be condemned, but all should be viewed critically. Here and there one might be useful. But since this use might become addictive, it is wise to remember that, as with other addictions, avoidance is better than a cure.

AN ORAL ARGUMENT

Everyone knows what an oral agreement is—one entered into by the spoken word. And everyone knows what a verbal agreement is—the same as an oral agreement. Certainly lawyers consider *oral* and *verbal* synonyms; if a contract is not written, it is verbal. Current usage, too, generally equates *verbal* and *oral* as meaning "something unwritten."

On a formal level, however, the definitions of *oral* and *verbal* should be distinguished. *Oral* denotes "by mouth"; *verbal,* "in words." The meaning of *oral* is clear; the meaning of *verbal,* since it refers to words that may be either spoken or written, is inexact and confusing. This would not be so if *verbal* meant communication by words as contrasted with other kinds of communication— the nod of a head, the squeeze of a hand, the twinkle of an eye. Unfortunately, this is not true.

In many contexts, *verbal* is quite ambiguous. For example, in "The President verbally took the Secretary to task," whether the admonishment was by writing or by spoken word is simply a guess.

A tag on: Talking about other kinds of communication, a symbol that transmits an idea without words is called a *glyph.* For example, an arrow showing direction is a glyph, as are many roadside signs.

122

IS THE PRESENT EVER PERFECT?

The tense known as the present perfect combines a past participle and a present form of the auxiliary verb *to have*. It is neither a simple past nor a simple present tense. Aptly called a retrospective present, it is a form that delves into the past and connects it with the present. For instance, "He *has passed* his bar examination" is a statement of the present effect of an action that occurred in the past.

Although many grammarians define the present perfect tense simply as a "past action extending to the present," the following, more comprehensive definition may better explain its various applications.

The tense expresses an action or a condition (1) begun in the past but continued into the present—"The Institute *has been working* on the code for over two years"; (2) begun in the past but ending in the present—"We *have* at last *finished* the manuscript"; (3) completed in the past but with consequences extending into the present—"The court *has held* that there can be liability without fault"; (4) completed in the past but at an indefinite time —"He *has tried* many difficult cases."

INTERROGATORY

Why does *ex-Governor* take a hyphen when *ex officio* takes none?

The *ex* in *ex-Governor* is a stressed prefix, which requires an accompanying hyphen. The *ex* in *ex officio* or, for that matter, in other Latin phrases, such as *ex post facto* or *ex libris,* is a preposition meaning "from or out of." Prepositions, even Latin ones, take no hyphens.

Decimate has wandered far afield from its original meaning, "to execute one in ten." Conquerors, it is said, made sport of the vanquished by killing every tenth man chosen by lot. During the days of the Roman legions, *decimate* was commonly used to describe a method of punishing rebellious or cowardly soldiers. Here again, one of ten warriors, chosen by lot, was put to death.

The definition of *decimate* has evolved to mean "to destroy a large or greater part of it"—it now conveys the suggestion of a loss greater than 10 per cent. That gory term, however, should always refer to something thought of in numbers. For example, "to decimate the health of the populace" is incorrect, as is "to decimate the resistance of the opposition." And it is just as improper to say "The Texas Aggies simply decimated Navy's line," except for football announcers who sport their own lingo.

Unless *decimate* is correctly used, it might detract extensively from the sentence—much more than 10 per cent.

DON'T FLOUT CLOUT

Probably no two words with such distinctive meanings are interchanged as frequently as *flout* and *flaunt*. And yet their only point in common is a phonetic resemblance.

Flout means "to mock" or "to scoff at"; *flaunt*, "to show off," "to display boastfully." *Flout* is properly used in "Although indicted, the defendant continued to *flout* the law" (he scoffed at it); *flaunt*, in "Counsel *flaunted* his interrogating skills" (he boasted of his skills).

Flout and *flaunt* are confounded not merely in everyday use but in writings of importance as well. The United States Supreme Court has misused those words in several written opinions. In fact, the frequency of their misuse suggests a caution: Before employing either word, play safe and be sure of its meaning.

RARE, MEDIUM, OR WELL-DONE

To do well by *well* words, two rules should be borne in mind. First, *well* needs a hyphen if it accompanies a past participle that precedes a noun: a well-prepared brief, a well-dressed woman, a well-managed office. This position is called attributive. However, when *well* and the participle follow a verb, a predicate position, *well* is not hyphened if those two words can be reversed without affecting sentence thought: "The brief is well prepared" (or, as reversed, "The brief is prepared well"); "The office is well managed" (reversed, "The office is managed well"). But a hyphen should be used in those compounds in which the intended meaning is affected if *well* and the past participle are reversed. For example, "Jonathan is well-read" makes no sense as *read well.* When this occurs—as it does with *well-manicured* or *well-founded*—a hyphen is necessary in either position: "He is a well-mannered child" (attributive); "The child is well-mannered" (predicative).

Second, when *well* and a present participle form an adjective, a hyphen is required regardless of the position of the noun: the well-meaning judge, the judge is well-meaning; my well-wishing friend, my friend is well-wishing.

One thing more, on a different tack: Well may serve as an adverb of quality between a past participle and an adverb of degree such as *very.* "We are very pleased with the verdict" if changed to "We are very *well* pleased" says it well.

APPRAISE THYSELF

What one knows seems simple; what one does not is another story. Consider the words *appraise* and *apprise*. Though their meanings are distinct and the words are unrelated, they are sometimes confused, one for the other.

Appraise, and its synonym *evaluate,* refers to judging or setting a value: "The auctioneer appraised the property at $10,000." The first caution with both *appraise* and *evaluate* is to avoid the common expression "appraise the value of." Since an appraisal sets a value, that phrasing is redundant—and to evaluate the value of a property sounds even sillier. *Assess* is another word with a similar meaning, but it becomes bothersome only once a year; *assess* means "to value for tax purposes."

The word *apprise,* "to inform or notify"—and here is the second caution—should never be replaced by *appraise:* "I will not make a statement," the defendant muttered, "until I have been appraised of the verdict." He meant notified, or apprised, of course.

Apprize is a little-used variant spelling of *apprise.*

SUBSTANTIALLY DIFFERENT

What is the practical difference in meaning between *essentially* and *substantially?* If a critique, when comparing two works, said the subject matter was treated essentially or substantially the same, would there be a difference? It would not seem so. The fact is that those adverbs are freely interchangeable in ordinary usage, each connoting the idea of "basic" or "of the essence."

When used as adjectives, however, their meanings take on different hues. For one thing, what is essential is

126

indispensable. Further action ceases without it: "The Committee's report is essential to its future conduct." On the other hand, what is substantial need not be indispensable, although in some cases it might be. *Substantial* connotes a great size, a fine quality, or a large amount—all important characteristics, but not necessarily vital. For example, in "A substantial part of the report was prepared by the chairman," only quantity is being referred to, not importance. And sometimes quantity is not essential—may not even be desirable.

A MUTUAL CONCERN

Do lawyers have a common respect for each other, or is it mutual? Do the partners have a mutual friend in the new jurist, or is he a common friend?

Common has the sense of a *sharing* by two or more persons (a common interest, a common heritage); *mutual,* of an *interaction* between two persons, a reciprocity (a mutual respect, a mutual agreement). *Mutual* usually refers to what each of two persons does or feels toward the other: "Allen Schmitz and Willie Meyer have a mutual admiration for each other."

Ordinarily *mutual* indicates a reciprocal relationship between only two persons, but the phrase *a mutual friend,* now widely accepted even by careful writers, may extend to a third person. Popularized by Dickens through his novel *Our Mutual Friend,* the expression, though grammatically inaccurate, has a good basis for acceptance. First, *common,* the appropriate word, carries unsavory connotations—shoddy, coarse, vulgar—and second, *mutual* is the only other word which can adequately express that particular three-way relationship.

127

MIGRATION IS FOR THE BIRDS

Does a person *emigrate* or *immigrate* to the United States —and if he is unsure, must he go back and start over again?

Careful writers use *emigrate* to describe a movement *from* a place of departure—hence a person *emigrates from*—and *immigrate* to describe a movement *to* a destination—a person *immigrates to.* "Knute Rockne emigrated from Norway in 1921. He immigrated to the United States."

Someone who leaves his country to reside elsewhere holds a double status: He is an emigrant when leaving his homeland and an immigrant upon his arrival in the host country. If he keeps moving about, however, he will lose both tags and become a mere migrant.

Return visit: If a writer does not mention the country of exit or entry, he may employ either term, *emigrate* or *immigrate,* depending upon his point of view. For example, "Madame Shupak *emigrated* (or *immigrated*) in 1894."

O SAY CAN YOU SEE

The interjection *oh,* which is used to express different emotions—surprise, pain, disapproval, or even nervousness—is capitalized only when it begins a sentence. But it always requires a following comma: "I must read that brief, and, oh, what a job."

The vocative *O* is handled quite differently on both scores. It is always capitalized, regardless of its position in a sentence, and it takes no punctuation: "Sail on, O Ship of State!"

EXHORT NOT THY COHORT

A *cohort* is not a colleague, not an associate, and not a companion. In fact, no individual can be a cohort. Therefore, a sentence such as "My cohort will assist me in this case" is faulty.

In the time of the Romans, a cohort, numbering between 360 and 600 soldiers, was one of the ten divisions of a legion. Today *cohort* is a nonmilitary term, referring to a large group or company, especially one united for a contest or struggle. To retain the sense of the word, the group must be so large as to be countable only with difficulty: "A cohort of legislators fought the battle for a reform act." "The President was unable to reach all his cohorts before election day."

In the reporting of criminal cases, *cohort* appears frequently as a substitute for co-conspirator, confederate, accessory, henchman, or plain fellow-criminal. This is a misapplication of the word, for *cohort* is not their synonym. A sentence like "The fugitive and his two cohorts were apprehended today" is improperly stated. This misuse of *cohort* is not confined to the criminal field. *Cohort* is often mistakenly used as a synonym for assistant or associate. And assuming that the *co* in *cohort* is a prefix as in co-trustee is erroneous; *cohort* is a solid word.

INTERROGATORY

Is *fellow worker* correct, or is a hyphen required?

Hyphens are not needed with *fellow* compounds: fellow American, fellow student, fellow citizen, fellow traveler. In those examples *fellow* is an adjective. If the noun following *fellow* has only one syllable, the two words should preferably be consolidated: fellowship, fellowman.

129

IS THERE AN ESQUIRE IN THE HOUSE?

Now that lawyers are doctors—it says so on the diploma—what should they call themselves? Doctors? Certainly lawyers qualify for that title. According to the dictionary definition of *doctor,* their right to the title equals that of others who earn it. A doctor is one who holds the highest academic degree awarded by a university in any specific discipline. This means that neither the medical profession nor others who have earned or have been honored with these high degrees have exclusive hold on that title. The training of lawyers and the degree conferred comply with the proper definition in all respects.

Nevertheless, the title *doctor* has become deeply entrenched in American minds as applicable only to members of the healing arts. From a practical point of view, calling lawyers *doctors* could create turmoil in the general public—for instance, who would respond to the terrified shout, "Is there a doctor in the house"? To avoid such misunderstandings, and because they do not seek that kind of recognition, many academic doctors—doctors of philosophy and holders of honorary degrees—prefer the simple title of respect *Mr.* In Great Britain, not even all medical practitioners are called *doctor*—surgeons, for example, are called *mister.*

A related question concerns the use of *esquire,* now that so many women have become members of the legal profession. Since the Middle Ages, *esquire* has referred to males only. From the Norman Conquest onward, the term was used to indicate those persons whose social position was higher than that of tradespeople. Naturally, lawyers were included in this elevated group, but people in many other occupations were also called *esquire.* In America, however, it became customary to accompany

130

only a lawyer's name, sans *Mr.*, with *esquire* or its abbreviated form.

To return to the question, Does the entry of women into the legal profession affect the continued use of *esquire?* Time will tell. Some female lawyers want only the label "Ms." Others think that since in the United States the word *esquire* is synonymous with lawyer, the term is devoid of sexual connotations, and therefore should embrace all lawyers. Of course, another possibility exists—a new word not yet conceived.

FLOTSAM AND JETSAM

The useless accumulations that always seem to overload the supply cabinet or attic might be labeled flotsam and jetsam. Perhaps a more apt name would be junk.

Flotsam and jetsam is a phrase used metaphorically to describe all kinds of debris, human or other, from vagrants and drifters to the excrement on barn floors. It makes for good description if not overused.

At one time *flotsam* and *jetsam* had distinct meanings; they were not, as they are now, a single coinage. *Flotsam* referred to that part of the wreckage of a ship still afloat; *jetsam*, from the Latin verb "to throw," was that part of a cargo tossed overboard to make the ship more seaworthy. From that action arose the word *jettison*.

Once upon a time, the story goes, the king of the realm owned all the flotsam, all the wreckage still afloat. The debris that washed ashore, the jetsam, belonged to the lord on whose property it beached. And there were other terms, too, that pertained to this wreckage, such as *lagan* and *findals*. But no one ever saw fit to make metaphors out of them.

ENDORSEMENTS TO THE REAR

Everyone knows that when the captain of the team endorses a hair lotion, he approves it. That is because *endorse* and *approve* are considered synonyms today.

Years ago, however, it was different. The word "to sanction" or "to have a favorable opinion of" was *approve*. The word meaning "to inscribe on the back of" was *endorse*—which developed logically from the root *dorse*, meaning "back." In fact, two spellings evolved. The other, *indorse*, is a word still in good graces, although less frequently used.

When a person asks where to sign, the answer usually is "Endorse it anywhere on the back." That advice is, of course, a redundancy to be avoided in formal writing. But *endorse on the back* is so widely accepted that it does not even deserve the flick of a fin—a *dorsal*, that is.

A further thought: Advising a person to *endorse on the back* could be helpful if some papers were to be signed on the back and others on the face.

HYPHENS KEEP THEM APART

Many writers use the hyphen to accommodate particular wordings. Through hyphenating unusual word combinations and eliminating hyphens to solidify words, some constructions are individualized and others made more forceful. But many uses of the hyphen are considered standard, and the following listing, with examples, covers those practices about which authorities agree.

A hyphen (1) connects the elements of compound modifiers preceding nouns: a so-called law, a profit-sharing plan, the above-mentioned rule, a happy-go-lucky fellow;

(2) indicates that two or more compounds have a single base—these are "suspensive" hyphens: long- and short-term notes, four- and five-volume sets, a family-owned and -managed business; (3) joins two or more words used as one-thought expressions: a know-how, the secretary-treasurer, a ne'er-do-well; (4) separates prefixes from roots to clarify intended meanings: re-form (not *reform*) the bylaws, re-cover (not *recover*) the book; (5) clarifies miscellaneous constructions: the years 1970-1972, the Chicago-New York flight, Afro-American, semi-invalid, pages 99-101, U-turn.

Of course, hyphens indicate the end-of line divisions of words. The rules governing such divisions are a subject unto themselves.

DILEMMAS KEEP HORNING IN

The word *dilemma*, because some writers consider it a synonym for *difficulty* and *perplexity*, is a problem unto itself. But how a *dilemma* can have its own problem is a puzzle.

Traditionally, *dilemma* has meant "a choice between two unpalatable alternatives." The complete expression, "to be on the horns of a dilemma," indicates graphically why two options are required—horns, of course, come in pairs. Being in a "bind," for example, might be a serious problem, but it is not a dilemma unless one is required to choose between two possibilities, both of which are unpleasant.

Substituting *dilemma* inappropriately achieves nothing but confusion. *Dilemma*, for example, should not be equated with *predicament* or *quandary* or *difficulty* or *plight* or *problem*. These good words are all related, but they need no horns.

A SPLIT INFINITIVE NEEDS NO REPAIR

Although many students have been cautioned against splitting infinitives—placing an adverb between *to* and a main verb—very few have been taught that splitting infinitives is permissible if emphasis is gained, if smoothness of phrasing results, and if meaning is unaffected. Sound peculiar?

Consider this example: "He hoped to quickly borrow money and build a new plant." By splitting the infinitive, *quickly* modifies both *borrow* and *build*, which is what the writer intended. He hoped to do two things quickly—borrow, and then build. If *quickly* was in any other position, it would be unsuitable if not downright erroneous. After *hoped, quickly* would make no sense; following *money*, it would not modify *build*, only *borrow*; placed after *plant*, it would no longer modify *borrow*. The splitting of the infinitive not only sounds right but also helps to clarify meaning.

So much has been written condemning split infinitives that further criticism is like adding a cup of water to the Atlantic Ocean. Indiscriminate splitting, of course, is not championed. In fact, it should be meticulously avoided because it not only makes a sentence awkward but also causes loss in clarity, as it does in this sentence: "Archibald Lipon, a fine lawyer, is able to, although he does not display such prowess on every occasion, exhibit pyrotechnics of oratory." Such foolhardy splitting can give the reader a splitting headache.

Nevertheless, splitting infinitives to avoid ambiguity or awkwardness has been a hallmark of many reputable writers. In "We begged our landlord *to* at least *paint* the outside" and "Efforts *to* amicably *include* dissenters were rebuffed," the splits are warranted and, in fact, encouraged. The unsplit versions not only lack force but alter meaning.

One further point: When an infinitive has an auxiliary—a part of the verb *to be* or *to have*—an adverb may stand between it and the main verb: *"to be* separately *handled";* *"to have* purposely *gone";* *"to be* genuinely *appreciated."* Such constructions are not splits. They should therefore pass muster even with extreme purists.

SANCTIONS HAVE TWO FACES

Homonyms are words that sound alike but have different meanings (*read, reed*). But why do some words carry within themselves two opposing meanings? That seems to be carrying things too far.

Take the word *sanction.* If a course of action is sanctioned, it is permitted or approved: "The court sanctioned the dismissal of the jury panel." Yet an imposed sanction, an economic sanction, for instance, is not a sign of approval, but an effort to discourage the continuance of an action. It connotes disapproval: "Sanctions against the aggressor were voted by the United Nations."

Another two-faced word is *moot.* Its most common meaning is "arguable" or "debatable," as in "Whether or not the death penalty deters criminals is a moot question." But *moot* also means that a question, when no longer relevant, merits no debate, at least not practically: "With the repeal of the law, litigation on its constitutionality has become moot." In other words, debate is now useless.

With all the words in the English language—some 450,000 of them—the need for one word to have two such contrary meanings is hard to fathom.

THINGS LOOK BETTER THROUGH CONTACTS

Lawyers, probably as often as others in professional and business life, use the verb *to contact*. "Please contact me after you've read the lease" or "I will contact you next week" are uses of *contact* heard almost daily.

The verb *to contact* was drawn from the noun *contact* to convey the thought "to get in touch with." Business and professional people find the verb particularly inviting because of its breadth; it leaves open the manner for getting in touch. The word, therefore, seems brisk and businesslike.

When a premium is placed on the number of words used, comprehensive *contact me* enjoys a handiness not possessed by "Telephone me soon," "Look me up," "Let's meet next week," and so on. But there also is a loss in preciseness. The phrase is so indefinite that it leaves one wondering exactly what steps to take. The English language provides other terms that are more specific: *confer with, get in touch with, ask, approach, consult,* and plain *see me*.

Despite the many choices, *to contact* will probably remain the convenience word of the future.

INTERROGATORY

Should the phrase *take place* be distinguished from *occur?*

Yes, but all dictionaries do not agree. Generally *occur* and *take place* are regarded as synonyms. But some authorities make this distinction: they consider what *occurs* as accidental or unforeseen and what *takes place* as scheduled or previously arranged. For example: "The induction will *take place* tomorrow if nothing unexpected *occurs*."

WHAT YEAR WAS IT?

Some abbreviations, despite their simplicity and brevity, are tricky to use. The expressions B.C. and A.D., for example, are properly employed only when they comply with long-established rules.

B.C., although it means before Christ, must *follow* the year: "The village was first inhabited in 93 B.C." A.D., which stands for anno Domini, must *precede* the year: "The city was first built in A.D. 460." B.C. is introduced by *in*, "inhabited in 83 B.C.," whereas A.D. bears its own *in—anno* means "in the year": "built A.D. 460."

A question arises whether A.D. may be used after a century: "The battle was fought in the eleventh century A.D." The abbreviation is more economical than the spelled out version—"the eleventh century after the birth of Christ"—but, one way or another, it violates its own literal meaning, "in the year of the Lord." A century cannot be in the year of anything. Nonetheless, it is common for writers, when it aids clarity, to use A.D.: "The octopus was first discovered in the fourth century A.D." If the period is clear, as is often the case, the era is preferably omitted: "The Declaration of Independence was signed in 1776."

Ancient Days: Many non-Christian writers use the abbreviation B.C.E., meaning before the Common Era, instead of B.C.

AS IF YOU DIDN'T KNOW

The basic point behind the use of *as if* and *as though* is that they introduce suppositions, and suppositions require the subjunctive mood. Although the subjunctive is no longer in favor—there are few uses for it in current writing—it still functions to express a contrary-to-fact condition.

The introductory words *as if* and *as though* signal that such a hypothetical condition is forthcoming. For example, "He handed out money as though he were a king" and "He ran as if he were pursued by tigers" describe unreal conditions. That is, although they could be true, they are not in those contexts. They therefore take a subjunctive form, *were*.

In formal writing, *as though* is preferred to *as if*.

HE'S GOT YOUR NUMBER

The rules governing the use of both *number* and *amount* and *fewer* and *less* are similar. Like *fewer, number* refers to separate units, countable things: "He is collecting a number of Blackstone editions." Like *less, amount* refers to quantity, unified mass—bulk, weight, or sums: "We need a larger amount of time, money, and humor to finish this job."

Although the *amount* of something is *less* than expected (*less patience, less sand*), the words *amount* and *number* are not properly modified by *less,* but by *small* (or *large*): "A small (not a *less*) amount of ink was delivered," even though less ink was received than expected.

Word savers: Since *a number* means "many," it is more concise to say that than to say *a number*. "A number of lawyers were in the courtroom today" can be shortened to "Many lawyers were. . . ." And "Here is a check *in the amount of* $25" usually needs only *of* or *for:* "Here is a check *of* (or *for*) $25."

THE FEWER, THE MERRIER

If people paid even less attention to the distinctions between *fewer* and *less* than they do now, the meanings of those words would merge and a useful term, *fewer*, would vanish from the English language.

It is not uncommon to hear "Slim Bread has less calories than its nearest competitor" or "Fifty persons are on the panel, ten less than we normally have." *Fewer* should replace *less* in both sentences.

Fewer refers to number, countable units, items that are distinguishable: fewer books, fewer clients. *Less* is applicable to quantity that can either be measured, such as material in bulk—less debris, less sand—or regarded as a unit, such as weight, money, time, and distance—less than 50 pounds, less than ten dollars, less than two years old. It is also employed in an abstract sense (less pain, less honor).

The question that *fewer* answers is How many? *Less* answers How much? A summarizing example might be "The fewer mistakes we make, the less time we'll spend." *Fewer* takes a plural noun; *less,* a singular.

Less is normally accompanied by *than: less than. More,* the antonym of *less,* differs from it in usage, embracing both number *and* quantity—more clients, more sand.

IN ALL LIKELIHOOD

If there is a likelihood of something happening, any one of these three words—*likely, apt, liable*—may be used to express it. But each has different applications.

The most common of these words is *likely.* It is always suitable to express simple probability: "The code is likely to (probably will) be adopted soon."

The term to express "habitual or natural tendency" is *apt*: "The judge is apt (has a tendency) to stutter when he loses his temper." *Apt* means "to have an inherent inclination toward, or an aptitude for"; hence the word *aptitude*: "An apt student of physics has an aptitude toward that study." Generally *apt* and *likely* are regarded as interchangeable when meaning "probable or tending toward," although *likely* is more widely accepted on a formal level. Used in these senses, the words are followed by infinitives.

Liable, when employed to mean "probable or likely," is informal. It invariably implies an unpleasant sense—exposure to something unwanted: "You're liable to get (exposed to the risk of getting) hurt if you're not careful." The inherent meaning of *liable* pertains to legal responsibility: "If you don't pay, you're liable to suit."

UP-TO-DATE IS CURRENT

The reason for the quandary over whether to hyphenate *up to date* is that sometimes it is properly hyphened and sometimes not. When *up to date* is used as an adjective, it always takes hyphens: "We have an up-to-date Manual." "Our Manual is up-to-date." But when used adverbially, it needs none: "Up to date nothing has been received." As an adverb, *up to date* answers the question *When?*

When *up to date* follows the verb *bring* or *keep,* it may be considered an adjective or an adverb and treated either way: "The professor keeps his material up to date" (adverb, no hyphens) or ". . . keeps his material up-to-date" (adjective, hyphens). There is a shade of difference between these uses. Which shade is more comfortable is for the writer to decide.

WHAT'S AT THE TOP?

A *climax* is the highest point reached through a scale of increasing, ascending gradations. It implies a series of steps or values resulting in a culmination: "The climax of his career was his election as president." A rhetorical climax concludes the ascending order of phrases or sentences. "I met her, I wooed her, I won her hand, I married her—all in one year."

Acme means "summit," the highest point. From this peak, physical or other, there can be no continuation. *Climax* should not be used as a synonym for *acme* because *acme* does not contain within it the sense of a continuous series. The acme is the culmination itself, the highest point of perfection or utmost attainment: the acme of his career, the acme of its power.

An *epitome,* derived from the Greek *epitimos,* "cut short or abridged," is a summary, a condensed account, or a characteristic sample; it is not an acme or a climax. It is incorrect to say, for instance, "Skelly's appointment to the bench was the epitome of his career." It was the high point, the pinnacle, the apex, perhaps, but not its summation. *Epitome* in less formal usage means "a condensed or ideal representation": the epitome of fashion.

INTERROGATORY

Is there a difference between *unfrequent* and *infrequent?*

Yes and no. As adjectives meaning "not occurring often," they are interchangeable, although *infrequent* is more usual: "The warden's visits were *infrequent* (or *unfrequent*)." But when used verbally to mean "not regularly visited," only the form *unfrequented* is proper: "Since the closing of Alcatraz, the island has been unfrequented."

TOO MUCH SEASONING

As a matter of style, the four seasons and the four terms designating academic years should be lowercased despite their importance. That they are so often capitalized reveals a reluctance to deemphasize what many consider to be key words.

Most style manuals favor lowercasing the seasons unless they are personified: "The Spring is dancing through all the countryside." Normally they should be written thus: "The four seasons are spring, summer, fall, and winter." The urge some writers have to capitalize a season accompanying a year, as in "The seminar will be held in the Winter of 1980," should be restrained. The capital letter is uncalled for: "the winter of 1980."

Although the names of college classes are capitalized—Freshman Class—the names of academic years—freshman, sophomore, junior, senior—are not. Even academic degrees are written in lowercase when referred to in general terms: "He received his *bachelor's* degree from Cornell." "Elsie expects her *doctorate* in the spring." When the name of an academic degree follows the holder's name, however, it should be capitalized: Herbert A. Watson, *Doctor of Philosophy;* Herbert A. Watson, *Ph.D.*

When referring to a century, the number should be written out in lower case: "The Dred Scott decision was a *nineteenth* century landmark."

XEROX IS A COPYCAT

If Jim said, "I'm sending you a xerox of that letter," everyone would know what he meant. Xeroxing, in common usage, is equated with making a copy of something. Yet his statement raises some problems. First, a letter cannot be xeroxed; there is no such verb. Second, *xerox* is not a generic word, and so one cannot send a xerox of a letter.

The word *Xerox* is a proper noun, a trade name of a copy machine manufacturer. Since nouns may always be used adjectivally, it is correct to say that a Xerox copy of a letter will be sent, if a Xerox machine is available—which is another issue. If the reproduction is from a machine made by another company, it certainly cannot be "xeroxed," correctly or incorrectly.

The answer to all this, if the letter is not a Xerox copy, is to use another term—reproduced copy, photographed copy, or copy. The last is probably the best. It has the advantage of brevity.

AD NAUSEAM

Is the commonly heard remark "Yesterday I felt nauseous" proper? The answer is no. *Nauseous* means "causing nausea," which was not what the speaker meant. The word wanted was *nauseated*, meaning "feeling sickness." The remark should have been "I felt nauseated."

A nauseous substance causes people to become ill. For instance, fumes from a gas main break are nauseous; they can cause sickness. People who inhale the fumes may feel sick, that is, become nauseated.

It is also possible to be intellectually nauseated. A repugnant speech, an abhorrent play, or a disgusting news article—any of these may be so repulsive as to be "nauseating." They may bring on a queasy feeling in the pit of the stomach, a nausea.

143

THE EGOTIST AND I

The words *egoist* and *egotist* are often considered synonyms; they sound alike; they look alike; and they both refer to preoccupation with oneself or one's ego. In some instances they are equally applicable to the same person. But here their similarity ends, for, precisely speaking, they are not synonyms.

An *egoist* is a person who thinks only of himself; his own interests are paramount at all times. He may or may not be selfish or conceited, but self-interest is his prime motivation. To an extent, he is a pragmatist, viewing matters both as they are and as they bear upon him. Such a person fires his imagination with thoughts of performing great accomplishments. In short, he sees himself as a pivot.

The *egotist*, a less complex creature, belongs to a more common breed than the philosophically minded egoist. An egotist is simply a conceited, boastful person. He delights in extolling himself in speech and in writing. An egotist loves himself to excess; an egoist refers to himself in excess.

Sidelights: Egotism and its derivatives, *egotistic* and *egotistical*, are more commonly used than the derivations of *egoism*. The antonym of *egoism* is *altruism;* of *egotism, modesty*.

THE ISE HAVE IT

Everyone agrees that only by using a lexicon can correct spelling be assured—memory is bound to slip. And what is worse is that no set rules govern the spelling of some classes of words.

Consider terms ending in *-ance* and *-ence,* for example.

The guideline on selecting one instead of the other is so complex, so difficult to remember, and so shot through with exceptions that it serves no purpose. The best advice, when confronted with this problem: consult a dictionary.

And then there are those commonly used words ending in -ise and -ize, whose spelling is guided by no rule at all. Consider *exorcise* and *organize; compromise* and *analyze; advertise* and *legalize.* Most of the words end in -ize rather than -ise, if that information helps any.

One set of suffixes that was doubtless created just to confuse is -able and -ible. That there is no sensible need for both endings is beside the point. The spellings continue to confound everyone. Look at *includable* and *deductible,* for instance, or *discernible* and *creditable,* or *capable* and *collapsible.* Better yet, look again at the first sentence in this article.

THE OPTIC OF THE BEHOLDER

Names designating those involved in the field of eye care are distinctive in that they pertain to the kind of expertise each person possesses. The four commonly used terms are *oculist, ophthalmologist, optometrist,* and *optician.*

The first two are physicians who specialize in the treatment of diseases and disorders of the eye. Some *ophthalmologists,* however, unlike *oculists,* do not prescribe corrective lenses. They diagnose and treat diseases only. An *optometrist* is not a doctor of medicine, but a doctor of optometry. These doctors examine eyesight and prescribe corrective eyeglasses. An *optician,* akin to a pharmacist, is trained only to fill optical prescriptions.

EVEN PRONOUNS HAVE SEX PROBLEMS

Webster partially defines the word *he* as "one whose sex is unknown or immaterial . . . 'he that hath ears to hear, let him hear'; used as a nominative case form in general statements . . . to include females, fictitious persons . . . and several persons collectively." The recent feminist movement, however, has thrown this use of the pronoun into disfavor, for it considers *he* acceptable only when referring to a male. Since writers have traditionally used *he* or *his* if either the sex of the antecedent was unknown or if both sexes were being referred to, how to avoid sexism in language and still preserve the integrity of the written word is a distressing problem.

In some sentences, references to gender can be omitted. But in others, this is not feasible. The phrase *he or she* is awkward; using *you* lowers the tone of formal writing; and *one* sounds stilted and lifeless. Some words can be desexed by avoidance. For instance, *executrix* or *administrator* can be termed *personal representative*, although some information is then withheld.

Another possibility is to use a neutral plural. "An *attorney* should never arrive late for court; *he* should always be prompt" could read "*Attorneys* should never arrive late for court; *they* should always be prompt." This latter device is not usable in all cases, however; for instance, in "Each is entitled to their own views," *each* requires a singular pronoun. *His or her*, as stated previously, can be employed here, but clumsily.

INTERROGATORY

Is there a simple way to differentiate the spellings of *discreet* and *discrete*?

Discrete means "separate" and the *e*'s are separated. This is not so with *discreet*, which means "prudent."

146

THE ART OF RHETORIC

Rhetorical devices, most bearing Greek names, are useful stratagems to add variety and effectiveness to writing. Their names are unimportant; but they can, in some instances, fire up otherwise drab sentences with word pictures.

Metonymy is the substitution of the name of one thing for the name of another, the names having a close relation to each other, or the use of one word for another which it suggests—"The White House" for Office of the Presidency; "The Crown" for the ruler of the realm.

Synecdoche is a species of metonymy. They differ only in that synecdoche names a part to represent the whole— "mouths to feed" for children; "prow" for ship. It is sometimes difficult to distinguish synecdoche from metonymy.

Litotes is an affirmative statement, expressed by denying the contrary: "not bad" for good; "not a few" for many; "far from correct" for incorrect. "Clarence Darrow was not a bad lawyer."

Oxymoron is a combination of contradicting or incongruous words. The expression is paradoxical: a wise fool, sweet sadness, or Elizabeth Barrett Browning's "thunder of white silence."

Hyperbole is exaggeration for emphasis, often humorous. Even in serious writing this figure of speech is not designed to be taken literally: "The books on his desk were piled a mile high."

Metaphors and *similes* are sister devices in that both are forms of comparison. A *metaphor,* derived from a verb meaning "to ferry across," is an implied comparison, one that does not use *like* or *as:* "He is a lion" or "His words were bolts of lightning directed at each juror." A *simile* uses *like* or *as:* "He roars like a lion." "Her smile was as warm as a summer's day." These figures of speech appear frequently in almost everyone's writings and in everyday conversation. They are useful devices because they conjure up instant pictures. Original metaphors and similes are effective; trite ones—clinging vine, big as a house, green-eyed monster, sharp as a tack, budding genius—and mixtures—the hand of authority stepped in, it is bad luck to change horses after setting sail—should be shunned. The latter fault, known as mixing metaphors, results from a failure to stay with one image. It is like not letting your left hand know that you should step off with the right foot.

SIMILAR IS NOT THE SAME

Similar is not a proper substitute for either *same* or *identical:* "ALI-ABA's distribution of books through the first six months of 1978 was 10 per cent greater than in a *similar* (should be *the same*) period last year." "Prescott's uncle was killed in battle, and his cousin met a *similar* (should be *the same*) end."

The use of *similar* should be restricted to its meaning "having likeness or resemblance, especially in a general way": "Amory's problems with that judge were similar to mine." And it should not be used adverbially for *similarly*.

The adjective *analogous* refers to a partial similarity between things essentially different. Since they correspond in some particular, one item clarifies another: "His experiences with lecturers are analogous to mine with authors."

148

REPLICAS ARE REAL

A *replica* is a technical term in the fine arts. It refers to a facsimile or duplicate of a work made either by the creator of the original or made under his supervision. Reproductions that do not conform to those standards should not be designated *replicas*. Other suitable words are available.

Of this group, the most common and appropriate word is *copy*. And since a copy is a reproduction of an original, the word *reproduction* may also serve. A *facsimile* is an exact reproduction, ordinarily produced by photostatic or photographic equipment. Then there is *duplicate, model, miniature, print,* and *counterpart,* among others.

If *replica* is applied loosely to mean any duplicate, the English language will suffer the loss of a useful term. *Replica,* for example, should not be used in this sentence: "Our waiting room is a replica of the anteroom in Independence Hall." As has been aptly said, "There is no such thing as a modern replica of an ancient original."

RESPECTIVE OF ORDER

Respectively, meaning "each in the order named," serves to tie members of one series to a following descriptive series: "Williams, Benton, and Sager studied in Michigan, Connecticut, and Maine, respectively"; "In 1962, 1965, and 1973, Willoughby was elected district attorney, commissioner, and judge, respectively." Without *respectively,* it might be assumed in the first example that each person studied in all three different states and, in the second, that Willoughby won three elections in each of three years. In such sentences *respectively* serves a useful purpose.

149

If only one series is set out, however, *respectively* is unnecessary because nothing is being matched. For example, *respectively* is pointless in "Those three are practicing physicians in Michigan, Connecticut, and Maine, respectively." No one would imagine that each doctor was practicing in all three states.

The use of *respective* parallels that of *respectively* in that it also is used to sort out items in a series as they relate to one another: "New York and Chicago lawyers know far too little of their respective bar associations." However, *respective*, unlike *respectively*, is seldom useful. In fact, in many sentences it is sheer surplusage, as it is in the following examples: "Students will be interviewed for the respective jobs now available" and "Counsel for both sides returned to their respective seats." If *respective* is believed to be necessary, think twice. Most sentences show improvement without it.

WHO'S ELDER?

Sentences like the ones that follow, which actually appeared in print, are not uncommon: "Prince Rainier has announced the engagement of his eldest daughter." "Prime Minister Trudeau introduced his wife Margaret to the President." These statements, of course, were inaccurate, and each could have been embarrassing. As is well known, the Prince has only two daughters and the Prime Minister just one wife. The announcements implied, however, that Prince Rainier had fathered at least three girls and Mr. Trudeau had acquired two or more wives.

When describing or speaking of only two persons, as in the Rainier example, the form to use is the comparative, *elder* in this case. The superlative, the *est* form, is required when discussing more than two persons or things. An easy way to choose correctly between the *er* and *est* forms is to remember that *er,* with two letters, should be used when comparing two objects; *est,* with three letters, should be employed when there are three or more.

In the Trudeau statement, the problem is one of punctuation; commas should have enclosed the wife's name. The heart of the matter is the difference between restrictive appositives, which are not set off by commas, and nonrestrictive appositives, which are.

Once a family relationship is mentioned—his wife, my son, your daughter—whether a name that follows should be set off by commas depends upon the number of people in that particular family category. If there is only one person, then the name is merely descriptive, and it should be set off. If there are two or more persons, no commas should be used. For example, in the sentence "Mildred's daughter Janet is here," *Janet* is not enclosed in commas, indicating that Mildred has at least another daughter. But in "Mildred's brother, Seymour, is here," the commas betoken only one brother. If Seymour's name had been omitted entirely—"Mildred's brother is here"—the statement would still have been accurate.

INTERROGATORY

An article discussed *elder* and *eldest.* Are these words still used?

Yes, although they sound archaic. In current writing, both formal and informal, *older* and *oldest* are preferred. The phrase, *elder statesman,* however, seems to have carved a permanent niche for itself.

KNOW THY COLON

The use of the colon, like that of other marks of punctuation, is set by convention. Almost everyone uses a colon on occasion; those who do not may consider it too formal for their style of writing.

A few constructions mislead some writers into employing a colon where none belongs. The two most common errors are to use a colon to separate a verb from its object—"After examining the collection, he selected: taxation books, UCC bibliographies, and tort treatises"—and to separate a preposition from its object—"After examining the collection, he selected books about: taxation, the uniform commercial code, and torts." The colons in those examples should be deleted.

A useful rule to remember is that a colon should not immediately follow a form of the verb "to be." In fact, it should not directly follow any verb, but the predominant error involves "to be." In the following sentence, the colon should be omitted: "Among the suggestions for good writing in *The Elements of Style* are: revise and rewrite, do not overwrite, and do not overstate."

A *final caution:* The uses of the colon and the dash should not be confused. A colon introduces a list or an explanation; it promises something to come, as in *"The following is a list of our faculty:* Kenneth James, Elaine Townsend, and Marie Simmons." A dash introduces a summarizing clause that emphasizes what preceded, for example, *"Federal Tax Liens, Basic Accounting for Lawyers, Lifetime and Testamentary Estate Planning*—these are our bestsellers."

The last word: A colon is placed outside quotation marks.

MOSTLY INCORRECT

"Most all books on taxation have a ready market" is a sentence that needs correcting. It contains a colloquialism, *most all*, that does not belong in careful writing. The phrase should be reworded *"Almost all* books . . . have a ready market." *Almost* is an adverb meaning "approximately" or "very nearly."

Most is sometimes misused by itself, that is, without an accompanying *all*. In "Most any day now we should receive an offer," *almost any day* was meant. *Most* is an adjective, the superlative degree of both *many* and *much*.

A somewhat similar situation arises in this sentence: "What is amazing in retrospect is that lawyers are almost never commended for the many good things they do." The phrase *almost never* consists of two incompatible words. *Almost* means "very nearly"; *never*, "not ever." The example would read satisfactorily if *hardly ever* were used instead. *Almost never* is properly used in a few contexts, but they are so rare that it is better not to search for them.

THIS TOO SOLID FLESH

The adverb *too* means "also"—"We, too, will be attending the meeting"—and "more than is desirable"—"The lawyer seems too tired to continue."

When *too* follows *not*, as in "His performance was not too good," it means "very" and suggests sarcasm by understatement, that is, "His performance was awful." A better wording would be *not very good* or *none too good*.

Too in "He was only too pleased to come early" functions as an intensive, meaning "in excess." In this construction, idiom requires that *only* accompany *too*. Also, *too* should not serve transitionally, that is, as a conjunctive adverb, even though its synonym *also* may be so used: "Too, this matter needs attention" should read "Also, this matter. . . ."

Whether to enclose *too* in commas is a matter of taste; some stylists consider such punctuation old-fashioned, but each instance must be decided on its own merit. In formal writing, commas are preferred unless they interfere with sentence rhythm. In "That argument we will handle, too," the comma aids clarity.

Too awkward: "We know that the plaintiff, and his witnesses too, *is* to be present today" reads better, "We know that the plaintiff and his witnesses, too, *are* to be present today."

DOES AU COURANT ALTERNATE?

Although the adjective *alternate* is defined as "an action by turns or step-by-step," dictionaries list it as a synonym of *alternative*, a word with the basic meaning "a choice between two (or more) possibilities." Interchanging these terms serves no purpose except to weaken the language by destroying precision.

In "The office received alternate proposals," the meaning is that the proposals were received one after the other or "each in turn." If they were alternative proposals, several would be delivered for a choice to be made. *Alternative* implies "one *or* the other."

Alternate as used on highway signs—Alternate Route—although inaccurate, is more concise than *alternative* and hence serves better as a signpost. Routes offering a choice are actually alternative routes, but *alternate* has taken its place with other eye-catching sign words.

DON'T PASS THIS UP

No one confuses the meanings of *passed* and *past*. Their misuse is usually just a matter of misspelling.

To avoid this mix-up, two points should be kept in mind. First, *passed,* and not *past,* is the past tense of the verb *to pass*. Second, when action is indicated, a verb form of *pass* is called for: "He passed the ammunition."

Past serves as several parts of speech—adjective (the past months); adverb (he walked past); preposition (it is now past the hour); noun (shades of the past)—but not as a verb. Hence "The judge's best years have past" should be *passed*.

THIS IS WORTHWHILE

One caution about *worthwhile* immediately comes to mind. *Worthwhile* has a built-in temporal sense—*while* means "a short time"—and it should therefore be used only when time is being considered.

Something worthwhile is, by definition, worth the consuming of time. Hence various activities, sports, for example, may be worthwhile—worth the time they take. Although a briefcase or a file cabinet or an automobile may be worth owning, they should not be described as worthwhile.

Worthwhile is sometimes used in a vague sense. For instance, "The business venture was *worthwhile*" does not tell whether it was profitable, challenging, or even socially advantageous. A seminar might have been worthwhile, but it would be helpful to know whether the lectures were informative, entertaining, well-presented, or merely tranquilizing.

Two other matters worth considering: spelling and sentence position. First, spelling. *Worthwhile* is usually spelled solid, as in this sentence, though in the past it commonly was hyphenated. Whether or not to hyphenate is a matter of style and a writer's choice. Second, position. Traditionally, *worthwhile* was used only predicatively: "The job is worthwhile." Today it may be used attributively: "It is a worthwhile job."

No double trouble: It is correct to say a task is worthwhile or worth doing—but not worthwhile doing. Make it one or the other.

SOME FOUL WORDS

Two rather unimportant words that surface occasionally in some writings, and then usually in error, are *fulsome* and *noisome*. They both look like what they are not. *Fulsome* does not mean "full of" and "noisy" is not the definition of *noisome*.

Fulsome means "offensively excessive." It describes remarks so extravagant as to lack good taste, particularly in that they are patently insincere. Those who use the expressions *fulsome praise* and *fulsome oratory,* thinking they are commendatory terms, are well intentioned but mistaken. *Fulsome* should be reserved instead for remarks of disparagement: "Shaw's summation was so pretentious as to be almost fulsome."

Noisome is unrelated not only to noise but to any sound, for that matter. It means either "unwholesome," as in "It is a noisome environment," or "offensive to smell," as in "The prison at Dartmoor was infamous for its noisome air." Come to think of it, a certain sound may be associated with *noisome* after all—a sound of revulsion.

PLUS AND MINUS

Plus is an accepted preposition in the sense of "added to." For example, "Three plus two equals five." "Their projects plus our finances make a good combination." The number given a verb following *plus* is determined by the subject. In the examples, *three*, construed as a singular, takes *equals*, a singular; *projects* (plural) takes *make* (plural).

The use of *plus* as a conjunction is not acceptable on a formal level: "Carlton has fine stage poise, plus he is cooperative and bright" needs a change to *and* or *besides*.

Minus, the opposite sign to *plus*, serves as a preposition, too. "Five minus two equals three" exemplifies its primary meaning, "diminished by." Another meaning, but one not entirely accepted, is "without" or "having lost." Some authorities do not approve of this sense except when used facetiously, as in "They always said Keeney forgets everything. He even went to be sworn in as a judge minus his robe."

INTERROGATORY

Some dictionaries list *include* as a definition of *comprise*. An article stated that *include* is not synonymous with *comprise*. Which is right?

Unabridged dictionaries report all definitions in use—the good, the bad, the indifferent. The inclusion of a definition in such a dictionary does not, ipso facto, equate common meaning with good usage.

It is better, and certainly more precise, to use *comprise* when all parts of something are being named and to reserve *include* for occasions when only some are.

157

A PERSPICACIOUS PERSON

It is difficult to understand why writers use the words *perspicacious* and *perspicuous*. Both these pompous terms are easily replaced by suitable, shorter synonyms. Be that as it may, the words are nonetheless used, and sometimes confused—not only by writers but by some dictionaries as well. Webster, for instance, considers *perspicacious* a synonym of *perspicuous*.

Perspicacious means "shrewd; keen, sharp-witted"; *perspicuous*, "clear, lucid, easily understood." *Perspicacious* is used of people: "A perspicacious person will make a good trader." *Perspicuous* is applied to things, like a treatise or a debate.

A general guide: The shorter the word, the clearer the message.

GET THE POINT?

Lawyers frequently are called upon to provide opinions. If they respond to these requests with personal appraisals, rather than with opinions from other sources, they may preface their remarks to indicate that they are expressing their own attitude. A customary way of doing this is to say, "From my *point of view* (or *viewpoint* or *standpoint*), the idea is. . . ."

All three expressions convey the same meaning, but is any one term preferred? The answer, according to the usage of most respected writers, is no. Although some hardline grammarians contend that *viewpoint* is a colloquial contraction of *point of view*, that viewpoint has not taken hold.

Point of view may be somewhat more formal than *viewpoint*, but the latter term is still acceptable in formal writing. And the narrow objection that *standpoint* is an impossible word because no one can stand on a point is so silly as not to merit serious consideration.

One caution is that these words may become tiresome if overworked. They may be replaced by *opinion* or *view* alone, and more economically.

DEADWOOD IS FOR BURNING

Many words mean the use of too many words—*wordiness, verbosity, prolixity, verbiage*, and plain *long-windedness*. In addition, several rhetorical terms denote a use of more words than are required for clear meaning. *Tautology* is the needless repetition of the same thought in different words: "It is visible to the eye"; "necessary essentials." *Pleonasm*, which means "to be more than enough," also indicates repetition, especially of two words used for the same grammatical function. It is an unnecessary fullness of expression: "My teacher, *he* told us to skip that lesson." *Redundancy*, a more general term, is the use of more words than are strictly needed, an excess or superfluity: "all *of* the members"; "equally *as* good."

No matter which term properly describes a particular fault, the overriding concern is to avoid the use of unnecessary words. In fact, their inclusion violates a basic principle of good writing: meaning should be conveyed with precision and economy. Needless words, like deadwood, should be lopped off.

> A sentence should contain no unnecessary words, a paragraph no unnecessary sentences, for the same reason that a drawing should have no unnecessary lines and a machine no unnecessary parts.
>
> *The Elements of Style*
> —WILLIAM STRUNK, JR.

NOUNS ARE REPLACEABLE

Substituting nouns for verbs makes for static, murky writing, especially when the nouns refer to actions, events, and activities. For example, "The *solution* was the result of a careful *inspection* of the prothonotary's records" is improved as "He *solved* the problem by carefully *inspecting* the prothonotary's records." "Outside the courtroom *violent arguments* frequently occurred" is better as "Outside the courtroom the litigants often *argued* violently."

Almost any singular noun can be easily converted into an adjective. But using more than one noun to modify another noun should be scrupulously avoided in the interest of fluid writing. The sentence "In the third circuit, the lawyer-judge relationship is unusually cordial," for example, is stilted. Formations such as "the criminal procedure study committee," those in which a noun modifies two or more polysyllabic nouns, are particularly awkward. "The committee for the study of criminal procedure" is much more readable.

Unquestionably, the practice of using nouns as modifiers is established and permissible in reputable writing. Whether to use a noun or an adjective, however, is in many instances the writer's decision. Ordinarily the adjective form is preferred—*governmental* action, rather than *government* action—if meaning is not distorted. But an ethics teacher, for instance, is not necessarily an ethical teacher, any more than a sanitation director is a sanitary director.

The use of nouns as modifiers, however, is so common that sometimes it is difficult to determine whether the qualifier is an adjective or a noun: a trial manual, a loose-leaf book, a research scholar.

160

FREE ADVICE IS WORTH IT

Advise, a verb, means "counsel or warn": "Pagano should advise his client not to sign." But using *advise* in the sense of *notify* or *inform* is incorrect. For example, "Please advise Timothy of your decision" should be changed to *notify,* and "My secretary just advised me it is raining," to *informed.*

Everyone must know by now that an expression like *beg to advise* is old-fashioned and that *be advised,* when a person makes a simple statement, is pretentious. But phrases of that kind nevertheless sometimes appear in correspondence.

Advice, a noun, means "a recommended opinion"; the sense of *opinion* is an essential ingredient in *advice.* The statement "the present *advice* is that the courts will close tomorrow," for instance, needs rewording. Forecasts, statements, and announcements are neither advice nor opinions.

One thing more: What is done advisedly is done deliberately, after careful consideration. It is a step back—a consultative step back—from what is done intentionally.

An angry client might intentionally pound the witness dock, but it is unlikely that he did so advisedly.

Another thing: The noun formed from *advise* has two spellings—adviser and advisor. The first one is preferred.

ARE ALTERNATIVES CHOOSY?

A question sometimes raised is, Are there *alternatives* or only an *alternative?* If the choice is between torts and criminal law, are the alternatives torts and criminal law or is there only one alternative, torts or criminal law? Traditionally, *alternative*, derived from the Latin *alter*, has pointed to the second of two possibilities. It is still used in that sense by writers who defer to its Latin origin. But many careful users of the English language have strayed far from that established meaning; they equate *alternative* and *choice*. Today one may safely choose between the singular form *alternative* and the plural form *alternatives*. Both are now commonly employed and both are now equally accepted. *Alternatives* must take a plural verb and the conjunction *and*—"The alternatives are pleading *and* (not *or*) remaining mute"—*alternative*, a singular verb and the conjunction *or*—"The alternative is pleading *or* (not *and*) remaining mute."

Additionally, the meaning of *alternative* and *alternatives* has been enlarged to embrace a suggestion of more than two. In fact, *alternatives* today may be any number: "The armed services offer three alternatives—the army, the navy, and the air force."

One consideration is the difference in connotation between *alternative* and *choice*. A *choice* is made of a person's free will from several possibilities—he may join several bar associations or reject them all—but an *alternative* implies that a choice must be made—the alternative is paying tuition or dropping out of school.

INTERROGATORY

Please comment on the sentence "If he would have called the plaintiff first, he would have won the case."

The premise of a supposition should not contain the word *would*. Stated in another way, *would* does not belong in an *if* clause. Corrected, the example would read: "If he *had* called the plaintiff first, he would have won the case."

TO BE CONTINUED

In everyday conversation *continue* and *resume* are treated synonymously. "Let's continue" and "Let's resume" mean the same thing—"Let's go on."

In writing, however, those verbs should be distinguished because they ordinarily are not interchangeable. *Resume* suggests "a taking up again" after an interruption: "The negotiations resumed after a short break." *Continue* implies no interruption: "The negotiations continued until they ended." It would be proper to say that a trial continued all morning and then resumed after lunch.

Alert: Continue should not be immediately followed by *on,* since continue means "to keep on." When *resume* means "a summary," it should be written with accent marks to indicate pronunciation—résumé.

RESTLESS THOUGHTS

The related words *restive* and *restless,* both derived from the Latin term "to remain standing," imply uneasiness. They should not be equated on that account, however, for the words are not synonyms, and each enjoys a long history of distinctive usage.

Restive, defined as "resistant to control," connotes an impatience under restriction that borders on unruliness. Animals that are restrained—caged, leashed, corralled—might become restive. A person, too, might become restive if imposed restraint and delay are intolerable: "Prison rules make prisoners restive."

Restless implies an uneasiness of mind, an emotional disturbance; it does not suggest any physical restraint. A restless person fidgets: "Lawyers may become restless while waiting to go to court."

163

SPECTATORS, LISTEN TO THIS

Today an *audience*, as listed in many dictionaries, is a group that listens, watches, or even reads; an audience may listen to a lecture, watch a sporting event, or read a bestseller—even a worstseller. The etymology of *audience*, though of little practical consequence, is nonetheless informative for those concerned with precise meanings of words.

Audience is derived from the Latin *audire*, "to hear." Many English words stem from that source: audio, auditory, auditorium. However, when the primary activity is watching, as at a display or an exhibition, those attending are more accurately called spectators. *Spectator* originates from another Latin verb, *spectare*, "to look at," and it too has been the fountainhead of many related English terms: *spectacle, inspector, retrospect.*

In formal writing, *audience* should be restricted to listeners, and *spectators* to lookers. If both looking and listening are involved, however, the preferred word is *audience*. The group watching a play, for example, is aptly named an audience, but calling a readership an audience strains one's hearing a little too much.

WHAT IS SO RARE?

Scarcely and *rarely* in some constructions are probably as synonymous as any two adverbs can be. For example, the meaning of the following sentence is the same, regardless of which word is used: "We *scarcely* (or *rarely*) see them anymore."

But the adjectives *scarce* and *rare* never mean quite the same thing. Although each word suggests a short supply

164

or something "hard to come by," something rare is valuable in itself because its source is diminishing: "Precious gems are so named because they are rare."

What is rare is in permanent short supply. Scarce items, on the other hand, have no lasting value in themselves; they simply are not plentiful at the moment: "The supply of foolscap is scarce today, but a delivery will arrive tomorrow."

A book in insufficient number to accommodate present needs is in scarce supply at this time. A rare book, however, since only a few copies exist, will be rare at any time.

DO YOU REMEMBER?

When a person summons something from memory, does he *remember* or does he *recollect?* Both words imply "a putting oneself in mind of something." The difference between them refers not to the end result, but to the amount of time and effort required to reach that result.

To remember denotes a spontaneous memory. The person experiences a prompt, effortless recall, undisturbed by even a momentary lapse. This kind of memory is popularly termed instant recall.

To recollect suggests an endeavor to recall—a conscious searching of the mind. The process is not instantaneous; it takes time. A person trying to recall is aware of his efforts. He may even feel frustrated until the recollection works its way through. Recollecting is re-collecting (same word but pronounced differently) what was stored in memory. This mental process is what Coleridge speaks of in his well-known statement: "Beasts and babies remember . . . man alone recollects."

GERUNDS VERBALIZE

Probably only pedagogues find it important to know that in "I prefer jogging," *jogging* is a gerund. What is important to understand about gerunds, as a practical matter, is their proper use.

First, a little background. A gerund is a verb ending in *-ing* that functions like a noun; in fact, it is generally called a verbal noun. A gerund may act as the subject of a sentence, "Jogging is my favorite sport"; the object of a verb, "I enjoy jogging"; the object of a preposition, "Bill Dreshner devotes his days to jogging"; and a predicate nominative, "His favorite sport is jogging."

The chief concern with gerunds is whether to abide by the old rule that the subject of a gerund should be expressed by a possessive. Authorities agree that proper names and other nouns linked with a gerund must be in the possessive case: "We object to McCabe's coming." But all do not agree that all *pronouns* should be in the possessive. Although "We object to his coming," for example, is a correct construction and best suited for formal writing, some grammarians would also approve "We object to *him* coming" if the person is to be emphasized rather than the action. There is even greater endorsement of this use of the objective case with plural nouns: "We heard the *children* singing at Christmas."

If a sentence with a gerund seems awkward, either idiom must prevail or the sentence should be restructured. One solution is to use a prepositional phrase when feasible. For example, "The dean discouraged *her attending* class today" could read "The dean discouraged *her from attending* class today."

All this means that considering the flexibility of the rules, good judgment and a finely attuned ear must govern.

TWO DIFFERENT OPPOSITES

Although *reverse* and *converse* have a similar sense, "that which is opposite," they are used in different contexts. *Reverse* is defined as "opposite, inverted, the contrary": "Bibliographies list the names of authors in reverse order —Penico, Frank." *Converse* suggests the turning about of the terms of a statement or proposition. For example, "Grizzwold knows the forest ranger" is the converse of "The forest ranger knows Grizzwold." "The relation of wife to husband is the converse of the relation of husband to wife."

JUST ENOUGH

Just has "just" too many meanings: "precisely" (just perfect), "narrowly" (just missed being struck), "recently" (just left), and "only" (just a morsel).

The term is colloquial when used as an intensive meaning "very" (just fine), "truly" (just great), and "simply" (just grand). The expression *just about* makes no sense; the words are contradictory. And *just exactly* is repetitious. The phrase *just as* takes no intervening *the:* "He was selected just as the others were" (not *just the same as the others were*).

INTERROGATORY

Is it being prissy to prefer *soon* to *quickly* in this sentence: "We asked them to do it quickly"?

The answer depends on the context. To do a thing *quickly* is to do it with speed. To do it *soon* is to begin without delay. That difference could be significant.

167

AS IT OUGHT TO BE

A common word that expresses obligation is *ought*. If something should be done, then it ought to be done. *Ought*, although more imperative than *should,* does not indicate an out-and-out requirement, but it does convey a sense of responsibility. When a sense of compulsion is meant, *must* is the word to express it.

Ought is always followed by an infinitive in affirmative sentences: "We ought to leave" (present tense). "They ought to have followed suit" (past tense). But the infinitive may be omitted if the sentence is clear without it: "Will the judge now charge the jury? He ought to" (charge the jury). In negative statements the sign of the infinitive, *to,* may always be omitted: "It is so late that the judge ought not (*to*) charge now." Whether to use the *to* in such sentences is a writer's decision, but its omission is favored.

An alert: Ought needs a *to* in affirmative sentences unless one is supplied by a following verb. In "Many lawyers ought and some do engage in pro bono activities," *ought* needs its own *to*.

ONE OF THESE DAYS

Some constructions sound more natural when mis-applied. Consider these sentences: "It has been one of those trials that exhausts every juror" and "He is one of those lawyers who wants to litigate all the time." Query: The verbs *exhausts* and *wants* are singular, but should not the relative pronouns *that* and *who* be construed as plurals since they refer to *trials* and *lawyers?*

Although, grammatically, plural antecedents require plural verbs, some respected writers ignore logic and "play it by ear" with this particular *one of* construction.

168

They use a singular verb when in their opinion it makes the sentence sound better. Nonetheless, it is wise to observe customary rules of grammar and to use plural forms in sentences like those in the examples. To be one of those who follow (follows?) the practice of the years will stifle unnecessary criticism.

The following sentences will bear the same analysis: (1) "That is just one of the articles that *make* (not *makes*) this magazine successful." (2) "One of the things which *have* (not *has*) fascinated us most is the new index system." (3) "Peckham is one of those lawyers who *are* (not *is*) dramatic." These constructions are proven when inverted: "Of those lawyers who *are* dramatic, Peckham is one."

Of course, in a sentence like "Jackson is the only one of those lawyers who wants to litigate," the singular verb *wants* is correct because only *one lawyer* wants to litigate.

IN BACK OF THE FRONT

It may seem illogical, but grammarians who reject the expressions *back of* and *in back of* in formal usage do not quarrel with *in front of*. In any event, shorter terms can serve in each instance. Simple substitutes might be *behind* or *rear* for *in back of*—"The law school is *behind* (not *in back of*) the auditorium" and *before* for *in front of*—"The defendant stood *before* (not *in front of*) the judge," even though *in front of* is not grammatically objectionable.

A little behind: The phrase *at the back of*, which has a *the* in it, is proper even in formal usage: "The boy is at the back of the house," but not "in back of the house."

169

THE INTRODUCTORY COMMA

Whether or not to use a comma to set off introductory material can be a vexing problem. In some instances there are no guidelines; where to place a comma is simply a writer's personal decision. In other introductory constructions stylistic rules are well established.

First, the established rules. Commas should set off participial phrases—"Slowed by the death of a negotiator, efforts to reach an agreement made little progress"; infinitive phrases—"To provide an incentive to study, the Board established a series of awards"; nominative absolutes—"The speech having been concluded, we all left"; and dependent adverbial clauses—"After Bocke left Washington, the office functioned better."

Now, a questionable rule—whether or not to set off introductory prepositional phrases. No firm convention governs this usage, but a good suggestion is to use commas only after long phrases, those containing at least seven words. Shorter phrases, unless governed by another rule, should not be followed by a comma. In counting the seven words, hyphened compounds—"semi-invalid," for example—should count as one word. One exception to this rule would be in this example: "In Florida, weather prophets are dismissed daily." Without a comma, one might imagine the sentence meant "In Florida weather. . . ." And in "In 1967, 107 men left the employ," removing the comma runs the numbers together.

A comma in the following sentence is justified because of the length of the phrase: "On account of recent changes in the law, the manuscript had to be rewritten." Some editors, however, lavish commas on introductory prepositional phrases, no matter how short. They would punctuate as in the following sentences: "In the fall, we find seminar attendance at its peak." "During the night, the police searched for the fugitive." Most of today's writers omit these commas.

SPRINKLE THE AGENDA WITH DATA

Some words, like nature, adapt to the times at different rates. English adopts foreign terms slowly.

Take *agenda,* for example, a Latin plural form meaning "things to be done," usually at a meeting. Time has reduced the expression to a singular, so that now the meeting program itself is commonly referred to as the agenda. An example might be "The agenda for tomorrow's convention was mailed yesterday." Because of such usage, *agenda* has developed its own plural—*agendas.*

Data, also a Latin plural, is treated differently from *agenda.* For one thing, *data* has a recognized singular form, *datum,* which, though seldom used, could be. *Agendum,* on the other hand, does not exist in English.

Understandably, many writers purposely avoid using the odd-sounding *datum,* as in "An important datum is now being presented." They get around it by switching to the plural: "An important item in the financial data is now being presented."

Although *data,* in formal writing, needs a plural verb— "The available data *are* subject to review"—in informal writing a singular form is generally used—"Precise data *has* not been offered." In fact, that usage is receiving such ever-widening recognition that its acceptance into formal English may be just a matter of time.

171

SUCH . . . AS IT IS

As functions as a relative pronoun following *such* when *such* is an adjective preceding a noun. This means that it is an error to use *which, that, who,* or *where* as a replacement for *as* in those instances. *Such . . . as* is the correct combination. All this may sound complicated, but examples should clarify any misunderstanding.

Consider the following: "We shall render such assistance that the circumstances allow." "It was meant for such lawyers who contemplate attending." "We condemn such terrible conditions which exist in the inner city." In each example, *as* should have been used instead of *that, who,* and *which.* To repeat—the key to this long-standing convention is that *as* must be the relative pronoun when *such* is used as an adjective before a noun.

Some writers object to the *such . . . as* convention, not on grammatical grounds, but because they think it sounds awkward, as in "Lawyers should carry to court only *such* documents *as* are needed." If this construction is bothersome, it can be cured by changing *such . . . as* to *the, those,* or *that:* "Some lawyers carry to court only *those* documents *that* are needed."

A *related fault:* It is incorrect to say "We taught only in *such* areas *in which* facilities were available." It should read ". . . *such* areas *as those in which.* . . ."

HARANGUE-A-TANG

For the sake of emotional stability, it is best to avoid engaging in either a *harangue* or a *tirade.* But if an oratorical outburst does develop, at least it should be properly labeled. Although both are denunciatory speeches, *harangues* and *tirades* are neither delivered in the same forum nor directed at the same audience.

A *tirade* is a long, intemperate speech, defined as "a prolonged outburst of denunciation." It may be directed to or at a few people or one person only, and it may be made anywhere. A *harangue* is also an intemperate speech—usually vehement, passionate, noisy—but it differs from a tirade in that it is delivered before a large group, usually a public assembly. It need not attack or be vicious, even though its tone is violent. A tirade is a verbal assault; a harangue is scolding rather than vindictive. The following examples are typical: "The Senator engaged in a two-hour harangue on the misuse of federal funds." "Mr. Wilson screamed a tirade of protest and rage at poor Sam."

INTERROGATORY

An article pointed out that a word which follows and is common to two or more complementary or antithetical phrases should be preceded by a comma. Would you give a few more pertinent examples?

Here are some of each. "The report contained many, if not all[,] of the newly acquired exhibits." The words *of the* are common to *many* and *all*. "He plans to, and probably will[,] confer with Sharpe." *Confer* is common to *plans to* and *will*. "This meaningless, though demanding[,] situation must be confronted." *Situation* is common to *meaningless* and *demanding*. "His presentation was more articulate, more informative, more provocative[,] than any of the others." The words *than any* are common to *more articulate, more informative,* and *more provocative*. All bracketed commas are required.

173

OBSTACLES IMPEDE PROGRESS

When a person's progress or action, whether literal or figurative, is seriously hampered, is the interference an *obstacle* or an *impediment?* The answer depends upon the effect the hindrance has on further advancement.

An *obstacle* stands in the way of progress or action, and blocks it. Unless the obstacle is removed or surmounted, further development will cease. For example, "The road-block and police cordon were the obstacles that trapped the fleeing criminals"; "His poor credit was an obstacle the loan officer could not overcome."

An *impediment*, on the other hand, is something that hinders or delays rather than stops, bars, or obstructs. Its root, *ped*, offers a key to its meaning—an impediment causes foot dragging. It hinders by being a burden. In other words, an impediment, unlike an obstacle, does not terminate further movement, but simply makes its continuance more difficult.

IT'S NO USE

It is amazing how often the little word *use* is ignored for a longer and sometimes inappropriate word—*utilize* or *usage*. If *use* were used more often, there would be less general misuse.

Consider *utilize* first. Dictionaries list *utilize* and *use* as synonyms, as indeed they are. *Utilize*, however, connotes "put into use," as in "If we plan better, we can utilize our old inventory after all." In this sense *utilize* suggests the making of some practical use, possibly a profitable use.

Utilize, however, is ugly-sounding and a waste of syllables besides. Leaders in the field of writing recommend employing it only when *use* cannot serve—which is seldom.

Usage, like *utilize*, often incorrectly jolts *use* out of a sentence. But *use* and *usage*, unlike *use* and *utilize*, are not even synonyms—*usage* is a specialized term pertaining to a customary way of doing or a long-continued and adopted practice: "These law books have had hard usage." When referring to language, *usage* commonly means a standard of use that results from word frequency and patterns. But it is often misused in sentences like "The price of the product will drop as its usage increases." *Use* would be the correct word there, as it is in most instances.

X-RAYED WORDS

The term *X ray*, of German origin, was so called because its exact nature was unknown. Whether to capitalize and hyphenate *X ray* depends on how the word is used —as a noun, a verb, or an adjective.

The noun *X ray* is preferably spelled as in this sentence, with a capital *X* and no hyphen. But when it is a verb or adjective, a small *x* followed by a hyphen is standard: "They x-rayed his arm"; "Liza is an x-ray technician."

The expression *cross reference* is similar as far as hyphenation is concerned. In fact, it is sometimes spelled *X reference*. It, too, is not hyphened as a noun—"These cross references are available"—but is hyphened as an adjective or verb: the cross-reference pages; please cross-reference all pages.

Since no consensus on style exists on these expressions, writers may select their own.

175

SMOOTH AS (S)ILK

The word *ilk* has long been accepted as a disparaging term meaning "kind." "We don't need people of that ilk" means that those people are not a wanted kind, not socially acceptable, for instance. The pejorative sense that *ilk* implies is now recognized as standard by some dictionaries.

In Scotland, *ilk* has no such connotation. "Thomas Walters of that ilk" does not mean "kind" or "breed." Instead it relates a personal name to a clan or place, as in "Thomas Walters of that ilk, that is, of Walters."

Despite all this, the meaning of *ilk*, as understood by most people in the United States and as noted in dictionaries, is "breed, class, stripe, or kind"—all used uncomplimentarily. Misuse by the many does not, however, preclude proper use by the few.

A CARAT HAS NO RED TOP

A *carat* is the unit of weight for precious stones and metals: "The sapphire weighs two carats." Gold, however, is measured not in *carats*, but in *karats*, a spelling that arose just to distinguish gold from all other metals. Gold jewelry customarily bears a karat marking, such as "18k," to indicate the fineness of the gold content. One karat is equal to $\frac{1}{24}$ part of pure gold in an alloy; a 24-karat ring, then, is a ring of pure gold.

A *caret*, an inverted v-shaped mark used by writers and editors ($\wedge$), indicates an insertion in a manuscript or printed material. It is an old, standard mark, even appearing on the original copy of the United States Constitution.

NUMBERS CAN COUNT

Numbers always add up and many languages have contributed to the numbering systems used throughout the world today. The *Arabic* figures—1, 2, 3, 4, and so on—enjoy universal acceptance. *Roman* numerals—I, V, X, L, C, D, M—are also widely used, primarily for special purposes: numbering the preliminary pages of books, marking commemorative dates, indicating volume numbers of books and magazines.

In contrast to the ten symbols of the Arabic system, the *Roman* numeral system uses only seven letters. A number is increased by placing a letter *after* another letter of greater or equal value—for example, 13 is a combination of 10 plus 3—X plus III = XIII. A letter placed *before* a letter of greater value decreases the number—40 equals 10 from 50—L minus X = XL. A dash over a numeral multiplies it by 1000—$\overline{V}$ = 5,000; $\overline{L}$ = 50,000.

The *metric* system is based on multiples of ten, and uses two languages—Greek prefixes for multiples and Latin prefixes for divisions. The list below sets out how the prefixes change the meaning of the word *meter*; other terms, such as *gram,* are also modified by these syllables.

Number	*Greek*	*Value*
Ten	*deka*meter	10 meters
Hundred	*hecto*meter	100 meters
Thousand	*kilo*meter	1,000 meters
Million	*mega*meter	1 million meters

Number	*Latin*	*Value*
Ten	*deci*meter	1/10 meter
Hundred	*centi*meter	1/100 meter
Thousand	*milli*meter	1/1,000 meter
Million	*micro*meter	1/1,000,000 meter

THE CLIENT'S MAN

The listing in some dictionaries of *client* and *customer* as synonyms is an unnecessary blurring of definitions.

A *client*, from the Latin *cliens*, originally was a hearer, a listener to advice. Hence it is logically used to describe a person seeking advice from a lawyer. At one time *client* was applied to "a lawyer's customer only," but its use has been extended to include those who seek other kinds of professional advice.

A *customer* is a buyer. By customarily purchasing from a shop, buyers came to be called *customers*. Today the term is applied to all purchasers even though their buying patterns fluctuate. Loyal buyers, on whom shopkeepers can depend, are called *regular customers*.

From any view, the terms *client* and *customer* are not interchangeable. No lawyer, for example, would hang a sign saying, "The client is always right."

THE RIGHT PHRASE

The smallest combination of related words without a subject and predicate is called a phrase. Some phrases have only two words. Since phrases are the backbones of sentences, it is helpful to be able to recognize them and to understand their functions.

Phrases are classified according to the way they are introduced: by prepositions—*after* the seminar, *on* the desk; by participles—*having rushed* into the courtroom, *seated* on the bench; by gerunds—*controlling* the corporation, *governing* the state; by infinitives—*to comply* with the rules, *to sit* quietly; by nouns—*Governor* of Nebraska, *Attila* the Hun; and by simple verbs—*has been appointed, had agreed.*

A phrase functions as though it were a single word—a noun, a verb, an adjective, or an adverb. Functioning as a noun, a phrase may be either the subject of a sentence—"*His major case* was settled," or the object—"He settled *his major case*"; as a verb—"Allen *may help* Roger, but he *cannot help* everyone"; as an adjective—"Fulton is a man *of many talents*"; and as an adverb—"Hawkins always arrives *on time*."

Verbal phrases—participles, gerunds, infinitives—function in different ways. A participle acts as an adjective, modifying a noun or pronoun—"The person *reading over there* is my teacher" (present participle), "The man *struck by the car* was a neighbor" (past participle). Gerund phrases serve as nouns—"Rowing is good exercise" (subject of the sentence); "*By swimming*, he develops his physique" (object of the preposition *by*).

Infinitive phrases may be used in several ways: as an adjective—"It is time *to leave to eat*"; as an adverb—"Wobensmith was impatient *to begin the lecture*"; and as a noun—"The Institute decided *to buy the building*."

How should one differentiate between *economic* and *economical?*

Confine *economic* to the science of economics and to the necessities of life: an economic formula; economic reasons. *Economical*, defined as "saving" or "not wasteful," suggests prudence in management: "That method is economical." "The efficiency expert recommended a more economical way to transmit data." When "thrifty" is the thought, use *economical*.

NEVER SAY NEVER AGAIN

The defendant, when he promised the judge he would *never ever* steal again, was trying to be emphatic—and possibly he impressed the court with his earnestness. But sincerity alone does not deliver good grammar.

Never is defined as "not ever," "at no time whatever," or "on no occasion." It does not aptly refer to a single action, but rather to action occurring over a period, as in "During the three years he attended law school, he never visited the library" or "During De Francesco's many years of practice, he never applied for ABA membership." But when the action is particular rather than extended, *never* is unsuitable. It should not be used, for example, in "Although Tom Fleron went to court yesterday, he never approached the judge." A proper recast would replace *never approached* with *did not approach*.

The antonym of *never* is *ever*. It means "always, any time, or in any case." In negative statements, *ever*, not *never*, is proper: "No one had *ever* (not *never*) filed so voluminous a brief." When a negative qualifying word is involved, such as *seldom, hardly,* or *barely,* whether to use *ever* or *never* is a writer's choice. For instance, it is correct to say either *"Seldom or never* or *seldom if ever* has there been such a turmoil"—though the *if ever* phrase is generally preferred.

IT AIN'T NECESSARILY SO

The dictionary definition of *obviate* is "to meet or anticipate and dispose of." The sense of the word, however, which is more easily kept in mind, is *to make or render unnecessary*: "His voluntary leaving obviated his eviction."

Occasionally *obviate* is misused to mean "make obvious" or "reflect." For example, "Their action in emergencies obviates (makes obvious) the thoroughness of their training" is incorrectly put. *Obviate* is also misused in the sense of *remove* or *eliminate,* as in "All the difficulties were obviated."

ICS IS ICKY

The number of the verb in a sentence must sometimes disregard the number of the noun. Often a verb must be trim enough to accommodate a singular sense even though the governing noun is enlarged to plural proportions.

Take *politics,* for example. Although plural in form, *politics* is frequently singular in meaning. This is so when it refers to a science or profession: "His business is politics." "Politics is a study in itself." But when *politics* means opinions or principles, it has a plural sense and takes a plural verb: "The President's politics are matters of public concern."

Scissors, too, though plural in form, may take a singular or a plural verb: "The scissors *are* (or *is*) on the table," but "A *pair* of scissors *is* on the table." Consider *athletics.* As a system of training, *athletics* is singular: "Athletics is good for all growing children." When referring to sports in general, it takes a plural form: "Intercollegiate athletics are forbidden to failing students."

The names of studies or activities that end in *ics* are normally singular: economics is; mathematics is. "Acoustics is a favorite course here." But "The acoustics have deteriorated" is correct, since no specific course is meant.

181

TRANSPIRE SHOULD EXPIRE

The word *transpire* appears in print so frequently in sentences like "The media discovered what transpired at the meeting" that it is drifting far afield from its original definition. As used here, and as used most commonly, *transpire* means "to happen or come to pass." Many usage authorities, however, reject these shaded meanings.

The definition of *transpire*, derived from Latin, is "breathe through." In its proper sense, it means "leak out or become known." *Transpire* implies an "escape from secrecy": "It soon transpired (came to light) that the accountant was embezzling." But even when used accurately, *transpire* is such a pretentious word that perhaps it belongs in the archives.

The enlarged, informal use of *transpire* is questionable on the ground of "convenience or necessity." Since many words accurately convey the desired meaning—*happen, occur, take place, befall, come to pass, present itself*—no patent need for it exists. Maybe *transpire*, except in botany, should breathe its last—it is pompous with one breath and inaccurate with another.

EXPECTING IS NOT ANTICIPATING

Anticipate and *expect* both refer to a future event, to something foreseen. But there the similarity ends. *Anticipate* suggests preparing or acting in advance of an event, whereas *expect* indicates a mere belief that an event will occur.

Anticipate is often mistakenly used for *expect*, the appropriate word in most constructions. Properly, *anticipate* is used (1) when an event is foreseen and (2) when something is done on its account, as in "Anticipating a

motion contra, counsel prepared a brief in support."
But in "Officials anticipate that the court's activity will
equal last year's" and in "The Commissioner anticipates
another normal caseload," *expect* should replace *anticipate*, since only the likelihood of the occurrence is being
considered and not the taking of measures in advance.

Addendum: The preposition that follows *expect* should
be *of* for a person—"The district attorney expects efficiency *of* his employees"; otherwise, it should be *from*—
"The clerk expects efficiency *from* his new machines."

Unlike *expect, anticipate,* when used in the passive voice,
is not followed by an infinitive: "A quick move was anticipated," but not "The move was anticipated to be quick."
When *expect* is used to mean "suppose or presume," as in
"We expect you want to see our new library," it is informal.

IMPELLED BEYOND BELIEF

The word *impel* implies a force or an urgency that drives
one on. *Induce* does not connote a compelling influence.
A softer word than *impel, induce* means "to lead or to
persuade."

Counsel might rightfully ask "What impelled him" or
"What induced him to ignore the court order?" The
answer depends upon whether an outside force influenced his decision—in which event he was impelled—
or an inner conviction prevailed—in which event he was
induced. Some further examples are "Counsel's fiery presentation impelled the jury to pay close attention." "An
offer of more money induced him to join the firm." "His
family's poverty impelled the student to seek a scholar-
ship."

PLENTY OF WHAT COUNTS

Plenty is used colloquially both as an adverb—"The judge was plenty mad"—and as an adjective preceding a noun—"He has plenty room to move." But its proper use is only as a noun meaning "abundance," normally followed by *of:* "He has plenty of room."

Although some writers use *plenty* as a predicate adjective, as in "The harvest was plenty," most writers reject that use in favor of *plentiful* or *plenteous*, two words with the same meaning, "having or yielding abundance." *Plenteous,* however, sounds literary and is unsuitable in textual writing.

The number to give *plenty* when it is being used as a noun is governed by the context: "Although there *were plenty* of reasons advanced, there *was* not *plenty* of thought behind them."

Are the words *whether* and *if* interchangeable?

No—at least not in formal writing. The conjunction *whether* introduces noun clauses; the conjunction *if* adverbial clauses. In some constructions, the use of one for the other has a drastic effect upon meaning. Consider the following examples:

(1) "Let me know whether this book serves your needs."
(2) "Let me know if this book serves your needs."

The first sentence asks for a reply in any event. The second, however, calls for an answer if, and only if, the book serves satisfactorily. In other words, no response is expected unless the condition created by the *if* clause (that the "book serves your needs") comes to pass.

184

AVERAGES CAN MISLEAD

In general conversation, the words *average, median,* and *mean* are loosely interchanged, with no attendant confusion. But when exactness in meaning is required, distinguishing these words becomes important.

An *average* is determined by adding a series of quantities and then dividing by the number of elements in that series. For example, in the sequence 1, 3, 5, 11, 15, the total of 35 when divided by 5 yields an average of 7. The *median* is the midway point—in an arithmetical series, it is the middle number. In this example, 5 is the median; two numbers fall above it, two below. To illustrate further, if the median dividend of a corporation is $3, the number of payouts above $3 equals the number below it.

The *mean* is also a middle point, but it is found by adding the two extreme series numbers and dividing by two (in the initial example, the mean is 8). The mean is commonly used with temperature statistics; the high and low temperatures of the day are added and divided by 2. For example, an 80° F maximum and 60° F minimum yields a mean of 70° F.

In a nonnumerical sense, *average* should not be equated with *ordinary, common,* or *typical.* An ordinary person or activity should be so termed, not described as average; "He is an average American," for example, could be worded more informatively. And the expression *on the average* is trite.

A FOCUS ON DICHOTOMY

Writers stirred by the novelty and impressive tones of scientific and academic vocabularies often draw from them for their own writings. Though these words arrest attention, they can boomerang disastrously if incorrectly used.

Focus, a term from optics and photography, is often used to mean "to direct attention to," a legitimate usage. But employing it to cover an area even larger than the view of a wide-angle lens is objectionable.

Consider the following two sentences: (1) "We should all now focus our attention on this one subject." No argument with *focus*, as we are being asked to direct our thoughts to a specific matter. (2) "Law students should focus on the many career opportunities available to them." An objection to *focus* there is not that it misleads—the direction to be taken is clear enough—but that it is a needless borrowing from a technical glossary. And the word is not apt anyway—focusing on an unspecified group of things is impossible; a person needs a sharp point on which to direct his attention. More suitable expressions would be *consider, review, evaluate*, or plain *look into*.

Dichotomy is an imposing but commonly misapplied term. In its proper sphere, the study of logic, it means "a division of a whole for analytical purposes into two mutually exclusive parts." It is difficult to transpose it logically into general English. It often simply displaces other words that would serve just as well. For example, in "Socialists hold that a dichotomy exists between the owners of the means of production and the workers," *separation, split*, or *division* puts the thought simply and precisely. And more accurately.

It is best to leave the scientific jargon to the scientists; grammarians have enough dichotomies to focus on.

186

A PERIOD ENDS IT

Ask anyone when a period is used as a mark of punctuation, and chances are he will reply, "At the end of a declarative sentence." That answer, as far as it goes, is correct, since that is its most frequent employment. But it has many other uses, for example, after initials and abbreviations—*id.*, C.O.D., H. W. Barnes; as a decimal point—$5.21, 6.72 grams; and in a group of three to indicate ellipsis—"Bill Farnsworth spoke . . . and went." Miscellaneous uses of the period are after a letter or number in an outline or enumeration and as an eyeleader in an index, but these are of no practical concern to most writers.

Perhaps a better question is when should periods *not* be used. They should not be used with the following: per cent; nicknames—Tom, Dick, Sam; well-known acronyms and abbreviations—UNESCO, FBI, WCAU, NBC; abbreviated common colloquial language—ad, bus, exam, photo; Roman numerals and contractions—George V, Vol. III, sec'y, ass'n; dollar denominations without cents —$50, $1,000; and sentences in parentheses within other sentences—"The president (he was just reelected) will chair the meeting."

CALCULATE THE RECKONING

Calculate is used so frequently to mean "to think, to suppose, to intend"—"He calculated that 10,000 spectators attended" or "He calculated to leave early"—that it is hard to believe the correct meaning is "to ascertain by a precise mathematical method." For instance, in "With our knowledge, we can calculate the velocity of light accurately," no guesswork is involved.

The word derives from the Latin *calculus*, which means

"pebble." During the Roman Empire, the cab drivers figured their fares through a hodometer, a taximeter. This consisted of a container of pebbles so set that the turning of the axle caused the pebbles to fall into a receptacle. At the end of the trip, the pebbles, the *calculi,* were counted to determine, or *calculate,* the fare. No guesswork.

Calculate and *reckon* are synonyms in the sense of computing or systematic reasoning. When used in any other sense—think, believe, guess—these verbs are colloquial and are not fittingly used on a formal level.

PRONE NOT TO MOVE

Since it is commonly said that "position is everything in life," physical position, as well as social status, merits consideration. A person lying *prone* is lying face downward, flat on his stomach. Lying on the side, even though face downward, is not good enough. In another sense, *prone* means "inclined": "He is prone to make quick decisions." The position opposite *prone* is *supine*— lying on the back with the face upward. *Supine* is often used figuratively in the sense of "passive or cowardly": "His supine reaction to criticism reveals his insecurity."

Prostrate and *prone* describe similar positions of the body—on the stomach with the head facing down. *Prostrate* additionally suggests a feeling of helplessness, submission, or fear. A person shooting a rifle may purposely lie prone, but "intention" is not ordinarily implied in *prostrate.* Someone falling prostrate is not acting with full control, and is probably helpless at that moment.

In general usage, *prone* has been enlarged to mean lying flat in any position, and some dictionaries, not caring how one lies, so define it.

APPARENTLY SO

In general writing, it is often difficult to distinguish between *apparent* and *evident*. It can even be troublesome, at times, to clarify the several meanings of *apparent*.

Apparent may be used in the sense of "appearing to be" or "not necessarily real or actual": "Doan's apparent anger proved to be only a joke." "The defendant's apparent unconcern didn't mislead the jury." In these examples, what seemed true was not. Another meaning of *apparent*, quite the opposite, is "capable of easy perception," that which is open, unconcealed. Something apparent is obvious, not hidden: "It is apparent that Lidstone's reelection is assured." "The Mayor's conviction for bribery makes it apparent that he violated the law."

Evident has a basic meaning of "clear to the understanding and satisfactory to the judgment." That which is evident is provable by external, demonstrable signs or facts: "Bregan's happiness was evident." "If we spend more than we earn, it is evident that we will bankrupt ourselves." In these examples, what was apparently true was evidently so.

INTERROGATORY

Which is right—*depositary* or *depository?*

They both are right, but are distinguishable. *Depositary* is applied either (1) to a person or institution entrusted with something of value or (2) to a place where something is held. *Depository* is used to describe only a place where something is deposited or stored, where things may be left for safekeeping or sale.

A DISCOMFORTING THOUGHT

The traditional sense of *to discomfit* is clear—"to cause utter frustration or defeat." More simply put, *to discomfit* means "to thwart, disconcert, or vanquish": "Beckett completely discomfited his adversary." "The ruling will discomfit counsel."

To discomfort means "to make uncomfortable." It connotes uneasiness, possibly pain. Since it is an ordinary word with no hidden meanings, it is discomforting to learn that some dictionaries equate it with *discomfit*.

WHETHER OR NOT YOU LIKE IT

In the expression *whether or not*, whether the *or not* should be omitted is a question on which writers disagree. In most instances the preference of the writer should prevail. If meaning does not require the *or not*, if it is just a filler, as in "We are not sure *whether (or not)* he will attend," certainly it may be omitted. But if the writer prefers emphasis, the *or not* is perfectly acceptable despite its redundancy. It may be superfluous but it is not objectionable.

When equal stress is given to alternatives, as in "The case will be tried whether or not counsel appears" or "The parade will take place whether it rains or not," the *or not* is indispensable. Those sentences without *or not*— "The case will be tried whether counsel appears" and "The parade will take place whether it rains"—make no sense.

A test to decide whether *or not* is required is to substitute *if* for *whether*. If the *if* changes the meaning, *or not* is needed—as is true in the examples in the preceding paragraph.

METICULOUSNESS IS A VIRTUE

Originally *meticulous* meant "exhibiting care prompted by fear or timidity." The word derives from the Latin *metus*, "fear." Today, however, *meticulous* is used to mean "overcareful or fussy about small details"; and neither fear nor timidity has to accompany it. On the contrary, among some writers *meticulous* now enjoys a favorable connotation—a sense of strictness, thoroughness, and preciseness, as exemplified in this statement by Mr. Justice B. N. Cardozo: "[We] no longer interpret contracts with meticulous adherence to the letter when in conflict with the spirit." Other writers, however, assert that *meticulous* still retains a sense of "overdoing," an excessive concern for trifles. These writers equate *meticulous* with *finicky*, not with *scrupulous*.

Scrupulous is the word to use when the meaning intended is "correct to the smallest detail." It describes a person who is punctiliously exact: "He reviewed the book with scrupulous care." Although both *meticulous* and *scrupulous* suggest painstaking effort, *meticulous* is preferably employed when the details are handled with fussiness; *scrupulous*, when they are handled with precision.

Principle: A basic meaning of *scrupulous*, not coming into play here, is "principled."

FACTORS AND OTHER NEEDLESS ELEMENTS

The following words are often used in expository writing to indicate the lines of the discussion. These words are *element, factor, aspect*, and *phase*.

An *element* is "a component part of a whole": an element of grammar, an element of nature. A *factor* is "one of the elements that contributes to bring about any

191

given result": a *factor* in the decision, the *factor* of hered-ity in general health. Essentially *factor* is a mathematical or commercial term, but it is often used as a synonym for *element*.

Phase means "a stage of transition or development." It connotes a temporary state or appearance. Its chief characteristic is "change": the phases of the moon, the different phases of a disease. *Aspect*, a more compre-hensive word, means either appearance to the eye or mind—"From a personal aspect it looks more inviting" —or a way in which a thing may be viewed or re-garded—"questions having many aspects."

Excise department: The foregoing words are sometimes used needlessly, just to pad a sentence. For example, "Another *aspect* of the situation that ought to be con-sidered is the delivery date" could be reduced to "We should consider the delivery date." *Phase* is sometimes misspelled *faze*, a colloquial verb meaning "to worry, dis-concert, or disturb."

What do you think of the expression "the foreseeable future"?

Most usage authorities condemn it on the ground that the future is a blank wall. They say the expression makes no sense—one cannot see into the future. But what the phrase normally means, and what one can sensibly infer, is the future as far as can be predicted. Though probably inappropriate in textual writing, the expression may be useful on other occasions. All this is apart, of course, from the principle of tort law that a person is responsible for the "foreseeable" consequences of his actions that cause injury.

192

NONSENTENCES MAKE SENSE

In general conversation, incomplete sentences, known as sentence fragments, are common. They are easily understood from context or from gestures. In formal writing, however, it is best to avoid them, since they look informal, are sometimes misunderstood, and, strictly speaking, are grammatically incorrect.

Now to reverse direction. Experienced writers use fragments for special purposes. In the hands of a skilled author, fragments can effectively arrest attention. Overuse is discouraged, but not occasional use.

Consider this example. "Why did the union agree to compromise? To end the strike? To end the company's financial decline? To supply the city a much-needed product?" A writer may combine these minor sentences and say instead: "Did the union compromise to end the strike, to end the company's financial decline, or to supply the city a much-needed product?" Complete, but less striking.

THE ADVERB CONFLICT

Some sentences are improperly expressed because of a failure to remember that an introductory adverbial phrase or clause modifies all verbs in the independent clause it precedes.

Take this sentence as an example: "When Albritton goes to court, he tenses and barks at his aide." The adverbial construction—*When Albritton goes to court*—properly modifies both *tenses* and *barks*. The entire clause has the same effect on the verbs as that of a single adverb: "*Usually* he tenses and (*usually* he) barks at his aide."

A problem with these compound predicates develops when the second verb and the introductory phrase are incompatible, that is, the adverb cannot service both verbs. Consider "During the fall term, Blackton fell ill and retired the following year" and "In 1978, the Chief Justice lectured in England and returned to the bench a year later." The first example says that Blackton retired during both the fall term and the next year; and the Chief Justice, in the second, returned to the bench simultaneously in 1978 and 1979. Very unlikely stories. Although the sense in these examples is clear, grammatically the sentences should be unraveled. The web untangles if the adverbial phrase is restricted to one subject—"During the fall term, Blackton fell ill. He retired the following year"—or is subordinated to its proper verb—"The Chief Justice lectured in England in 1978, and returned to the bench a year later."

A GOOD REFERENCE

The meanings of *allude* and *refer* have a basic difference—and also a basic similarity. First, the similarity: Both *allude* and *refer* mention something to which they direct attention. To allude to something is to name it indirectly—"When he mentioned criminality, we knew he was alluding to (meant) Section 12." To refer to something is to name it specifically—"He referred to (named) Section 12 as the section on criminality." Stated in another way, *allude* implies or hints; *refer* states directly. Something identified is not alluded to, but referred to.

Elusive spellings: (1) *Allude* is sometimes mistakenly confused with *elude* because of the similarity in sound. *Elude* means "to escape." (2) *Reference* has only one middle *r; referred* and *referring* have two.

194

TONY ADVERSE

Both *adverse* and *averse* express opposition, but not from the same point of view. *Adverse* means "opposed, contrary, or hostile": adverse rulings, adverse criticism. *Averse*, defined as "reluctant or unwilling," denotes a distaste or dislike for something and a tendency to avoid or spurn it: averse to crowds, averse to air travel. It may involve an emotional feeling—averse to telling a lie—whereas *adverse* reflects a mental state, which may not necessarily suggest dislike or disgust. *Adverse* is better suited to describe ideas and judgments rather than people. Laws may be adverse to some people's beliefs; people may be averse to obeying those laws. Certainly many people were averse to the Nineteenth Amendment.

An inclusive example might be "Although the state legislation was adverse (unfavorable) to the ERA, the women were not averse (reluctant) to continuing the fight." In this sentence, *to* follows both *adverse* and *averse*. Although *from* is occasionally used after *averse*, *to* must always follow *adverse*.

Throwback: Lawyers not averse to charging inordinate fees may have to tolerate adverse criticism.

GOING AROUND IN CIPHERS

The figure *0*, which by itself represents "nothing," can be described by so many words that it really must be something. Dictionaries list *aught, ought, naught, nought, zero,* and *cipher;* yet most people prefer just plain *0*.

Grammarians, on occasion, have tried to determine which of these words has the most distinguished history, proving that even nothing can be important. But such re-

195

search has been all to naught. In fact, it was discovered that *aught* and *ought* stemmed from a printing error— the initial *n* in *naught-nought* had been inadvertently omitted. The shortened spelling *aught-ought* caught on and many printers continued the tradition. Everyone did not recognize the validity of the decapitated *aught-ought,* however, and to this day some pedants do not.

Cipher is the word preferred in formal writing for the Arabic character *0,* but over the telephone *zero* sounds zippy and clear. The people's choice, however, is still just plain *0.* This confirms that, dictionary apart, the voice of the people ought to be heard.

And, oh, one thing more. Some writers distinguish between *aught* and *ought,* using *ought* only as a verb, as they ought: "He ought to know better." *Ought,* then, though still nothing, is nevertheless as important as *nought,* its serious competitor. According to Edgeworth "all Cambridge scholars call the cipher *aught* and all Oxford scholars call the cipher *nought.*" Which is just a lot of goose eggs in America.

Should either the prefix *ex-* or the suffix *-elect* be capitalized when joined to a title?

Neither *ex-*, unless it begins a sentence, nor *-elect* should be capitalized as part of a title. "After the ex-Governor addressed us, we heard from Senator-elect McFarlin."

Although *ex-* and *-elect* take hyphens, they are not italicized unless they are specifically being referred to, as in this sentence.

THE RIGHT SIGN

The words *emblem* and *symbol* are interchangeable in some, but not in all, contexts. Both are visible signs that suggest something invisible or intangible. They are distinguishable, however, in that a symbol might be any outward sign.

A *symbol* is described as a sign that stands for something spiritual or nonmaterial bearing a relationship to it: "The cross is the symbol of Christianity; the Star of David, the Mogen David, is the symbol of Judaism." "Theodore Roosevelt was a symbol of trust busting."

An *emblem* is a sign, too, but its meaning can be found in its Latin root *emblema,* meaning "inlaid ornament." An *emblem* is a design specially created to signify an idea or object usually associated with it: "A balance is an emblem of justice." "The spread eagle is the emblem of the United States." Ordinarily emblems are pictorial representations with mottoes appended to them. They used to appear on the family shields of old; today they are on flags, banners, school crests, and coins.

Symbolism: Symbols may be constructive. When the actual delivery of a sale or gift cannot be made because of its bulk or inaccessibility, a symbolic delivery can be made. Delivering the key to a box in a bank vault serves as a constructive, or symbolic, delivery of its contents.

DIFFERENT KINDS OF LAWYERS

In Great Britain, those engaged in the practice of law are called *barristers* or *solicitors.* The chief distinction between these lawyers is that one represents clients, whereas the other pleads at the bar.

A barrister engages in advocacy, conducting the trial or argument of cases in the superior courts. His nearest American counterpart is "trial lawyer." Barristers do not deal directly with clients; only solicitors do. The fees of barristers, therefore, come not from clients but from solicitors.

Solicitors represent clients and perform for them all general forms of legal work. They plead in the lower courts, in courts of chancery or equity, advise clients, and draft legal papers and documents.

Barristers are known collectively as the bar. Solicitors are not members of the bar; their official organization is called the Law Society.

IN IS OUT

Possibly no preposition surpasses *in* in introducing redundant or unwanted expressions. Any *in* phrase should be examined to see whether it is replaceable by a single word. For example, *in close proximity* is verbiage for *close* or *near, in lieu of* is better stated *instead of,* and *in possession of* can frequently be supplanted by *with.* Certainly *in the neighborhood of* can be shortened, when appropriate, to *about* or *around,* and *in the near future* to *soon.* Only in rare instances (*rarely*?) is the longer expression more suitable.

Inasmuch as should be spelled as in this sentence; better yet, simply replaced by *since.* A companion, also spelled as two words, is *insofar as.* Often it can be replaced by *as to* at the beginning of a sentence. But if *as to* is not wanted, *insofar as* need not be used either. The *in* can be omitted: "So far as we know, the bill has not been signed."

IT'S MINIMUM, TO SAY THE LEAST

Understatement, especially when unintended, can be as bad a fault as overstatement. The sentence "Ehrlich's worth cannot be underestimated" intends to extol him, saying that his worth is beyond expression. But the real sense of the sentence is just the opposite; it states that Ehrlich is worth so little that his value could not be smaller. The sentence should have been recast "Ehrlich's worth cannot be overestimated."

The same rationale applies to *minimize*. "His mastery of legal writing cannot be minimized" says that his mastery is so small that nothing can diminish it. Here again, *overestimated* or *overstated* would have been appropriate.

Minimal standards: Minimal means "smallest or least possible," not "just a little" or "not much." Hence "Our sales were minimal" does not mean that they were smaller than usual, but that they were the least possible. As an adjective, *minimal* is preferred to *minimum*—as at the beginning of this paragraph. The plural of the noun *minimum* is *minimums* or *minima*.

INTERROGATORY

When should "If he were . . ." replace "If he was . . ."?

"If he were" is a subjunctive form used to introduce a contrary-to-fact condition, one that is not true. "If he were (he is not) district attorney, he would prosecute vigorously."

When the clause introduced by *if* is a mere condition, however, one not necessarily contrary to fact, then the indicative should be used, as in "Counsel looked to see if the judge was (he might be) seated" or "If the Chief Justice was absent, no doubt he was ill."

UNAFFECTED SUBJECTS

A basic principle of grammar is that a verb agrees with its subject in person and number. Confusion sometimes arises, however, when a modifying or parenthetic phrase immediately follows the subject. The solution: find the true subject.

Consider these examples: "*Who* besides them *is* (not *are*) willing to provide bail?" "Present *counsel* and every other lawyer *knows* the difference." "The court's *closing* after all those continuances *delays* a final result." In each instance, the true subject is the italicized singular noun; hence the verb is singular, too.

Setting off by commas expressions like *along with, in addition to, together with, accompanied by,* when they immediately follow a subject, makes clear that no compound subject has been formed. The combination of the subject and such expressions, therefore, has no influence on the number of the verb: "The expert's drawing, in addition to his other exhibits, *is* most effective." "The mortgage, including the notes, *is* to be signed." "The testimony, together with the many witnesses, *makes* the case airtight."

The words *plus* and *with* create a different problem in that the phrases they introduce are sometimes set off by commas and sometimes not. It all depends on how they are used. When a phrase with *plus* or *with* is treated parenthetically, it is enclosed in commas; when considered restrictive, that is, an inseparable part of the subject, it takes none. For example, "The amount charged, *plus interest,* amounts to more than contemplated," but "The f.o.b. price *plus the shipping charge* is $2,725.50." "The transcribed copy, *with a complete set of instructions,* is now available," but "The copy *with the signature on the bottom* was the document received today."

200

APOLOGIA

Both *apology* and *excuse* admit having done or said something offensive to someone. An apology acknowledges blame and expresses regret. It admits that one has been wrong, and now seeks to make amends: "I sent him an apology for missing the affair." An excuse implies an intent to be released from blame, but makes no admission of guilt, seeking instead to avoid censure: "His excuse for filing late is that he was hospitalized."

Alibi is a commonly accepted colloquialism for *excuse*: "The lawyer offered no alibi for the verdict." On a formal plane, *alibi* should not be so used. Its legal meaning, "a plea of fact of having been elsewhere when an offense was committed," should be respected: "Chuck Ramsey's alibi was that he was in Baltimore during the Newark holdup."

MEET SUCCESS HEAD-ON

Meet and *meet with* should be interchanged cautiously because in some constructions they do not mean the same thing. For example, in the sense of "to come into the company of," the verbs are distinguishable.

Consider "The dean will meet the new members of the faculty" and "The dean will meet with the new members of the faculty." The first sentence suggests an opportunity "to make the acquaintance of"; the second, a get-together "to join the company of." In the sense of "to experience," *meet with* is required: "Counsel met with an accident as he was hurrying to court."

One common meaning of *meet* and *meet with,* however, is "to encounter": "Seldom do we meet the prothonotary anymore." "The proposal should meet with hearty approval."

DON'T PRESS THE IRONY

In some ways *irony* and *sarcasm* are direct opposites. *Irony* is a rhetorical device in which what is said is contrary to what is really meant. *Sarcasm* is a form of ridicule—its purpose is to hurt someone. For example, "What do you want, little man?" could be either sarcasm or irony. If the person being addressed jumped center for the Portland Trailblazers, the question would be ironic, perhaps tinged with sarcasm. But it would be pure sarcasm if the person was the pee-wee water boy.

Irony, to state it in another way, contrasts the literal with the implied. Of its three basic categories—dramatic irony (an actor commends his actress-wife's virtue just after the audience has seen evidence of infidelity); irony of circumstance (it storms on the day of the Weather Bureau's annual outing); and verbal irony ("This is a great day" is said when it is actually teeming rain)—the last one is the most common. The classic example of verbal irony is W. C. Field's epitaph, prepared at his direction: "Better here than in Philadelphia." Remarks that cloak a person's true feelings are not sarcastic; they are ironic.

THERE'S NOPLACE LIKE NOWHERE

It is not uncommon to see a sentence such as "Counsel went noplace today." *Noplace*, when used as an adverb, is a colloquialism; it should be replaced, at least in serious writing, by *nowhere:* "Counsel went nowhere today."

The rule applies equally to *anyplace, everyplace,* and *someplace.* They, too, should not be used adverbially for *anywhere, everywhere,* and *somewhere:* "I saw him *somewhere"* (not *someplace*).

But as nouns, those same *place* words are standard English. They may be written either open—*any place, no place, some place*—or closed—*anyplace, noplace, someplace:* "The parolee said he is heading for *anyplace* (or *any place*) far away." On a formal level, these words are preferably spelled open.

Two cautions: The *where* adverbs use no terminal *s.* Instead of "Though we looked, we could find him nowheres," it should be *nowhere.* The expression *nowhere near,* as in "The judge is nowhere near finished with his charge," is informal. It is better rephrased *not nearly.*

Final thought: Where should be used only if place is being indicated. In "Here is a book where your questions will be answered," the meaning of *place* is not intended. The sentence should read "Here is a book in which your questions will be answered" or, better yet, "Here is a book that will answer your questions."

BE CAREFUL—CONTAGIOUS

In everyday parlance, *contagious* and *infectious* are loosely interchanged; but they have discrete medical meanings. *Contagious* means communicable by contact; *infectious* means communicable by infection. A *contagious* disease is transmitted from one person to another by direct or indirect contact with the patient. An *infectious* disease is communicated by organisms—by air, by water, by insects, as well as by personal contact.

Contagion is derived from a Latin term meaning "touching." Some people believe, therefore, that only contagious diseases are transmitted by touch and that infectious diseases cannot be. This is not so. Diseases that are infectious may also be contagious.

AN ELLIPSIS CUTS IT SHORT

The word *ellipsis* refers to (1) an omission of words from a sentence, of sentences from a paragraph, or of paragraphs from a text, and (2) the punctuation mark (. . .) that indicates this omission. Usually the ellipsis is a purposeful omission of words to avoid repeating what was said in a preceding construction. In "The first shipment should arrive tomorrow, and the second by Saturday," the omission of *shipment should arrive* following the word *second* saves words, with no resulting confusion. In "All had developed as had been expected," *had been* can be omitted without corrupting the grammar: "All had developed as expected." These elliptical sentences say concisely what is meant. The omitted words are clearly implied.

An ellipsis is also used to eliminate part of an exact quotation that is not required by the main thought being expressed. The omission makes the retained part blend more smoothly into the sentence. For example, "Four score and seven years ago, our fathers brought forth on this continent a new nation, conceived in liberty and dedicated to the proposition that all men are created equal" can read, by eliminating phrases, "Four score and seven years ago, our fathers brought forth . . . a new nation . . . dedicated to the proposition that all men are created equal." The ellipsis does not affect the basic thoughts.

An omission from a quoted sentence is indicated by three dots (periods) or asterisks. Dots are preferred: "Friends, Romans . . . I come to bury Caesar, not to praise him." If a period would follow the ellipsis, a fourth period is required.

WHERE OR WHEN

Definitions that use *is when* or *is where* are faulty. The linking verb *is* should not introduce an adverbial clause, but rather a description of the subject by another noun or a noun with modifiers: "Incarceration is confinement in a penal institution," not "Incarceration is when a person is confined in a penal institution." "The Supreme Court is the highest tribunal of the United States" rather than "The Supreme Court is where nine jurists sit as the highest tribunal of the United States." *Pilferage* is not "where or when a person takes," but "the act of taking." The use of *is when* or *is where* to define is a mark of immature writing.

Where, O Where: Putting *is* aside, *where* is frequently misused for *when.* In the sentence "Where disputes occur, businessmen are reluctant to use legal sanction," *when* should replace *where.* *Where* represents place; *when,* time. *Where* is neither a proper substitute for *that* —"The reporter noted *that* (not *where*) counsel made a serious error"—nor for *in which*—"The office is trying a tort case *in which* (not *where*) contributory negligence is a major factor."

In what general official designations should hyphens not be used?

The most concise answer is from the United States Government Printing Office *Style Manual:* "Do not hyphen a civil or military title denoting a single office. . . ." Therefore, do not hyphen the following: Consul General, Editor in Chief, Lieutenant Governor, Vice President, Sergeant at Arms, Chief of Police, Judge Advocate General, Attorney at Law.

THERE IS LITTLE TO CONCISENESS

Brevity is the essence of *concise* and *succinct*. Both words indicate the using of as few words as possible.

Succinct derives from a Latin word meaning "girded." Its literal meaning, therefore, is "held up as by a girdle," which implies making something compact, tight, and well-knit: "A strict and succinct style is that where you can take away nothing without loss, and that loss to be manifest"—Ben Jonson. What is succinct conveys much with few words.

Concise refers to a style that eliminates all unnecessary words. It stems from a Latin term meaning "to cut." The meaning indicates the action taken by a writer— he cuts or lops off unneeded words: "The style of Sir Ernest Gowers was concise; he used few adjectives and adverbs and avoided expletives almost entirely."

Although both *succinct* and *concise* signify a style in which thoughts are conveyed by few words, strictly speaking only *concise* is a style—"That sentence is pithy because concise"—whereas *succinct* refers to content— "The brief is succinct; it contains no excess material."

DEPRECIATION MAKES IT SMALLER

Look-alikes, just because of their resemblance, can more easily be misapplied than words that do not take after each other. Two such look-alikes are *depreciate* and *deprecate*.

Deprecate means "to express disapproval of" or "to plead or protest against": "The manager deprecated Preston's leaving before quitting time"; "Every honest man must deprecate these deceitful methods." *Depreciate* means "to belittle" or "to lower in value": "He depreciated the importance of his attendance at the meeting."

Depreciate is rarely misused; *deprecate*, frequently. It is not unusual to hear *deprecate* applied in the sense of belittlement, as in "The dean is a modest man; he deprecated his contribution to the school" or "He analyzed his book in a self-deprecating manner." Both sentences need a form of *depreciate*. This misuse is so common that Webster now notes that *deprecate* has been influenced in meaning by *depreciate*. In precise usage, nonetheless, those words should be distinguished.

Depreciate, considered here in the sense of disparagement, has another primary meaning, "to become less in value or price," a commercial term. When so used, the words *in value* should not follow it.

Postscript: *Appreciate* is an antonym of *depreciate*. Therefore, appending *in value* to it is also redundant.

EFFECTIVE WHERE IT COUNTS

Ineffectual is sometimes applied in psychology to mean a person incapable of performing sexually. In general usage, however, an ineffectual person is totally incompetent; he is simply not competent in any undertaking.

Like *ineffectual*, *ineffective* means "not effective, incompetent, futile": "Although Hunt cross-examined well, he was ineffective before a jury." Unlike one who is ineffectual, an ineffective person may be incompetent in one undertaking but completely effective in others: "On a golf course, Lucas was a dud, but with a client he certainly could drive a point home." Lucas was effective where it counted.

207

BLONDES ARE COLORFUL

In Romance languages, adjectives agree in gender with the nouns they modify: *un homme sérieux* (masculine); *une femme sérieuse* (feminine). In English, such words are neutral and serve both genders: *a serious man, a serious woman.*

English has borrowed many foreign words, retaining, in some instances, both the masculine and feminine forms for adjectives and nouns. These imports should bear the label "Handle with Care" to avoid the promiscuous intermingling of the genders. For example, "blonde protégé," a phrase found in a recent magazine article, is inconsistent—*blonde* is feminine and *protégé,* masculine.

The march to anglicize foreign words has moved at different paces. *Protégé,* for instance, the French masculine spelling, is the accepted English spelling, as is *protégée,* the feminine spelling. This applies equally to *fiancé* and *fiancée,* and *blond* and *blonde.* However, in its adjective use, the *e* in *blonde* has been steadily disappearing so that *blond* has become, at least in informal writing, a bisexual word. Some writers use *blonde* when referring to a woman (the blonde Cara) and *blond* in all other cases: "Her blond wig." "The blond wood." As a noun, *blond* is used only of a man, and *blonde* of a woman: "She is a blonde." *Brunet* and *brunette* bear the same distinctions, the first masculine and the second feminine.

Confidant, a masculine form, may be used of either sex according to some respected writers. But not everyone agrees. Many writers still prefer the form *confidante* when referring to a woman.

BETWIXT AND BETWEEN

Consider this sentence in which *between* plays a key role: "There is much in common between the English and the American system of jurisprudence." Is singular *system* correct or should it be "between the English and (no *the*) American *systems*"? The answer is that either form may be used. When *between* precedes two items, each clearly pointed to by a modifying word such as *the*, the construction may be either singular or plural. The writer must decide which conveys his message more clearly or with greater impact.

If the modifiers of the noun are possessives—"An understanding between *their* and *our* attorneys was reached"—a plural noun (*attorneys* here) must be used. Possessives tend to unite rather than separate, and a plural bears the weight of both possessives.

An alternative in these cases is simply to advance the noun, as "between the English *system* of jurisprudence and the American" or "between their *attorney* and ours."

LEAVE THE TILL ALONE

Some writers shy away from *till* because they fear the word is unacceptable. Not true. *Till* is a good word, readily interchangeable with *until*. Both words mean "before," "up to," or "when," and either may properly begin a sentence. Although rhythm should determine the choice between them, *until* is commonly preferred at the beginning of a sentence.

The abbreviated form *'til* is a variant of *until*, frequently seen in advertisements and informal writing. It is a useless abbreviation, however, since it has as many characters as *till*. *'Till* is substandard.

209

APPROXIMATE IS NEAR ENOUGH

Consider this sentence: "The house is about 200 yards from the road." Is *about* properly used, or should *approximately* replace it?

In a strict sense the better choice is *approximately*, a word whose meaning is more precise than *about*'s. But many respected writers prefer *about*, even in formal writing, because it sounds less pompous and is considered synonymous with *approximately* by many dictionaries.

The same question is sometimes raised with the words *though* and *although*. They are interchangeable except for the obvious constructions in which only *though* can serve, such as *even though* or *as though*.

IT'S ALL WRONG

Wrong functions as both an adjective and an adverb. Hence in many constructions *wrong* is right. Before a verb, however, the proper adjective form is *wrongly*: "Two words were wrongly spelled in that brief." When functioning as a verbal modifier in other positions, either *wrongly* or *wrong* is permissible, but *wrong* is preferred: "In that brief, two words were spelled wrong."

INTERROGATORY

What terms are used to describe the two sides of a coin?

Since coins are losing their value, perhaps these descriptions will disappear, too. At the moment, the face is called the *obverse;* the back, the *reverse.* As kids, we always called them *heads* and *tails.*

EUPHEMISMS SAY IT SOFT

Euphemisms are mild, polite, agreeable expressions used to replace a word or words that might be considered blunt, indelicate, or offensive; for example, *expectorate* for *spit*. Although euphemisms are sometimes warranted —to avoid offending someone or to lessen a deep sadness—the better style is to call things by their right names and not to evade exact words.

Beyond that advice, personal taste, dictated in part by local customs, is bound to play a part in the selection of words. What is considered profane in one area, for instance, may be accepted wordage in another. Abstaining from affected forms of writing is still a mark of good style, however.

Euphemisms are frequently applied to matters of death, old age, and bodily functions. Common ones are *to pass on, enter into rest,* and *go to one's reward* for *to die.* There is *halitosis* for bad breath; *abdomen* for belly; *limbs* for legs; *unmentionables* for underwear; *intoxicated* for drunk; *indolent* for lazy; *remains* for corpse; *expecting* for pregnant; and *social disease* for syphilis or gonorrhea.

Bankruptcy becomes *straitened financial circumstances,* stockbrokers are now *account executives,* and the poor are the *underprivileged* or the *disadvantaged.*

Euphemisms have gone so far that waitresses are called *hostesses;* undertakers, *funeral directors* or *morticians;* fortune tellers, *clairvoyant readers;* file clerks, *research consultants;* and plumbers, *sanitary engineers.*

To be tactful is laudatory, but selecting words merely for "respectability" should be viewed with narrowed eyes, or a sense of humor.

CONSEQUENCES COME LATER

The reason for confusion between *subsequent* and *consequent,* probably, is the odd relationship each bears to the other. It is all a matter of sequence. A subsequent event is not necessarily a consequent event, but a consequent event is always subsequent.

Subsequent denotes "succeeding" or "following in order of time." What is subsequent happens later: "Subsequent to his release, Arnold Vivian found himself in difficulty again." Vivian's trouble was not a consequent one—it did not stem from his release—but was simply a later or subsequent happening. *Consequent* means "following as a natural result or effect." A consequent happening develops from a previous occurrence and, therefore, is clearly subsequent to it: "Gatner was indicted for embezzlement; consequent trial will establish his guilt." "The flood and the consequent devastation disrupted the life of Wilkes Barre for years."

Variety department: A substitute for *consequent* is "resultant"; for *subsequent,* "later."

MORTALS SHOULD BE MORAL

Possessing no sense of morals can be described by three words—*amoral, unmoral, nonmoral.* Pedants find some slight distinctions among them, but, practically speaking, they are synonymous.

Amoral is defined as "not aware of moral standards." The definition is applicable to animals, infants, and the mentally deficient, who, since they cannot comprehend moral standards, should not be judged by them. *Unmoral* means "having no morality," which is virtually what

212

amoral means. The distinction between *nonmoral* and its sister words is just as nebulous. *Unmoral* and *nonmoral*, both perfectly good terms, are less commonly used than *amoral*.

Immoral may be applied to persons who are depraved or wicked. Their behavior is "contrary to accepted principles of right and wrong." Immoral persons—burglars, murderers, rapists, for example—are willful violators of moral standards. They realize that their conduct invades the rights of others. In a narrower sense, *immoral* often is equated with sexual license—engaging in illicit sex relations.

Button down: It is said that Robert Louis Stevenson originated the word *amoral* when he said "There is a great deal in life and letters which is not immoral, but simply amoral."

GET ON WITH IT

There is little to say about the distinction in use between *upon* and *on*. In almost every instance, based upon today's parlance, either word is correct. *Upon* is more formal and still is the preferred word to indicate upward motion or to connote "on top of": "The defendant leaped upon the juror." "The files were stacked one upon another."

Some uses of *on* and *upon* are idiomatic, however. It is always *upon* my word, never *on* my word; always *on* my account, never *upon* my account. And in England *on* and *upon* have no rhyme or reason: Kingston *upon* Thames, but Henley *on* Thames.

ONE, TOO?

The idiom *one or more*, which begins with the singular *one*, takes a plural verb: "One or more of the witnesses *have* been prepared for today's trial." "One or more of the secretaries *are* looking for new positions." Yet the idiom *more than*, which begins with a plural sense, can take a singular verb if the following noun is singular: "More than one specification *is* ambiguous." And although "More than one dollar *was* spent," yet "More dollars than one *were* spent."

DEMEAN THING TO SAY

Some people may be surprised to learn that *demean* has two different meanings. Traditionally, it meant "to behave." College students, for example, were admonished "to demean themselves like gentlemen." And although still so defined, nowadays it is seldom used in that sense.

The meaning for *demean* in current favor is "to debase, degrade, or disparage." In fact, that is its only accepted meaning in the vocabulary of some respected writers: "No one thought that Etherton would demean himself by making such an unsuitable marriage."

With either meaning, however, *demean* as a rule is used reflexively—demean themselves, demean himself.

INTERROGATORY

In an article on *imply*, a meaning given was "to hint." Isn't *insinuate* a synonym also?

Both words mean "to hint," but "*to insinuate*" is "to hint slyly or subtly." *Insinuate* implies underhandness. The words are not interchangeable.

214

SUPPOSE NOBODY PRESUMED

Supposedly is defined as "in a way assumed to be actual, real, or genuine." What is *supposedly* so implies uncertainty. It does not suggest that the assumption is correct; on the contrary, it suggests a possibility of error: "Nikles is supposedly in line for a judgeship, but this information is simply hearsay."

Presumably means "probably," implying that a belief is justified by previous experience, sound practice, or logical inference: "Presumably the parade will pass right by our doorstep again this year." "Since the professor has had years of experience, presumably he is competent in his field."

What is *presumably true* is probably so, what is *supposedly true* is possibly so. *Presumably* implies likelihood; *supposedly* accepts something as true on insufficient grounds, and hence is doubtful or questionable.

INTERROGATORIES

Does *strictly* in *strictly forbidden* add to meaning?

No. It seems redundant. Something is either forbidden or not.

Is this sentence correct: "He is one of the best, if not the best, lawyer I know"?

It is not well stated because the comparison is incomplete. The meaning of a final part of a comparison should not depend on a preceding parenthetical phrase. Revised, the sentence would read: "He is one of the best *lawyers* I know, if not the best."

BIBLIOGRAPHIES LIST THEM ALL

A bibliography is an alphabetical list either of sources consulted to write a book or paper, or sources for further research. Unless definitive, a bibliography should list only items that have been evaluated for their suitability.

The style that governs bibliographic entries in footnotes is found in *A Uniform System of Citation:* Harvard Law Review Association, 1976. Publications listed in footnotes differ in many respects from those in bibliographies; for example, in bibliographies the names of authors are inverted.

The format for book entries consists of three units, each followed by a period. (1) The name of the author, inverted for alphabetizing: Leach, Thomas R. The names of coauthors follow in regular order: Leach, Thomas R., and Robert T. Harcar. (2) The title of the book in italics (underlined in typescript): Leach, Thomas R., and Robert T. Harcar. *Tax Problems Simplified.* (3) Facts of publication: Leach, Thomas R., and Robert T. Harcar. *Tax Problems Simplified.* Boston: Hanum Co., 1963. A revised or numbered edition should be noted after the title: *Tax Problems Simplified.* 2d ed.

Magazine and newspaper entries are encased in quotation marks, and specific volume and page numbers and dates are given.

In the typical entries that follow, each item begins flush at the left margin. Subsequent lines are indented.

Davenport, William B., and Daniel R. Murray. *Secured Transactions.* Philadelphia: The American Law Institute-American Bar Association Committee on Continuing Professional Education, 1978.

Rothman, David C., Editor. *Pension and Profit-Sharing Plans*. Philadelphia: The American Law Institute-American Bar Association Committee on Continuing Professional Education, 1978.

Rowan, Thomas. "Tax Problems Abroad." *Estate Planning*. August 14, 1976, p. 7, Col. 2.

Asterisks: (1) Authors' names should conform to the spelling on the title page, that is, if the name on the title page is John J. Boland, it should appear that way, but inverted, in the bibliography, and not "Boland, J. J." (2) Multiple items by the same author should be listed alphabetically by title (excluding *a, an,* or *the*), but the author's name need appear only with the first item. The name may be replaced by a dash for the other references. (3) Indentions should follow the style in the preceding paragraph.

Should a period be placed inside or outside quotation marks? How would, for instance, "In God We Trust" be punctuated?

In Great Britain, a final punctuation mark, even a period, follows closing quotation marks. In the United States, periods and commas are placed inside quotation marks; colons and semicolons outside, as in the following examples:

1. It reads, "In God We Trust."
2. When he said "In God We Trust," everyone nodded.
3. He pointed to "In God We Trust": it is the motto on every American coin.
4. He saw the motto "In God We Trust"; he then knew it was an American coin.

AND IN THE BEGINNING

Good writers sometimes use *and* or *but* or even *or* to begin a sentence. This placement of a conjunction shortens the pause occasioned by a preceding period, creates emphasis, and starts a summing up. It knits the thought that follows with the preceding sentence, or, at times, indicates an afterthought. And, too, those conjunctions avoid cumbrous formal connectives—*moreover, nevertheless, nonetheless, furthermore,* and *however.*

One thing more: A comma, unless otherwise called for, should not follow these conjunctions when they begin a sentence: "And the evening and the morning were the first day."

COSTLY BUT WORTH IT

A quartet of everyday words dealing with business and professional affairs are *price, cost, value,* and *worth.* They are all related terms because they are applicable, in many instances, to the same transactions.

The *price* of an article is the amount a person is willing to sell it for. The price is normally indicated by a figure on a ticket. The *cost* is what the purchaser actually paid for the article, which may be different from the figure on the ticket. The *value* of an article is judged by comparing it with a recognized standard. The article, when compared with other similar articles, may be so superior in quality that the price may be justified and the purchaser induced to spend that sum for it. Its *worth,* however, is subjective. *Worth* relates to a buyer's desire or need for an item. An article may be worth much to a collector, for example, but little to almost anyone else.

A HOUSE IS NOT A HOME

A *synonym* is defined as "a word having the same or nearly the same meaning as another": joyful, elated, glad. *Interchangeable* is defined as "capable of putting each in the place of the other." Books on word usage frequently use both terms, *synonym* and *interchangeable*, because those labels are accepted and concise. And yet "synonyms" do not have exact meanings, and the validity of interchanging them may be as questionable as their meanings.

The English language has so few true synonyms that hunting for them may be futile. The best that can be said for synonyms is that, despite subtle shades of difference, they retain similarity in meaning: *multitude, throng, crowd, mob; agreement, contract, covenant; enterprise, project, venture; decline, reject, spurn; char, scorch, sear, singe, burn.* Synonyms all, but not identical.

More important than knowing many synonyms, however, is an awareness of the effect particular words have on the reader. Skilled writers select words not simply for their meaning but for their connotation as well. Connotations are the associated meanings the words evoke—the pictures they conjure up. These implied meanings may be different, depending on the experience, education, and social level of the reader, but some similar emotional reactions are expectable. For example, though both a *house* and a *home* are defined as "dwellings," a *house* suggests a structure, and usually no more, whereas a *home* is associated with warmth, serenity, security, parents, children—maybe a dog. In choosing words, therefore, significant attributes are of importance.

Almost all synonyms, no matter how nearly identical their definitions, differ in connotations. *Cheap* and *inexpen-*

sive, for instance, are synonymous, but *cheap* suggests "inferior," whereas *inexpensive* implies nothing about quality. An inexpensive article may be valuable despite a low price. *Unwise* and *foolish* both indicate poor judgment or a lack of common sense. Describing a venture as *unwise* does not, however, imply scorn or ridicule of the persons involved, whereas calling it *foolish* would expose them to ridicule.

And so when two words are described as interchangeable, what is really meant is that their connotations in a particular context are so similar as to call up the same, or nearly the same, images.

DON'T GET PERSONAL

Writers and speakers use the terms *personal* and *personally* to emphasize or to bestow importance. "My personal opinion" sounds more impressive to some people's ears than "my opinion" alone. But ordinarily *personal* is unnecessary because an opinion is a personal viewpoint. In rare instances, an opinion may be described as *private* if it differs from a public or official opinion, but calling it *personal* is seldom justified.

The common expressions "Personally I think" and "Dudley is someone I know personally" are open to similar criticism, since *personally* serves no purpose. Omitting *personally* will not affect the sense of those messages. Likewise, *personal* is useless in "a personal friend of mine"; without *personal,* the phrase "a friend of mine" is succinct, complete, and personal.

But business and social relationships can be distinguished. Someone may be a "personal friend" in contrast to a "business friend": "Mr Hughes is a business friend of the controller, but a personal friend of the director."

A COMPLEMENT COMPLETES THE MEANING

Almost no one confuses the meanings of the sound-alikes *compliment* and *complement*. But they are sometimes misspelled, each for the other. Their spellings are distinguishable by remembering that complement means "to complete" and that *complete*, like *complement*, has two *e*'s.

In grammar, a *complement* is an element of a sentence that completes the predication of a verb. The complements of action verbs are called objects: "Hopewell dismissed his *attorney*" (direct object). The complement of a linking verb *be, seem, feel, smell,* and the like—is either a noun or an adjective. These complements describe a subject: "Furthermore, *Robertson* was a *negotiator*" (predicate noun); "*Warren* looked *bad*" (predicate adjective).

One kind of complement, the objective complement, is sometimes confusing. An objective complement completes the sense of a transitive verb and refers to the direct object: "The committee called the project (object) a *failure*"; "With such testimony, the defendant dug his hole (object) *deep*"; "Counsel labeled the charges (object) *ridiculous*." In each instance, the objective complement follows and modifies a noun, which is itself the direct object of the verb.

NOT EQUAL

Since *equal* is an absolute, it is an incomparable adjective. Nothing can be *more, equal* than *equal* itself. A *more equal* distribution of assets, for example, means a *more equitable* distribution, which is the correct way to say it.

Equally and *as* are not companionable; they should there-fore not be coupled. In "His approach was equally as nonsensical," *as* should be deleted. When comparing two persons or things, *as . . . as* is the proper construction, not *equally . . . as.* For example, *equally* should be omitted in "He writes equally as well as his partner" and in "His language was equally as bad as hers." But if only one person is named, *equally* is then the word to use: "His partner writes equally well."

When *equally* introduces two choices, it takes *and,* not *or.* In "It was equally difficult to believe that he had no defense to offer or that he intended not to establish one," the *or* should be *and.*

YET IT SHALL BE

Yet, in the sense of "up to the present," is a temporal adverb. It refers to the time between an occurrence and the moment when the occurrence is being discussed.

To encompass this span of time in a negative statement, *yet* requires a perfect tense, not a simple past tense. In "He has not arrived yet, so I did not go yet," time, in the first clause, with a present perfect, is properly con-tinued to the present; but in the second, with a simple past tense, it is not. The second clause needs correcting: ". . . so I *have not gone* yet."

Still more yet: When serving as a conjunction, *yet,* like any other conjunction, may begin a sentence: "Yet it will come to pass." In this use, *yet* means "but." The ex-pression *as yet,* meaning "so far," is good English at the beginning of a sentence—"As yet we have not received the manuscript"—but not at the end. "We have not received the manuscript as yet" needs its *as* deleted.

222

FLOATING STATEMENTS

Ordinarily the adverbs *such, too,* and *so,* as well as the demonstrative pronoun-adjectives *that* and *those,* should be followed by a completing clause, one that defines the preceding thought. In colloquial speech, completing clauses are frequently omitted, as in "It was such a hot day today." This construction. and others like it, is now considered standard English by some dictionaries.

Nevertheless, in formal writing that kind of statement should not be allowed to float in mid-air. It should be anchored to a completing thought, like those in italics following the quoted examples. "He was *so* angry"— *that I feared for his health.* "We didn't think he was *that* sick"—*to warrant medical examination* (better stated, *so sick as to warrant medical examination*). "It was just *too* good"—*to be true.* "They had *such* an experience"—*as comes to few people.* "It was one of *those* drawn-out sessions"—*the likes of which everyone is subjected to on occasion.*

An easy escape when either *so* or *such* is used for emphasis is to replace it with *very:* "It was *very* (instead of *so*) hot today."

INTERROGATORY

I have seen *worthwhile* spelled as one word and as two words, with and without a hyphen. Which spelling is correct?

Originally the word was spelled *worth while,* as two separate words, and some purists still spell it that way. But an irresistible trend is developing to spell it solid—*worthwhile.* A writer may therefore take his pick.

PREPOSITIONAL IDIOMS

No rules have been formulated that point to the proper combination of verb and preposition to convey an intended meaning. Idiom governs these constructions, and idiom is illogical. When a verb requires an accompanying preposition, then one must resort to memory or else consult a good dictionary.

The problem with relying on memory is that there are innumerable prepositional idioms, combinations of verbs and prepositions. Consider the word *agree* as an example: (1) "The members of the society *agree in* principle." (2) "The bar associations *agree with* the governor's committee." (3) "General Motors will *agree to* RCA's plan." (4) "The congregants now *agree among* themselves to close admission." (5) "The jurors could not *agree on* a verdict."

With so many possibilities, no wonder it's so hard to agree.

DON'T JETTISON THE COMPARISON

Comparisons are made in almost everyone's writings—comparisons of persons, comparisons of things, comparisons of ideas. Formal English requires that comparisons be complete, that is, the terms must not be left to inference. In informal settings, the reader or listener must often use his ingenuity to discover what is being compared.

Frequently, in newspaper promotions and in television commercials, products are advertised as "being better." Better than what? Only seldom is the question answered. In casual conversation, expressions such as "Norton has more gall" (than who or than what?) or "We attended the most fascinating trial" (of Old Bailey? of the year?) are commonplace. These comparisons dangle.

A complete comparison needs either a comparative form, like *more* or *better,* between at least two elements— "Lawrence is a better trial lawyer than Eagelson"—or a superlative form, like *most* or *best,* within a group of three or more elements—"Of the many legal education awards in America, the most prized is the Harrison Tweed." These comparisons are so explicit that nothing need be inferred from the context. And this is as it ought to be. Even comparisons readily understood should be completely spelled out. For example, "After reviewing the file, we knew at once we would need more time and personnel" requires a complement, such as *than we had anticipated.* A comparison cannot go it alone; like a tango, it takes two to compare.

ACCENT THE POSITIVE

Normally thoughts are expressed more clearly in the positive than in the negative. A reader more easily grasps what is than what is not.

The simplest way to assert the positive is to avoid the negative *not* when a positive word will suitably serve. For example, instead of *was not pleased,* say *disappointed;* for *did not encourage, discouraged;* for *was not dependable, untrustworthy;* for *not sane, insane.*

Sentences should contain no more than two negatives, as they then become too hard to follow. In a statement like "Bracelen did not regard the disappointment as unimportant," sorting *not, disappointment,* and *unimportant,* and arranging them logically in the mind, is an unwelcome chore. From so many negatives, nothing positive can develop.

A DISAGREEABLE SUBJECT

Although verbs should agree in number with their subjects, they frequently do not—probably because they are attracted by a noun nearer than the subject. This error can be avoided by remembering that the verb should agree with the *true* subject, not an intervening noun—most often an object of a prepositional phrase modifying the subject.

Consider these sentences in which the true subject is italicized and the correct form of the verb is in parentheses. (1) "A *group* of three files were reviewed" (*was*). (2) "A large *amount* of general information and citations are in that book" (*is*). (3) "A new *set* of rules and regulations have been adopted" (*has*). (4) "The increasing *rate* of cases in the U. S. Supreme Court were viewed with alarm" (*was*). (5) "A *committee* of five ALI members and three ABA members are to represent the organizations" (*is*). (6) "The *total* of the bills charged to the various printing companies were exorbitant (*was*). In these examples the plural nouns in the *of* phrases need watching, for they can obscure the true subject.

Inverted constructions (those in which the verb precedes the subject) raise havoc with some writers, since the logic of the sentence is not always readily apparent. But the rule is clear: A verb must agree in number with its subject, not with a predicate nominative. The true subject is italicized in these examples; the correct form of the verb is in parentheses: "From these extracts are gleaned one single *thought*" (*is*). "Among those in attendance was the *Chief Justice* and *members* of the cabinet" (*were*). "It was a verdict in which is seen two *areas* of hope" (*are*). This type of sentence can often be restructured to avoid awkwardness. For instance: "Two *areas* of hope *are* seen in that verdict."

> Some writers are as easily drawn off the scent as young hounds. They start with a singular subject; before they reach the verb, a plural noun attached to an 'of' or the like happens to cross, and off they go in the plural; or vice versa.
>
> <div align="right">A <i>Dictionary of Modern English Usage</i>
—H. W. Fowler</div>

WRONG TYPE; FIND ANOTHER

An expression that omits *of* in a sentence like "This type article is unpublishable" is colloquial. *Type* should always be followed by *of* when used with a noun. Although such omissions are not uncommon, the *of* is as necessary here as in "This kind of lawyer will make a good judge." The sentence "This kind lawyer will make a good judge" would never be tolerated, unless the attorney's humaneness was being considered. And just as "This kind of a lawyer" is an impropriety, so is "This type of a letter" or "This type of an article." The *of* is required, but not the *a* or *an.*

Converting nouns into adjectives by using *type* as a suffix is becoming widespread: practice-type manuals, question- and answer-type programs, estate planning-type seminars. These expressions are unidiomatic. Good writers shun them as inappropriate and needless; certainly less wordy, more suitable constructions are available. A "subsidy-type payment," for example, is just a "subsidy"; a "martinet-type man" is "a martinet."

Worth ignoring: "I deliberately went on an issues-type campaign." —Richard Nixon

A MATTER OF HISTORY

Both *historic* and *historical* are adjectives derived from the same root. The words are not interchangeable, however; in fact, they are distinguishable.

Historic means "memorable" or "important in history." It refers to history-making things: a historic declaration, a historic building, a historic moment. "The surrender of Cornwallis to Washington at Yorktown was a historic event."

Historical has the sense of "pertaining to history." It is the general adjective and refers to what is concerned with history: a historical record, a historical play, a historical point of view. "*Gone With The Wind* is a historical novel."

ENOUGH IS ENOUGH

Whether to use *enough* or *sufficient* depends first on the part of speech called for. *Enough* generally functions as a noun, as in "We have enough for our needs." Saying "We have sufficient for our needs" not only sounds odd but is incorrect besides. *Sufficient* is an adjective.

But in some instances—and this might at first seem contradictory—*sufficient* may not properly serve as an adjective, although *enough* may. For example, in "We have a sufficient quantity," *sufficient* is correct but not *enough.* Yet in "We have enough paper," *sufficient,* though correct, is not so idiomatic as *enough.* The explanation is that *enough* is a pseudo-adjective which has won its spurs as an "adjective of amount." In fact, *enough* is the word to use whenever simple amount is involved.

When, on the other hand, quality or kind is being considered, *sufficient* is the word to use. In "The honor bestowed was sufficient to satisfy him" and in "Warren has developed sufficient skill to become lead counsel," *enough* does not qualify.

Further amplification: A companion word, *ample*—"Our resources are ample for our needs"—means "more than enough." In that definition the comparative form *more* modifies *enough,* as it does in "The number of assigned personnel is more than enough to handle the study." But *ample,* the key word, cannot be compared. Something cannot be more than ample, for it then would be more than "more than enough." In fact, properly, it can't even be "barely or hardly ample." *Ample* is quite enough.

THERE'S NO HOPE WITHOUT IT

Hope, when used in the passive voice as an impersonal verb, must take *it* as its subject. This means that the parenthetical expression *it is hoped* cannot properly be written without *it.* For example, "The statutory amendments are creating what is hoped will be only a few problems" should read ". . . what *it* is hoped will be only a few problems." The subject of *is hoped* is the indefinite pronoun *it,* not *what. What* is the subject of *will be.* In "The case was not listed today, as was hoped might be possible," *was hoped* needs *it.*

Not hopeless: The noun *hope,* when it follows *no,* should be in the singular, not the plural: "The defendant has no *hope* (not *no hopes*) of a favorable verdict."

PSYCHE, OR THE 50-MINUTE HOUR

A *psychologist* is a person trained to analyze the human mind—its processes, functions, powers, and reactions. His skill is often directed toward the study of mental phenomena, especially in matters involving social maladjustment. Psychologists frequently are employed by industry for individual guidance.

A *psychiatrist* is a physician specially trained in the diagnosis, treatment, and prevention of mental illness. There are three sorts of psychiatrists: the so-called A.P. (analytic-psychological) type; the so-called D.O. (directive-organic) type; and the eclectic type. A.P.'s predominate in private practice; D.O.'s in state and county institutions; and eclectics in teaching hospitals, research facilities, and private patient-care services.

Psychoanalysts are psychiatrists who have engaged in the further study of psychic content and mechanisms. In accordance with principles first defined by Sigmund Freud, they probe below the level of consciousness for diseases reflected in emotional disturbances. These physicians analyze dreams, inhibitions, complexes, and similar manifestations, ultimately discussing them openly with patients to treat the mental difficulty.

ANTECEDENTS OR UNCLES?

The noun or noun construction to which a pronoun refers is its *antecedent*. Unless the pronoun refers unmistakably to its antecedent, meaning may suffer. For instance, "Mary told Alice she had made a serious mistake" is ambiguous because the pronoun *she* could refer to either *Mary* or *Alice*.

The following alerts may help avoid the misplacing of

pronouns. (1) A pronoun should follow, not precede, its antecedent. "When he wrote his first opinion, Justice Kolb was living in Missouri" is more clearly stated: "When Justice Kolb wrote his first opinion, he. . . ." This rule need not be followed if, in spite of the early placement of the pronoun, meaning is immediately clear. (2) The antecedent of a pronoun should not be a possessive: "In *Amsterdam's* book *Trial Manual for the Defense of Criminal Cases*, he offers many practical suggestions." The example should be reworded: "Amsterdam in his book . . . offers . . ." or even "In his book . . . Amsterdam offers. . . ." This is the permissible exception to No. (1), in which the pronoun precedes the antecedent. (3) An antecedent should not be a verb: "The sheriff *subpoenaed* him but he ignored it" should be changed to *but he ignored the subpoena*. (4) A pronoun such as *this, that,* or *which* should not be used if it vaguely refers to the general idea of a preceding clause or sentence: "He joined the bar association, *which* was expected and pleased his partners" is better stated "His joining the bar association, which was expected, pleased his partners."

Would you criticize the sentence "This lecture is better than any lecture I have ever heard"?

The example needs a small but important addition—the word *other*. Corrected, the sentence would read: "This lecture is better than any other lecture I have ever heard." Idiom requires *any other* when elements of the same kind are being compared.

231

QUOTE IT RIGHT

Quotation marks are marks of punctuation that indicate quoted matter. A quotation is by definition "something that is quoted, especially a passage referred to or repeated," and quotation marks are used to designate the beginning and the end of that material.

The conventions governing the use of quotation marks to enclose direct quotations can be summed up in five rules. (1) Capitalize the first word of the quotation if it begins a complete sentence. (2) Use commas to set off explanatory expressions that are outside the quoted material. (3) Place periods or commas inside quotation marks. (4) Place colons and semicolons outside quotation marks. (5) Place a question mark or an exclamation point inside the quotation marks if it belongs to the quotation; otherwise, outside.

Examples of these five rules follow:

(1) "Obtaining manuscripts is not our only problem," the director declared. "Prompt editing is equally important." But "Obtaining manuscripts," the director declared, "is not our only problem." (The *is* is not capitalized.)

(2) "The problem is not only obtaining manuscripts," the director declared, "but also editing them promptly" or "Our problem is not only obtaining manuscripts but editing them promptly," the director declared. (The person making the statement is not part of the quotation.)

(3) The preceding sentences are examples of the proper placement of periods and commas—inside the quotation marks.

(4) "We will beat them every time": that became our

motto. It is advisable to read the folio "Vesting"; it is succinct, yet clear. (Major midsentence punctuation marks are placed outside the quotation marks.)

(5) He bellowed, "I will never give up!" (The exclamation point is part of the quotation.) Who is the author of "Basic Rules of Arbitration"? (Only the name of the book is quoted.)

Some miscellaneous rules are (1) use single quotation marks to designate a quotation within a quotation, (2) use no quotation marks if the entire quotation is indented, sometimes called a block extract, (3) do not enclose single words such as *yes:* "He replied yes to my question," and (4) do not use quotation marks to enclose indirect quotations, those usually beginning with *that*— not "He said that 'They would leave soon,'" but "He said that they would leave soon."

A FORCEFUL STATEMENT

Forcible and *forceful* share an element of meaning, "the application of force." But the words should be distinguished because each is proper under different circumstances.

Forcible applies to something done by force—a forcible entry, forcible ejection, forcible invasion—whereas *forceful* suggests the effectiveness or the potential of force—forceful personality, forceful plea, forceful approach. *Forceful* is preferred for abstract use.

Forced and *forcible* are interchangeable in such expressions as "forced entry," mentioned previously, but generally *forced* is reserved for the application of *outside* influence upon persons or things, as in "forced labor," "forced air," or "forced march."

AN ACTIVE VOICE SHOULD BE HEARD

Good writers prefer the active to the passive voice almost all the time. The passive voice, however, does serve a purpose, though limited.

A verb is in the active voice when the subject does the acting: "The district attorney won the case easily." "The police found the runaways in a garage." The passive voice consists of a form of the verb *to be* and a past participle: "The case was won." "The runaways were found."

The active voice is customarily used because it is more forceful and direct than the passive. Consider "A fair trial was prevented by the judge's evident bias" (passive voice) and "The judge's evident bias prevented a fair trial" (active voice) or "De Rensio was reprimanded by no one" and "No one reprimanded De Rensio." The active-voice examples are natural, vigorous, concise— the active voice always requires fewer words than the passive.

When the subject is unimportant or unknown, the passive voice is preferable. "The Bar Association reelected Arnold Taylor chancellor" reads better in the passive, "Arnold Taylor was reelected chancellor by the Bar Association," since the Bar Association, the original subject, is of lesser importance here than the name of the person who was reelected. Another instance is "Trespassers will be prosecuted," in which the emphasis is placed where it belongs. The *we* in "We will prosecute trespassers" weakens the effect. Who the *we* is, is inconsequential.

Writing tip: Avoid shifting voices within a sentence. For example, "The manual is inexpensive, and yet so much is learned from it" should be reworded "The manual is inexpensive and yet teaches so much."

PART AND PARTIAL

The words *partly* and *partially* are interchangeable in the sense of "in part" or "not entirely." For example, "The chamber door is *partly* (or *partially*) ajar." Some authorities recommend that only *partly* be used when "in part" or "not entirely" is meant; they argue, with merit, that *partially* is an inelegant word and that the extra syllables are superfluous. But that viewpoint probably goes a little too far—in football no sportscaster worth his mike would dare say "a partly blocked punt"; it is always "partially blocked."

In other constructions, however, *partially* might be ambiguous, for it has the further sense of "with bias" or "inclining to take one part." For example, how did the arbitrator decide in "The arbitrator ruled partially for the plaintiff," or what happened in "The debate was partially documented"?

The adjective *partial* as a rule raises no such problem. It may properly be used in the sense of either "biased"—"It is inconsistent with justice to be partial to an adversary"—or "not totally"—"France made a partial payment on her war debt."

ALL CATHOLICS ARE NOT PAROCHIAL

A Catholic can be a protestant and a Protestant enjoy catholic beliefs, and yet neither be a renegade.

A *protestant* is merely an objector, or protester, either vociferous or silent. If *catholic* is not capitalized, it is an adjective meaning "universal," "of interest or appeal to many." The word *catholic* does not refer to any religion. A person who has catholic interests or tastes has a wide vision and a broad mind. His attitudes and concerns are far-ranging, not parochial.

WHAT'S YOUR PREFERENCE?

Idiom requires that the object of *prefer* be followed by *to* and not *rather than:* "Seltzer prefers litigating *to* (not *rather than*) negotiating." "The bar association prefers Alden M. Black *to* (not *rather than*) Thomas J. Scanlan for judge." And *than* cannot serve alone when *prefer* is being used to compare two things. In "The board prefers issuing a new stock than increasing the old," *to* should replace *than*.

Frequently *prefer* is followed by an infinitive: "Mason prefers to leave early." However, in a more complex sentence, where normally two infinitives are required, *rather than* must be used; for example, "Mason prefers to leave early rather than to arrive late." Theoretically, the sentence should read "Mason prefers to leave early *to* to arrive late," but that awkwardness is intolerable; hence *rather than*.

INTERROGATORIES

Should we discriminate between *systemize* and *systematize?*

Not really, although *systematize* is more common. Both words mean "to reduce to system" or "to formulate": "Lawyers who *systemize* (or *systematize*) their daily workload are bound to succeed."

A sentence in a newspaper read "He is unmindful about those things that bother us most." Is *unmindful about* a proper expression?

No. Idiom requires *unmindful of.*

PERSONS UNKNOWN

A newspaper might headline a story "An unknown spectator died in court today," and the report would not be wrong. But strictly speaking, that person really was not *unknown* unless absolutely no one knew him—which, though possible, is unlikely. A more precise report would refer to an *unidentified* man. Only hermits are truly unknown.

A FEAT IS NOT A FOOT

Much has been written about peculiar idioms that combine singular and plural modifiers, such as the phrase *many* (plural) *a* (singular) *man.* Idioms involving measurement are equally odd and sometimes even misleading.

Take the word *foot.* Its meanings are simple, primarily "a part of the body" and "a unit of length." A question, however, is whether idiom approves both "a three-(plural) foot (singular) wall" and "a wall three (plural) foot (singular) high." The latter—"a wall three foot high"—is unacceptable; idiom requires "a wall three feet high." One may properly refer either to "a six-foot man," or to "a man six feet tall," or even, in shortened form, to "a six-footer," but not to "a man six foot tall." Which all shows what the English language can do to a good song: "Five foot two, eyes of blue."

Inching along: Foot is employed in compounds like clubfoot, barefoot, flatfoot; *footed* in terms like heavy-footed, slow-footed, sure-footed. Most *foot-* compounds are spelled as one word—footnote, footlocker, footpad—but not foot soldier; that needs two words, just as a soldier needs two feet.

237

SUCCESSIVE INTERESTS

Consecutive and *successive* have similar meanings—both mean "following one another." But the continuity of the movement may differ. These words are akin to *continuous* and *continual* in that their use depends upon whether an interruption occurs.

Consecutive, like *continuous,* implies an uninterrupted progression; *successive,* like *continual,* indicates a broken sequence. Although *successive* means "following in a regular sequence," so that the items relate to one another, it tolerates interspersions. For example, Monday, Wednesday, and Friday, although not sequential, are successive days. Three consecutive days signify three days in a row: Monday, Tuesday, Wednesday. Whatever is consecutive must be successive, but the converse is not necessarily so.

IF AND WHEN THIS IS READ

"I will handle this matter if and when I receive your check." The cliché *if and when,* if cut in half, loses nothing in meaning or emphasis. Although the purpose of the phrase is to indicate extreme doubt that something will happen, in most instances using both words is unnecessary. *If* expresses possible consequence—"If the calendar is overloaded, we will not be reached"—and *when,* time: "We are bound to be reached when the calendar clears."

Unless and until, a phrase usually used for emphasis in negative statements—"We will not try the case unless and until we are paid"—is also hackneyed. Either *unless* or *until* should be excised. "We will not try the case unless we are paid," for example, says it all.

238

THE WORDS STICK TOGETHER

Adhesion and *cohesion*, both derived from the Latin *haerere*, describe a physical phenomenon—the sticking or clinging together of two substances. They differ, however, in that adhesion applies when two dissimilar substances are joined and cohesion when the joining is of similar substances. Through the use of glue, surgical tape adheres to the skin and a stamp adheres to an envelope. Molecules of iron cohere and, figuratively speaking, so do tribal groups or free nations.

When used in a figurative sense, the nouns *adherence* and *coherence* are completely unrelated to the nouns *adhesion* and *cohesion*. *Adherence* suggests "the giving of belief and support," as to a political party or a religious sect. *Coherence* relates "to the order and consistency of thoughts or of statements": the coherence of an outline, of an argument, of a report.

The surgical term for the sticking together of tissues is *adhesion*.

BE WISE, NOT OTHERWISE

Discriminating between *other* and *otherwise* is a mark of a careful writer. The less sensitive disregard the adjective *other* in favor of *otherwise,* an adverb. *Other* means "different"; *otherwise,* "in a different manner or in other respects." They are not interchangeable.

Consider these typical sentences: "Baldwin is experiencing many problems, financial and otherwise, that have seriously depressed him." "Rawley's income, earned or otherwise, could not meet his expenses." "The facts appear otherwise than as reported." In these examples, *other*, not *otherwise*, is called for. In the first two, *other-*

239

wise, an adverb, is incorrectly paired with the adjectives *financial* and *earned.* In the last example, *appear* is a linking verb, which takes adjectives, not adverbs.

The adjective *other,* though not quite the malefactor that *otherwise* is, can be misused, too. For instance, in "The warden could not stare other than with chagrin at the condition of the cell," *other* should be replaced by *otherwise.* Otherwise it's all wrong.

Other material: The preposition following *other* is *than,* not *but* or *except.* In "The Institute has no other books *but* (or *except*) these to offer," *than* should be substituted. However, the phrase "other than" should not be used if the simpler word *except* or *unless* expresses the meaning suitably: "North Dakota lawyers, *unless* they have specialized in estate planning, will not be invited (not *other than those who have* specialized). "All prisoners, *except* those in solitary confinement, will receive extra recreation time" (not *other than those* in solitary).

FATUOUS ENOUGH TO BE FOOLISH

If one had to elect between being *foolish* and *fatuous,* foolish though it seems, the better choice would be *fatuous.* Foolish people usually cannot help themselves; fatuous people can.

A foolish person has no sense; he lacks good judgment and may even have a weak mind. His actions evince folly and nonsense. He acts injudiciously.

Fatuous means dullness and stupidity accompanied by complacency. A fatuous person is highly self-satisfied. Although such a person may be unaware of his silliness or stupidity, he could be made to realize that his judgment or attitude needs correcting.

IT'S WHOLLY WRONG

Lawyers, especially, should be sensitive to the idioms *in part* and *as a whole,* since those expressions are not strangers to legal documents. Neither idiom is inherently wrong; their combined use, however, can mislead if care is not taken.

Consider these sentences: "The administrator announced that one half of the listed cases have been consolidated in whole or in part" and "It was agreed that the compensation in whole or in part was subject to no further review." The magnetic pull of parallelism lured these writers to a faulty balance—"*in* whole or *in* part"— whereas it should have been "*as a* whole or *in* part." The same error is seldom made when the expressions are reversed. That is, *in part or in whole* are so patently illogical as to immediately arrest the writer's attention.

One way to avoid this error is to use *wholly* or *partly:* "The administrator announced that one half of the listed cases have been wholly or partly consolidated."

WHAT A HEADACHE

Everyone agrees that *what* may be either singular or plural when it serves as the subject of a sentence or clause. Its number is based solely on the context. If a construction is ambiguous, so that the proper number is not readily apparent, the following guideline might resolve the question.

If *the thing that* or *that which* can sensibly replace *what,* the verb should be singular; if *the things that* or *those which* can replace *what,* a plural verb is required.

A common error occurs in this type of sentence: "The new

suite has ten offices *painted in what appears* to be ten decorator colors." *Appears* should be *appear*, for "painted in what" is equivalent to "painted in things (colors) that," which takes a plural verb. Consider "Here are *what* seem to be the reasons" (*the things that* seem); "*What* were fairly good arguments were ignored" (*those which* were); "*What* seems to be the problem is the many offers received" (*that which* seems to be the problem is).

If unusual constructions involving *what* arise, consult a grammar. It'll tell you what is what.

IT AIN'T ORDINARILY SO

To achieve variety, many writers reach promiscuously for *ordinary, common, usual, customary,* and *habitual* as though those words were readily interchangeable. They are not.

Common is defined as "possessed or shared by all alike": common errors, common goals, common property. It does not mean "commonplace," and so should not be confused with the term *ordinary. Ordinary,* in addition to commonplace, suggests routine, everyday activity: an ordinary day at the office, an ordinary campaign speech, an ordinary function. *Usual* implies accustomed use, the way things are done normally. It indicates what is expected—the usual November meeting of the ALI-ABA Committee. *Customary* refers to established practice—that which a person or group normally follows: customary working schedules, customary dress, customary legal procedures. *Habitual* suggests a fixed practice resulting from habit: her habitual grin, their habitual courtesy, his habitual position by the door.

PERIODIC LOOSENESS

Declarative sentences are of two kinds: loose and periodic. A *loose* sentence is arranged in normal order—subject, predicate, object—so that the main thought comes at the beginning. A *periodic* sentence completes its meaning near or at the end of the sentence. Ordinarily loose sentences predominate; periodic sentences are used occasionally, for emphasis, and primarily in formal writing.

Examples of both sentences are "Ms. Churchville returned to court at 3 P.M. after a luncheon at a nearby restaurant" (loose); "At 3 P.M., after a luncheon at a nearby restaurant, Ms. Churchville returned to court" (periodic). Loose sentences are natural, unfolding the way people speak and write. The major statements are expressed quickly, with additional or minor matter tacked on. Periodic sentences are contrived. Their full meaning is not apparent until the end. They create suspense by holding a thought back, making the reader continue in expectation: "Though Beethoven composed music all his life, during his last ten years when he wrote some of his greatest works, he heard not a note, for he was totally deaf."

INTERROGATORY

It was helpful to learn the correct way to use *hopefully* ("it is hoped that" and "we hope"). Are other adverbs so misused?

Yes. *Thankfully* is, for one. In "Our lawyer—thankfully—was excellent," *thankfully* should be changed to *we are thankful to say*. And in "Regrettably, the offices closed early," it would be better to say *we regret that*.

243

ZOOMING IS FOR SPEED

The term *zoom* derives from aeronautics, where it means a brief, sharp-angle climb by an aircraft. Today, because of popular usage, *zoom* has expanded to indicate both upward and level movement. It therefore is proper to refer to a kite that zooms (into the sky) or a car that zooms (along the highway). *Zoom* may not, however, signify downward movement. "The gulls zoomed down on their prey" is incorrect—the gulls did not zoom, they swooped.

A CHORD FROM MUSICAL TIMBER

One thing *timbre* and *chord* have in common is that they refer to sound, usually the quality of sound. One thing *timber* and *cord* have in common is a wooden background. In spite of all that, there is one thing they all have in common—frequent misspellings.

Timber is "wood from growing trees suitable for structural uses": "Dawson bought the timber he needed to build the lean-to." *Timbre* refers to the quality of sound produced by a particular instrument or voice: "The timbre and range of that colortura soprano are almost unbelievable."

A *chord* is a combination of tones in harmonic relation played simultaneously: "The closing chords of the etude swayed us." A *cord* is a unit of measure for cut wood. *Chord* and *cord* are sometimes misspelled when used in other senses; a cord may be a raised rib on fabric, an electric wire, or a string or rope. In this sentence, the wrong word is being used: "The obstetrician dexterously severed the umbilical chord." At the end of that cord sounds a weak-timbred cry.

SUCH TROUBLE

The adverbial use of *such* is in disfavor with many grammarians, and almost all would avoid it in serious writing. But it has been deeply absorbed into most people's vocabulary, adding fluidity to otherwise stilted constructions. Consider these everyday sentences: "He never saw such ugly cars" and "I don't think he's in such good shape." Each expresses its meaning clearly and naturally. Nevertheless, on a formal level, the sentences need restructuring, with *so* replacing *such:* "He never saw cars so ugly" and "I don't think his shape is so good." Good grammar, but not the way people talk.

The intensive use of *such*—"He's such a good negotiator"—is never acceptable unless followed by a result clause. The proper construction is "He's such a good negotiator *that we all expect a settlement.*" Of course, another adverb, like *very*, could replace *such* and eliminate the problem: "He's a *very* (not *such a*) good negotiator."

TORTUOUS IS NOT THE WORD

Tortuous and *torturous*, when hastily written, are often misspelled, one for the other—not that that is difficult to do, considering their similarity in spelling. Both words derive from the same Latin verb, *torqueo*, "to twist," but they have no connection in current usage.

Tortuous means "winding," "crooked": "The road is tortuous and dangerous and frequently impassable." It is used derivatively to mean "not straightforward" and hence "deceitful" or "devious." *Torturous* denotes "full of, or causing, pain or torture": "My tight shoes were torturous." "The torturous interrogation led to a full confession." Remembering that *torture* has two *r*'s will help *torturous* both in spelling and in correct use. Webster surprisingly lists *torturous* as a synonym of *tortuous*—a torturous confusion of two distinct words.

GIVE IT YOUR ALL

All serves as an adjective, an adverb, and a pronoun. In careful writing, different rules of usage attach to each part of speech.

Adjective *all* is ordinarily problem-free: "All files should be reviewed today." "The trial lasted all day." As an adverb, *all* is also problem-free; it signifies "completely" or "wholly," as in "The statement was not all true" or "It's all gone." It should not be used, however, in this informal construction: "It is not all that difficult to resolve the problem."

When *all* is used as a pronoun, it may be either singular —"All he learned was from experience"—in which *all* is the equivalent of *everything*, or plural—"All are here"— in which the meaning is *each one of a group*. When *all* precedes a pronoun, *of* invariably follows it: "All of us have read the report." When *all* precedes a noun, no *of* is needed: "All the members are eligible." Whether to use *of* is simply a writer's decision. Preferably, *of* should be omitted—*all the members* is certainly more formal and less redundant than *all of the members*.

Roundup: Some dictionaries equate the expressions *all-around* and *all-round,* but the latter is preferred. "He is an all-round trial lawyer" means he is versatile, fully capable in all matters. The expression *all the farther* is colloquial. "This is all the farther we go until we get paid" is far gone and should read "This is *as* far *as* we go. . . ."

FLOUNDERING ISN'T FISHING

Whether one *flounders* or *founders,* trouble is brewing. Both words suggest distress, but an SOS is applicable to only one of them.

Flounder means "to struggle." A fish out of water or an animal mired in mud flounders, thrashes about. The sense of *flounder* is to stumble, to make mistakes, or to manage badly; *founder* implies complete failure or collapse: "The project has foundered." Derived from the Latin *fundus,* meaning "bottom," *founder* suggests its original meanings, "going to the bottom."

Founder, in the case of ships, means "to fill with water and sink." But since *sinking* is inherent in foundering, saying "the ship foundered and sank" is redundant.

THE DISORGANIZED ARE UNINVITED

Although *un-* and *dis-* are classic negative prefixes, equating them can lead to confusion. The prefix *un-* is generally passive, whereas *dis-* is generally active. A group that is ununited, for example, never became cohesive; its members remained separate. A *disunited* group has undergone positive actions to disjoin or to sever its affiliations. Likewise, to be *uninvolved* means "to have no involvement," whereas to be *disinvolved* is to have taken definite steps to withdraw from further participation.

Unorganized means "lacking system or order," as in "The files in this cabinet are unorganized" or "Before unionization, the workers were unorganized." *Unorganized* suggests the absence of a systematized whole. *Disorganized* also implies a lack of organization or orderly arrangement, but it further implies disarrangement, the overturning of an existing system. A disorganized office, for example, has had its established organization disrupted; an unorganized office would not have been systematized in the first place.

To be *uninvited* may be painful, but there is some salve in the thought that possibly the invitation was merely overlooked. There is no balm for being *disinvited*, however. No one likes his invitation recalled.

TOWARD SHORTER WORDS

Some English words have two equally acceptable spellings, although one may be preferred to the other. British spellings sometimes differ from those used in the United States.

Afterward and *afterwards* and *toward* and *towards* are all acceptable forms. In Great Britain *afterwards* and *towards* are favored. In the United States the shorter words are preferred, simply because they are shorter.

The adverb *upward*, for the same reason, is preferred to *upwards*. But as an adjective, the only acceptable spelling is *upward:* "The *upward* (not *upwards*) lurch of the elevator surprised us."

The adjective *onward* is always spelled that way: *an onward thrust, an onward movement.* Used adverbially, either *onward* or *onwards* is acceptable: *moved onward* or *onwards, climbed onward* or *onwards.* Here again, the shorter *onward* is preferred.

Backward and *backwards* are indiscriminately used, but a good rule is to use *backward* as an adjective—"He shot a backward glance"—and *backwards* as an adverb—"He fell backwards."

A TRIFLING MATTER

That which is so small as to deserve no notice or consideration may be called *petty*, *paltry*, or *trivial*. Which word to use depends upon the strength of feeling wanted.

Petty implies unimportance or narrow-mindedness, accompanied by contempt or ridicule: petty complaints, petty arguments.

Paltry, a stronger term, is derived from the Scandinavian *paltrie*, meaning "trash." And the derivation of that word is *paltor*, "rags." Clearly rags are worthless, which is what *paltry* connotes: "Only a paltry fool would make such silly demands." It further suggests that in comparison to what should be, something paltry is ridiculously small: "This is a paltry donation, considering his wealth."

Trivial implies that something is insignificant or slight, especially when compared with that which is important. The term comes from the Latin *tri*, "three," and *via*, "roads," denoting a convenient place for people to meet and discuss unimportant matters—today called gossiping. Unlike the other two words, what is trivial is not always derisive. For example, working on a crossword puzzle while waiting for a doctor is a trivial, but useful, activity. It keeps one from worrying.

PRESENTLY HAS NO PAST

Presently can be confusing right now. It means either at the present moment—"Dr. Sylvester is presently examining Mrs. Arkwright"—or soon—"Dr. Sylvester will examine her presently."

The preference of most writers, and certainly the safest

course to follow, is to use *presently* only in the sense of "before long, in a short time, or soon." When the meaning "now" is wanted, *presently* can be replaced by "at the present moment," "currently," or plain "now."

Presently, as well as *at present* or *currently*, unless contrast is wanted, is redundant when used with a verb in the present tense. "He is presently teaching at Southern Methodist" needs no *presently*.

NOT AGAIN, AGAIN

Although some dictionaries do not restrict the use of *reoccurrence*, *recurrence* is the favored form. Since the prefix *re-* means "again," such words as *reprint, rebuild, refill*, or *repent* need no "again": "Let's refill it," not "Let's refill it again." Also, *again* in the expression *repeat again* is superfluous if "once more" is meant, though it is a good idiom if another repetition is being called for.

Prefix *re-* has the further meaning "backward motion." Hence in the sentence "Barnett said that if the money is not all spent the remainder will revert back to the donor," *back* is clearly redundant.

INTERROGATORY

The exclamation point receives little attention as a mark of punctuation. When is it properly used?

Rarely—only when no other mark of punctuation is considered adequate, and only in sentences of few words. An exclamation point is most frequently seen after startling statements (What a fool!), after commands (Leave at once!), after interjections (Bravo!), and after sarcasm (Beautiful weather! [muttered during a storm]).

A WAY TO SUCCESS

The words *strategy* and *tactics,* although primarily applicable to military operations, are used in many areas of life.

Strategy has to do with an overall plan; *tactics,* with the specific means by which the plan is put into effect: "Brower's strategy for handling the crisis is brilliant. His aides, we're sure, will use effective tactics to carry it out." In business, political, financial, or domestic life, strategy is the adept use of stratagems, tricks or schemes, to attain an end or to gain an advantage over an adversary. Tactics is the technique whereby strategy is implemented, that is, it secures or processes what has been planned.

It should be noted that *stratagem* has two *a's,* whereas *strategy* has only one. *Tactics* calls for a singular verb when it refers to the art or science of obtaining the desired goals: "The tactics of political strategy is learned in the school of experience." When *tactics* refers to the implementations themselves, the verb is plural: "The battle tactics of Colonel Klenk were masterly as usual."

RAMBLINGS

Both *entitled* and *titled* are acceptable verbs: "The book is *entitled* (or *titled*) *Basic Corporate Practice.*" Possibly *entitled* is more formal.

Before should not be followed by *first,* since *before* includes the sense of *first.* In "Before the proposal is voted upon, it must first be approved by Council," *first* should be deleted.

If *mighty* is used to mean "very or exceedingly" on a formal level, it is "mighty wrong." Adverb *mighty* is colloquial.

Adjectives referring to animals should not be converted

to nouns. *Feline* and *canine* are not nouns; they mean "catlike" and "doglike": feline habits, canine teeth.

One should carefully avoid such common misspellings as *accidently* for *accidentally* and *incidently* for *incidentally*. *Rack and ruin* for *wrack and ruin* can be ruinous.

A *casket* is a small box in which to keep jewels and other valuables. The term has euphemistically displaced *coffin*. Except to appease the squeamish, this change is difficult to justify unless people think they are burying a "jewel."

Superior and *inferior to*, not *than*, are proper idioms: "The operator of this machine is *superior to* (not *than*) that one."

Throughout means "from the beginning to the end."

Problem verbs: The past tense of *beseech* is not *beseeched* but *besought*. *Burglarize* is colloquial. No accepted verb form has developed from the noun *burglar*. The persistent use of *burglarize* to avoid awkward phrases, however, will eventually validate that verb. *Enthuse* also is a colloquial verb form, but its acceptance on a formal level is nonexistent. "He was enthused about the project" needs *enthusiastic*. And when necessary, do not say the river has *overflown* its banks, but *overflowed*. *Overflown* is an airplane that has passed the runway.

INTERROGATORY

If on page 99 a reference is made to page 98, is page 98 properly called the *previous* or the *preceding* page?

Since what *precedes* occurs immediately beforehand, whereas what is *previous* may have occurred at any earlier time, a precise reference to page 98 should be to "the preceding page." The page that comes immediately before the referent page is the preceding page; all other earlier pages are previous pages.

SOLECISMS ARE NOT ALONE

Obviously, all word usage is not approved word usage. Approved usage might be described as that which occurs in the speech or writing of most cultured persons. There may be some disagreement, but by and large their diction and style are safe benchmarks to follow.

Bad word usage violates approved usage. The opportunities for these violations are many, but the three principal categories are termed barbarisms, solecisms, and improprieties.

A *barbarism* is a word irregularly formed or not in good use and therefore alien to established custom: *enthuse* for *enthusiastic; someways* for *some way; complected* for *complexioned; nowheres* for *nowhere; irregardless* for *regardless.*

A *solecism* is a word or expression that deviates from good idiomatic usage: *these kind* for *this kind; between you and I* for *between you and me; different than* for *different from.*

A word used in an incorrect sense is called an *impropriety.* Simply stated, it is an improper use of a word or expression; *learn* for *teach; disinterest* for *uninterest; affect* for *effect.*

A *bad prop: A malapropism* is a ridiculous confusion of words that resemble each other. Their sounds are similar, but their meanings are unrelated: *delusion* for *illusion; progeny* for *prodigy; reversal* for *reversion.*

This misuse of words was characteristic of Mrs. Malaprop, a matron in Sheridan's *Rivals.* She gloried in misapplying words: "Sure, if I *reprehend* anything in this world, it is the use of my *oracular* tongue, and a nice *derangement* of *epitaphs.*" The italicized words resemble *apprehend, vernacular, arrangement,* and *epithets,* all of which should be used respectfully, er, respectively.

PRACTICALLY A VIRTUE

Two primary meanings of *practically* are "in a practical manner" and "for practical purposes": "Powell reviewed the matter practically." "Practically speaking, nothing can be done." Another meaning, but accepted only for informal use, is "very nearly or almost": "The jurors were practically asleep during counsel's summation."

On an informal level *virtually* is also used to mean "nearly or almost"; more strictly it means "just about," "almost entirely," "in essence": "The district attorney virtually (almost entirely) handled the case during his lunch-break." "He's famous today, but he was virtually (just about) unknown before his election."

In sentences such as "The case is practically open and shut," in which *practically* means "in effect," *virtually* is preferable. But when hypothetical or theoretical contrasts are being made, *practically* is preferable: "Theoretically, free legal service seems desirable; practically it does not work." In almost all other instances, it is *virtually* (or *practically?*) impossible to distinguish between those words. Of course, using *nearly* or *almost* would, as a practical matter, virtually eliminate the problem.

The real McCoy: Virtually and *actually* have a remote similarity—the former means "in effect"; the latter, "in fact." But what is true with one is not true of the other. For example, "When Ms. Client's lawyer speaks for her, she is *virtually* speaking herself, even though she is not *actually* present."

AUTOGRAPH THE BOOK, PLEASE

A person who signs his name, or makes a mark representing it, writes his signature. If the name is illegible but is customarily written that way, it nevertheless is his signature.

An autograph is a signature, too, but has distinctive features. It must, according to its Greek root "written by oneself," be written by the person himself. No one can write an autograph for someone else. Further, unlike plain signatures, an autograph cannot be mechanically reproduced. Ordinary signatures can, of course, be written by another person authorized to do so and can be duplicated by machine. These are customary commercial practices.

Play names: Celebrities autograph by using their stage names, not their actual names. They use their real names only when their signatures are required in business transactions. Among authors and poets, few use pseudonyms today. For those who do, their assumed names are called pen names, from a French coinage *nom de plume*.

INTERROGATORY

Is it permitted, for the sake of variety, to interchange the words *number* and *figure*?

It depends on the context. The Arabic 5 is both a number and a figure. The word *five* is a number only; it is not a symbol, and therefore is not a figure. All figures are numbers, but all numbers are not figures.

The word *number* is the all-inclusive term describing how people count—that is, by numbers. When a list of numbers is arranged for counting, figures, of course (1, 2, 3 . . .), are used.

SHEER DISGUST

It sounds silly, but it is not easy to be properly disgusted, grammatically speaking. *Disgusted* can take as many as three different prepositions, depending on the meaning to be conveyed, and that is a disgusting fact to remember.

Idiom has decreed that one be disgusted *with* a person or a person's actions—"Penza is disgusted with her careless work"—*at* some particular action—"Lawson was disgusted at the verdict"—and *by* a personal quality or act—"Everyone was disgusted by Mike's behavior."

Finis. We've all had a disgusting fill.

DIVULGE A LITTLE OR DISCLOSE IT ALL

Divulge and *disclose* are synonyms in that they both mean "to show." However, in many contexts the words are not interchangeable, thus requiring a choice between them.

Although both words imply previous concealment, *divulge* is applicable when a secret is revealed to a select group—"The committee member divulged the plans to the reporters." "The Federal Reserve Board would not divulge its change of policy even to the President." *Disclose* suggests a general sharing of information with others—"The FBI disclosed all its available material to the media." "The Senator's marriage arrangements were disclosed to the public."

Neither word is used frequently these days, possibly because other words *reveal* as much as *divulge* and *expose* as much as *disclose;* in fact, they all *say* or *tell* equally well. Hence *divulge* and *disclose* are being slowly decommissioned.

HITTING LOW C's

Criticize is a word to reckon with because it has two different meanings, one deprecatory. Its primary meaning is "to make judgments as to merits and faults." Used this way, *criticize* does not imply an adverse appraisal.

Second, and more commonly, *criticize* means "to find fault." A person who criticizes something is, in ordinary parlance, disapproving. Such a person is described as being critical, that is, faultfinding.

A review of a literary work is sometimes called a *critique*. Although considered pretentious—preferred synonyms are *criticism, notice, review*—a critique itself need not be unfavorable.

To censure is to express disapproval, to offer adverse criticism: a letter of censure, a resolution of censure. In some foreign lands, news reports may be censured, that is, condemned, which may lead to their being *censored*, that is, prohibited from being published. People, too, may be censured, but they cannot be censored.

Uncensored: The adjective form of *censure* is *censorious*, "given to censure." A *censor*, an examiner, should not be confused with a *censer*, an incense burner.

Is there a difference between *oblivious* and *unaware?*

Oblivious originally meant "forgetful of something known in the past." In this sense, *oblivious* implied a present unawareness of something once known. Today *oblivious* is used to mean "heedless, not conscious or aware of." This is a reference to the present, a meaning synonymous with *unaware,* as in "He is *oblivious* (or *unaware*) of what is happening."

257

IT'S A BEGGING MANNER

The only thing in common between the expressions "to beg the question" and "to the manner born" is their frequent misuse. Neither phrase is so useful that writings cannot survive without them. But if used at all, they should be used properly.

"To beg the question" does not mean that one thinks another's arguments are unfair, nor does it mean that the critical point of a discussion is being bypassed. The construction indicates that the truth of something not yet proved is being assumed in advance; in other words, the proposition being debated is being used to prove that same proposition. For example, in a controversy about the ethics of some lawyers, the argument "How can these lawyers be ethical when they cheat their clients while paying fees to the ethics committee?" begs the question. It is like saying "The jury system is a bad thing because the jury system is a bad thing."

The confusion over whether the correct expression is "to the *manner* born" or "to the *manor* born" is quite understandable. The proper word is *manner,* meaning "custom." But in this phrase *manner* is often incorrectly spelled *manor,* under the mistaken belief that it refers to a person born in a manor and therefore "accustomed by birth to high position." Though an apt expression, it was not Hamlet's response to Horatio's question about the custom of carousing under the new king, Claudius. He said, "Ay, marry, is't:/But to my mind, though I am native here/And to the manner born, it is a custom more honour'd in the breach than the observance." Hamlet, although born in a manor, meant by "the manner born" that he had been "fitted by endowment or birth for a certain position in life."

WHOSE TURN IS NEXT?

Purists maintain that *whose,* since it is a possessive form of *who,* applies only to people, not to things. Though that may have been true years ago, well-respected writing today disproves that tenet. *Whose* may function as the possessive case of either *who* or *which.*

The sentences "It is a project whose guidance requires experts" and "It is a project the guidance of which requires experts" are both proper. The second choice, *of which,* however, is awkward and therefore less desirable. Consider another: "These are the cabinets whose locks need resetting" and "These are the cabinets the locks of which need resetting." Again, the clumsiness of the *of which* phrase makes it unappealing. The National Anthem, consequently, is not in jeopardy, and the flag "*whose* broad stripes and bright stars . . . were so gallantly streaming" can continue flying unmolested by grammatical barbs.

Is there a surefire way to avoid confusing *regretful* and *regrettable?*

Just remember that only a person can be "full of regret," which is what *regretful* means: "He was quite regretful about his error."

Regrettable applies to situations and occurrences in the sense of causing regret. An unfortunate situation, for example, is one that is regrettable. In fact, if the word *unfortunate* can sensibly serve in the sentence, *regrettable* may replace it. "The witness's death was unfortunate" (or regrettable).

But remember that *regrettable* has two *t*'s; *regretful,* one.

ALL DIVERS DON'T GET WET

Men constantly differ from each other in many ways. As it is said, "That's what makes horse racing." But if the differences are expressed by the words *divers* and *diverse*, they should be distinguished.

"Men of divers views" means men of sundry or various views. "Men of diverse views" means men of opposite or conflicting views—points of view that are unlike and separate. *Divers*, since it sounds archaic, is fast being replaced by *diverse*, indicating that soon the word to express the sense of several or different in character will be *diverse*. And this comes from divers sources.

DOUBTS ARE ONLY FOR THOMAS

It is doubtful that everyone agrees on how best to express certainty or assurance. Probably the term *undoubtedly*, since it means "beyond doubt," is the most forceful. A close second is the phrase *without doubt*, which also conveys a high degree of conviction: "Without doubt, we will win the case."

Doubtless and *no doubt* suggest certainty, too, but are weak terms, since they connote presumption or probability: "The judge will doubtless rule in our favor." "No doubt counsel will want to rest after the trial." In both examples, a sense of "probably" is apparent.

Another choice is *indubitably*, which means "too evident to doubt": "Indubitably class action suits are the most complicated of all." *Doubtlessly* could also serve here, but neither word is recommended—the former is pretentious; the latter, cumbrous. The best choice undoubtedly is *undoubtedly*.

FLAIRS DO NOT ENFLAME

Before the days of the written word, when man drew pictures, spelling was not a concern. Today, though, since most methods of communication are through the printed word, spelling, in one sense, is more important than speaking. Consider the words *flair* and *flare*. They are so commonly confused that some dictionaries now equate them in certain senses. But they should not be; their meanings are entirely unrelated.

Flair, which literally means "keen scent," has come to connote an ability to "smell things out"; therefore, an instinctive taste, feeling, or aptitude. A person may have a flair for the dramatic, for painting, for catching the public's eye. One who exhibits a conspicuous talent is said to have a *flair* for that pursuit.

A *flare* is a sudden or swaying light or flame, a torch, but it also connotes an outburst of anger or passion. A common expression is "He flared up when he heard the news." *Flare*, by analogy, has also developed the meaning "to flutter," hence "to spread out," as a current of air blows an article of clothing. A skirt, for instance, may "flare out."

All this means that sentences like "The company's flare for capturing the retail market is amazing" is inappropriately worded—at least for those with a flair for using the right word.

THE MAJOR AND THE MINOR

Experienced writers normally stress major ideas in their sentences and subordinate minor ones. The major thought is normally emphasized by placing it at the beginning of a sentence (sentences that suspend emphasis to the end are called periodic sentences). Minor ideas, since they do not deserve, and should not receive, the prominence of the principal statement, are properly lodged midway or at the very end.

A clause or phrase coming at the end of a sentence unfolds naturally and, as naturally, is thus subordinated: "Judge Farum fell off his swivel chair and broke his hip after having served without mishap for 20 years." Such information is likewise subordinated if placed mid-sentence. But that placement is contrived; it must be planned: "Judge Farum, after having served without mishap for 20 years, fell off his swivel chair and broke his hip." Midsentence placements sometimes have a periodic effect.

The primary thoughts in effective sentences are not placed in (1) infinitive phrases (not "Send the books first class *to avoid delay*," but "Avoid delay by sending the books first class"); (2) participial phrases (not "Hansford lapsed into a coma, *dying two days later*," but "Hansford died after being in a coma for two days"); and (3) clauses beginning with subordinating connectives (when, while, since, because, if, though) or relative pronouns (who, which, that) (not "Hansford had been in a coma for two days *when he died*," or "Hansford, *who had been in a coma for two days,* died," but "After being in a coma for two days, Hansford died").

Introductory subordinate clauses do not violate the principle of prominence because they lead naturally to the important idea that follows: "After we visited the courthouse, Delinger treated us to lunch."

TAKE ME TO YOUR MASTER

Ordinarily it is easy to follow the crowd, and just as easy to blur the meanings of words confused by the crowd. Succumbing to popular usage is a weak, careless, and indifferent approach to maintaining the quality of the English language. Some dictionaries have said, "Let's surrender." Take *masterful* and *masterly* as a case in point.

Masterful denotes "domineering, imperious, powerful" and suggests force and authority: "The President is masterful." "Ann is ruled by her masterful husband." *Masterly* connotes skill and expertness; it means "possessing the knowledge or art of a master": "Janeway ended his cross-examination with a masterly stroke." "Horowitz's performance was masterly."

Masterly is seldom misused, whereas *masterful* is a common offender, as in "His summation of the case was masterful" (masterly). The error in "He writes masterfully" is occasioned by the absence of an adverb form for *masterly*. Only by recasting the sentence—"He writes in a masterly way"—or completely restructuring it—"He is a masterly writer"—can this absence be filled.

MS. QUOTED

Cite and *quote* are synonyms when they refer to the repeating of someone's words by way of authority, but *cite* is more appropriate when the sense is merely to mention or to refer to them, especially when exact wording is not being reproduced.

To quote is "to give the exact words of an author," even to the point of including errors in spelling and punctuation. The errors may be followed by the Latin *sic* in brackets [*sic*] to indicate that the flaw was original:

"Jimnie [*sic*] Carter." In printed material and in typescript, direct quotations are sometimes distinguished by their block form, that is, the text is indented with less spacing between the lines than in the regular style.

The summons: (1) *To cite* has other meanings, such as "to summon someone to appear before an official" and "to honor for gallantry." It is also synonymous, in some contexts, with *points out, observes,* and *notes.* (2) *To quote indirectly* is to give the substance of a passage, to paraphrase, but not to reproduce the original phrasing. (3) *Sic,* which means "thus" or "in this manner" is not an abbreviation. It therefore takes no period. (4) *Citable* is spelled that way, not *citeable.*

THE HEART OF MIDLOTHIAN

The sentence "Bella Heidel was loath to say she loathed anyone" causes no spelling problems because *loathed,* a verb, is used in the past tense. If the sentence had been "Bella Heidel is loath to loathe anyone," the distinction between the adjective *loath* and the verb *loathe,* with its final *e,* would have been more problematic.

The adjective *loath* means "hesitant," "unwilling." The verb *loathe* implies an intense dislike and is synonymous with *detest, abhor, hate.* Although the words originally shared the meaning of hatred, the passage of time has tempered the adjective. *Loath* no longer reflects deep emotion. Probably *disinclined* and *averse* are its strongest synonyms.

Be not loath to say: (1) The meaning of another adjective, *loathsome,* unaffected by the development of its sister word, *loath,* still means "repulsive, detestable, hateful." (2) *Loathe* may be spelled *loth.*

TO SILENCE ENVIOUS TONGUES

Although one may experience both *envy* and *jealousy,* differences between these terms about the begrudging of another's possessions and accomplishments do occasionally arise. The main distinction is that *envy* stresses covetousness, desiring what another person has. More fully stated, *envy* is "a resentful awareness of an advantage enjoyed by another and a desire to possess the same advantage." It is a discontented longing for what another has, accompanied by a feeling of ill-will: "His lavish style of living was the envy of all the juniors in the office."

Jealousy is used in two different ways—one bad, one good. The frequently heard "She is a jealous wife" is possibly its most common use. There the implication is of suspicion and fear of rivalry. The more desirable sense suggests protection of one's name and reputation: "The district attorney jealously guards his good name."

What rule governs the punctuation of *especially?*

Probably what is being considered is a phrase beginning with *especially* that adds nonessential information to a preceding clause. Commas set off these expressions. In "Easley likes to counsel tort cases, especially those involving defamation," the *especially* phrase is informative but not indispensable; hence the comma. All similar phrases, in fact, not only those introduced by *especially,* should be thus punctuated. Usually such phrases are prefaced by words like *despite, irrespective of, particularly, perhaps, preferably, probably, regardless of,* and *usually.*

IT IS HUMANLY POSSIBLE

All children at one time have said, "I don't care what you call me; just don't call me late for dinner." Apparently, the same indifference exists among many adults; they care little whether they are called *human beings* or simply *humans*. Some authorities now regard *human,* because of widespread usage, as standard English, to be fully accepted. Others, possibly the majority, disagree. They do not accept *human* as a noun, as in "Humans control their own destiny"; in fact, they severely criticize such use. The proper noun form is *human being*.

Adjectival *human,* which means "characteristic of man"— human existence, human events, or human conduct—is, of course, long established. A sister word, *humane,* refers to the qualities of kindness and compassion, as in "It is the humane thing to do"—a humane lawyer, a humane verdict, a humane warden. The term *humanitarian* suggests concern for human welfare: "The President's humanitarian proposals have made him a man of the people."

Human error: Many years ago *human* and *humane* were interchangeable. In fact, Pope's famous line was first written: "To err is humane, to forgive Divine."

LIVID AND LURID—TWO PECULIAR COLORS

No one seems to blink an eye anymore at a sentence such as "Brandt was so angry, he turned livid." The statement is taken to mean that Brandt turned red with anger, but that is a popular misapprehension. His face may have had a reddish tone, more of a violet, but *livid* means "black" or "leaden," not "red." A person's livid face is not flushed; it is probably ashen. But if anger is being referred to, the example could correctly say, "Brandt became livid," for *livid* has developed the figurative meaning "furiously angry." *Livid* also means "discolored by bruising."

Lurid is another color word often misconstrued. Flashing lights of many colors, in a discotheque, for example, are lurid only in the figurative sense of "sensational." *Lurid* means ghastly yellow, such as the color of flame through smoke. By extension, it has come to indicate pale, unearthly, and gloomy. Like *livid*, it signifies a color less than vibrant.

J'ACCUSE

Alleged, accused, and *suspected* all point to persons entangled in legal problems. These terms, which frequently appear in newspapers and magazines, are used in the hope that they will avoid defamation suits. Although this verbiage may not be a legal defense at a libel or slander trial, it may be considered mitigating evidence.

Commonly, reports speak of an *alleged rapist*, an *accused embezzler*, a *suspected murderer*. Usage authorities agree, however, that a rapist cannot be alleged. Strictly speaking, only a crime or a condition can be alleged, not the person involved. Likewise, *accused embezzler* is a misnomer—such a person is not an embezzler, accused or otherwise, since he has not been convicted of embezzlement. He is merely one who has been accused of embezzling. A *suspected murderer,* too, is not a murderer suspected of committing a murder; he is simply a person suspected of having committed that crime. Before conviction, words that arouse suspicions of someone's guilt are best avoided, especially since some of the strongest suspicions remain just that—mere suspicions.

REACTIONARY RESPONSES

Reaction, a technical term meaning "to display some form of energy in response to a stimulus," is used in chemistry, biology, and mechanics. It should not be used as a general synonym for *response, opinion, attitude, impression,* or *reply.*

A person can have a physical reaction upon touching a hot stove, for example, or upon hearing unexpected news. The response, if immediate and involuntary, might be described as a reaction: "When Agnes heard the news, she reacted by fainting."

But soliciting a reaction to an article or a book review invites an automatic response, not an intellectual one. Such a request, if points of view and judgments are sought, should be for an opinion. A person who responds to a proposal, for instance, and offers "a reaction," not "an opinion," may be hedging against a future need to justify that opinion. It is difficult to criticize a reaction.

INTERROGATORIES

An article used the word *ergo.* Does that mean it is still accepted usage?

Not generally. *Ergo* is archaic and *therefore* should ordinarily replace it. *Ergo* serves to draw attention to what follows, but, if used at all, should be used facetiously—and sparingly.

Are the words *dissociate* and *disassociate* freely interchangeable, or is one preferred to the other?

The words are interchangeable, both meaning "to disunite" or "separate from." The shorter word is preferred.

VERBAL EXCESS BAGGAGE

Authorities agree that clear and concise writing is effective writing. How to achieve this goal cannot be outlined—a sixth sense is really what makes a good writer—but some guidelines can steer one away from the pitfalls of poor writing.

One recommendation is to eliminate wordiness, especially the kind that attaches to drawn-out prepositional phrases. Ordinarily these inflated expressions can be shortened to single words. A list of common offenders and suggested remedies follows.

in terms of: *at, in, for, by, with*
in the event that: *if*
in routine fashion: *routinely*
in receipt of: *have received*
in excess of: *more than, over*
in connection with: *by, from, about, at*
in all probability: *probably*
in addition to: *besides*
in view of the fact that: *since, because, considering that*
on account of: *because*
on the part of: *by, among*
in spite of the fact that: *although*
in order to: *to*
in a manner similar to: *like*
in the midst of: *amid*
in the immediate vicinity of: *near*
on the basis of: *on, by, after, because, of*
on the grounds of: *based*
similar to: *like*
during the course of: *during*

LAPSES ARE BAD FOR MEMORY

Although it is unquestionably correct to say "We are disturbed because so much time has elapsed," whether it is proper to say "We are disturbed because of the elapse of so much time" depends upon the dictionary consulted. Most dictionaries consider *elapse* only a verb —"much time has elapsed"—and describe its noun use as archaic. Preferably an *elapse of time* should be converted to a mere *lapse*.

Both the noun and verb forms of *lapse* are derived from the Latin *lapsus,* meaning "fault or error." As a noun, *lapse* suggests (1) a slip or slight error—"The judge apparently had a lapse of memory"; or (2) the passing of time—"The lapse between the mailing of the package and receipt was unexplainable"; or (3) a miscarriage through fault or laxity—"It was an intolerable lapse of justice."

As a verb, the primary meaning of *lapse* is "to cease to exist or to disappear": "Since we had nothing to say, the conversation lapsed." "Failure to pay premiums as agreed will cause the policy to lapse."

INTERROGATORY

Are both *leastways* and *leastwise* acceptable words?

Neither word is in good standing. *Leastwise* has more acceptance, but it is nevertheless better to say "at least" or "at any rate," which is what *leastwise* means. A companion question might concern *lengthways* and *lengthwise* and *sideways* and *sidewise*. With these words, the better practice is to use the *-wise* suffix. Unlike *leastwise,* however, *lengthwise* and *sidewise* are in reputable usage.

TEEING OFF ON T-WORDS

It may sound like "teeing off" on *t*-words, but some words beginning with the letter *t—thereof, therein, thereto, thereat, therefor*—are pompous and archaic. Correspondence and texts alike should not be stamped with these antiquities.

Frequently *t*-words are used at the end of a sentence: "Cooper's authoritative work is informative to the very end thereof." *To its very end* or *to the very end* reads better. In "Counsel was informed about Bello's part in the burglary but not about Kolmer's part therein," either *therein* should be omitted or exchanged for *in it.* Some writers dislike concluding sentences with *of it, in it, to it,* and so forth, because these are "letdowns," weak endings; but a weak ending, if the sentence cannot be restructured, is better than a poor one.

Therefore means "for that reason" or "as a result." Its sister word, *therefor* (without a final *e*), means "for that" or "for it." But *therefor* is becoming obsolete and hence should be used cautiously. In "I am sending you the document and need a receipt *therefor,*" *therefor* could be either deleted or replaced by "for it." Better yet, the statement could be rephrased *for which I need a receipt.* No one would then misunderstand the sentence.

THE FORMER IS FIRST

Former refers to the first member of a pair—persons, things, or parts—*latter* to the second. They may be used together or singly if reference is made to two persons or things. If three or more are mentioned, the terms are inapplicable. References should then be made to the *first* or the *first-named* and the *last* or the *last-named,* as the case may be.

271

Former and *latter* are normally used to avoid repeating nouns, primarily names. However, that repetition often is preferable to having a reader reread the words to see what *former* and *latter* refer to. Especially if the reference is long, it is easy to forget which is which.

> The mountain and the squirrel
> Had a quarrel
> And the former called the latter,
> "little prig."

> *Fable*
> —RALPH WALDO EMERSON

AN INTRIGUING ARTICLE

The verb *intrigue* has intrigued writers as long as there has been intrigue to discuss. Writers are intrigued, yes; but word-usage authorities are less than enchanted.

Intrigue comes in two forms: a noun meaning "a plot or crafty dealing," and a verb from the Latin *intricare*, meaning "to entangle or perplex." As a verb, it has come to mean "arousing the interest by puzzling, novel, or other arresting qualities": "The Orient never ceases to intrigue the traveler." Although used properly here, *intrigue* is not favored by many writers, who feel that it has developed into a fuzzy, catch-all term. Unless used in the sense of "to perplex," they prefer the more precise wording of *mystify, enchant, pique, puzzle.*

When used as a noun, *intrigue* can be typified by the machinations of the unholy trio—Bogart, Lorre, and Greenstreet. The word should not be employed when the writer intends a passing curiosity. Consider the synonyms of *intrigue;* they imply more than casual interest: *plot, design, ruse, stratagem.* Unless such meanings are wanted, it is better to confine *intrigue* to the Casbah.

NUMBERS ARE ENDLESS

A recent newspaper report included the statement, "He handled yesterday's assignments, *innumerable* as they seemed, methodically and promptly." Probably what was meant was "He handled yesterday's assignments, *endless* as they seemed, ..." *Innumerable* means "incapable of being counted." The assignments might have been numerous, but it was unlikely that they were not countable.

What is endless is continuous, "without end." The books in the Library of Congress may be innumerable (in the sense of very numerous and therefore not readily countable) but they are not endless. *Innumerable* is often used figuratively to signify "countless," although really referring to what is countable but only with great difficulty: "The old man's face has innumerable wrinkles." With painstaking effort, the wrinkles could indeed be counted.

INTERROGATORIES

Which is correct—*oneself* or *one's self?*

Both forms are correct; however, *oneself* is more commonly used.

What, if any, distinction should be made between *despite* and *in spite of?*

None grammatically. They are both accepted terms. *Despite* is more formal, but not so strong as *in spite of*. *Regardless*, too, with its accompanying *of*, is available: regardless of. Another possibility is *notwithstanding*, which also suggests a deterrent.

GET TO THE POINT

Letters should be composed with a straightforward approach, one that reflects original thinking. Jargon and trite expressions should be meticulously avoided.

The following small list of stereotyped expressions contains meaningless time-wasters.

1. *According to our records, upon examining our records, our records show.* State the actual information from the records.
2. *May I take this opportunity to thank you, take the liberty of, take pleasure in.* "Thank" or "commend."
3. *Acknowledging your letter, answering your inquiry, referring to your letter.* If necessary, refer to the reader's letter incidentally, but not by hackneyed expressions in the opening sentence, a particularly important position.
4. *Good enough to forward.* "Please send." *Please accept our thanks.* "Thank you." *Please feel free to contact us.* "Please call upon us."
5. *Attached* (or *enclosed*) *please find, attached hereto, enclosed herewith.* "I am enclosing" or "Attached (or enclosed) is (or are)."
6. *At the present writing.* "At present." *Up to this writing.* "Up to now." *At this point in time.* "Now."
7. *At an early date.* "Soon." *As of this date.* "Today."
8. *Permit me to say.* Omit this meaningless construction. *That we have at hand.* Omit *at hand.*
9. *Do not hesitate to ask us.* "Please write us if."
10. Omit the expressions *favor, communication, kind letter, valued thought,* except for those situations in which their exact meanings are appropriate.
11. Omit *duly,* as in *duly noted; esteemed* or *valued,* as in *your esteemed comment.*

274

12. *Trusting this suggestion will.* "We hope that." "We are sorry that."
13. *Wish to thank you.* Don't wish; do it.

DINGLE DANGLE PARTICIPLE

Dangling participial phrases, like split infinitives, are the chief fears of many careful writers. Committing either fault, they feel, will stamp their writing inferior. Certainly dangling modifiers, which include participles, should be avoided at all cost to prevent confused or ludicrous meanings. Split infinitives are another matter.

A modifier dangles when it modifies nothing in a sentence; that is, it has nothing to which it can anchor. A dangling participle, gerund, or infinitive is eliminated when it is given a definite word to modify. Consider the following examples with suggested corrections. "Walking to court, an automobile accident was seen." *Walking* modifies nothing; it cannot logically modify *accident:* "Walking to court, *I* saw an automobile accident." "Taking our seats, the trial started." *Taking* seems to modify *trial*—an absurdity: "Taking or Having taken our seats, *we* watched the trial begin." "To be informed, books must be read." *Books* are already informed: "To be informed, *lawyers* must read books." "To write well, rules of grammar should be followed." *Rules* may be right, but they do not write: "To write well, *one* should follow the rules of grammar."

Dingle but no dangle: Participles do not dangle in absolute phrases: "Generally speaking, we close early on Fridays." "Weather permitting, the office picnic will take place on Saturday." Infinitives that introduce a general truth do not dangle: "To be brief, time waits for no man." "To judge from reports, all must be going well."

275

THE PENALTY OF VENALITY

Venal and *venial*, like so many other look-alikes, are confused for that very reason. If any doubt attaches to their meaning, they should not be used. It is safer to select from several available synonyms.

Venal means corruptible, mercenary, open to bribery—venal pacts, venal officials. A venal person can be bought; he ignores self-respect for dishonest gain. An elected government official who secretly receives money for private profit for illegal acts previously performed is venal—twice venal. *Venial* refers to oversights of no great consequence, to unimportant, easily forgivable slips. It means "excusable"—venial faults, venial offenses.

Memory guide: Since venal public servants belong in penal institutions, *venal* may be quickly associated with *penal* as a guide for correct meaning and spelling.

PRONOUNS CAN BE POOR SUBSTITUTES

"A properly placed pronoun clearly points to its antecedent—the person or thing to which the pronoun refers." In the following examples that principle has been ignored: "He told his lawyer that he (who is he?) should not go to court today." "After the warden brought the prisoner to the judge, the police photographed him" (the warden? the prisoner? or the judge?). Nouns could clarify the meaning of the first example: "Galiardi told Louderback that Louderback should not go to court today." Using nouns is always a possibility, but sometimes they are unwieldy. It makes for smoothness to rearrange the different parts of the sentence so that only one antecedent precedes the pronoun, or, failing that, to recast the sentence entirely. The second example is one in which omitting the pronoun and repeating the noun is called for:

276

"The police photographed the *warden* (or the *prisoner* or the *judge*) after the warden brought the prisoner to the judge." That keeps the picture straight.

Multiple antecedents can sometimes be distinguished by making one plural and another singular. For instance, "A lawyer should talk to his client in simple language if his vocabulary is limited" is a case in point. It could be restated "A lawyer should talk to his *clients* in simple language if his vocabulary is limited," which indicates that the lawyer, not his clients, suffers from a vocabulary deficiency.

SHORTENED VERSIONS

Abbreviations are customary in informal writing. For example, state names immediately following proper geographic names—cities, towns, air bases, Indian reservations, national parks—are abbreviated: Seattle, Wash.; Randolph Air Force Base, Tex. On a formal level, those names are spelled out.

But this does not mean that shortened forms or abbreviations are never permissible in formal writing. The names of organizations, for example, must be given completely, but only once; thereafter they may be abbreviated or their popular names used. For instance, the first mention of the Federal Communications Commission or the Federal Bureau of Investigation should be spelled out, but they may be subsequently referred to as the FCC and the FBI. Those abbreviations take no periods. Also, business firm abbreviations are freely used: *Corp., Co., Bro., Inc., Ltd., Ass'n*—as well as commonly known generic terms preceding proper names: Mt. Rainier; Ft. Monmouth. An abbreviation may begin a sentence only if part of a title: "A. E. C. Appliance Co. has just moved."

VARIATIONS ON DEATH

Traditionally, the adjectives *deadly* and *deathly* pertained equally to something having the aspect of death: a deadly pallor, a deathly pallor. But today only deathly is normally used in this sense. What resembles or suggets death is deathly: a deathly stillness, a deathly odor, a deathly complexion.

Deadly, meaning "death-dealing," refers to what is capable of causing death: a deadly weapon, a deadly disease, a deadly poison. It also means "relentless," as in "a deadly competitor" or "a deadly enemy."

As adverbs, *deadly* and *deathly* both connote "extreme." Their idiomatic uses are somewhat different—*deadly*, "to an extreme"—deadly serious, deadly earnest—and *deathly*, "very or extremely"—deathly sick, deathly afraid.

PRACTICALLY PERFECT

Practicable implies feasibility. A plan that is practicable is capable of being efficiently accomplished, capable of being put into practice: "The lunar project proved practicable." Something *practical* is efficient, when governed by actual, ordinary conditions. It is not theoretical or idealistic but useful or adaptable to use: "A practical approach always beats a theoretical one." *Practical* can apply either to persons—a practical man—or to things—a practical suggestion. But *practicable* refers only to things that can be put to use, never to people.

The negative of *practicable* is *impracticable;* of *practical,* either *unpractical* or *impractical,* with the latter preferred.

FLAGRANTE DELICTO

Flagrant and *blatant* are terms describing words or deeds that spurn social standards. They both suggest offensive conspicuousness.

Flagrant, meaning "openly scandalous, notorious, heinous," connotes wrong or evil. A flagrant action is conspicuous because it openly and willfully disregards societal standards of conduct: a flagrant miscarriage of justice, a flagrant breach of legal ethics.

Blatant means "offensively noisy": a blatant appeal to prejudice, blatant demands from the minority. Blatant people are loud, blustery, obtrusive. A related meaning of *blatant* is "brazenly obvious," such as a Nixon Lie. This second kind of antisocial behavior is just as offensive as the first, and more devastating.

EXPLETIVES ARE NOT FOR PRINT

Expletives are either sudden oaths or words, usually vulgar, or phrases used to fill out a sentence or a line, *there is/are* and *it is.* These latter words, although called "anticipatory subjects," serve no grammatical function; the real subject follows the verb, as in "It is a *matter* of money" and in "There are always other *witnesses* available."

Ordinarily a singular noun follows *there is*—"There is one book for each person"—and a plural follows *there are*—"There are three lawyers waiting." When multiple nouns follow the expletive, however, a problem in selecting the number of the verb may arise. In "There are two resource material books, a manual, and a textbook on the shelf," the plural *there are* naturally precedes the adjoining plural element. With a reversal in the sequence, placing "two resource material books" last, there is a choice—whether to say "There are a textbook, a manual, and two resource material books on the shelf" or "There is a textbook. . . ." The latter, with its singular verb, is probably more common, the number of the verb being influenced by the proximity of a singular element.

Expletive deleted: Expletives of all kinds are best omitted except when needed to structure a sentence. Beginning a statement with an expletive places a weak construction in an important position. At the least, these expletives should be silently watched, the way the other kind should be silently spoken.

SYMPATHY BUT NO TEA

It is a mistake to consider *sympathy* and *empathy* synonymous. Each word enjoys its own distinct meaning.

Sympathy has as a basic meaning "the act of entering into or sharing the feelings of another." This meaning is the commonly used sense when one expresses sorrow for another's affliction or misfortune: "My sympathy is with Mr. Fiske in this moment of bereavement." Companion words are *commiseration,* which is often a spontaneous and vocal expression, and *condolence,* usually a formal expression of sympathy.

Primarily *empathy* is "the capacity for participating in or a vicarious experiencing of another's feelings, volitions, or ideas." A simpler statement might be that *empathy* is "an emotional and intellectual understanding of and identification with another person": "Since Falk, as salutatorian, had forgotten half his speech, he *had empathy for* (or *empathized with*) the bumbling valedictorian."

THAT'S THE WAY

The conjunction *that* is customarily used in formal writing: "Counsel said *that* he would like to continue." In less formal writing, *that,* because it starches the clause that follows, is preferably omitted. Without it, sentence rhythm improves: "Counsel said he would like to continue." And since *that* is not grammatically required—it is merely stylistic—the writer's ear is the sole judge.

In two situations, however, the use of *that* is strongly recommended. First, when time is indicated following a verb, as in "The Chief Justice declared on May 30 the court's caseload exceeded all records." A *that* after *declared* would make clear that May 30 was not the date of the Chief Justice's statement but the date on which the caseload exceeded all records.

Second, if a sentence contains two clauses, the second being introduced by *and that* or *but that,* an initial *that* should be used for the sake of parallelism. "The court crier announced a change in courtrooms is necessary and that the new room number will be posted soon" should be restated, "The court crier announced *that* a change in courtrooms . . . *and that* the new room number. . . ."

INTERROGATORY

How can one be sure not to misuse *likewise?*

Use *likewise* not as a conjunction, but only as an adverb—modifying verbs, adjectives, and other adverbs. For example, in "His clear thinking, likewise his fine court demeanor, impressed everyone," *likewise* is miscast. It is being unacceptably substituted for *and. Likewise* is properly used in "I apologized; now you do likewise."

281

COMPRENEZ-VOUS?

Apprehend and *comprehend* are related in that both apply to a thought process. They differ, however, in that they are sequential—apprehension precedes comprehension.

To apprehend means "to come to know," "to lay hold of with the understanding" (its meaning "to place under arrest" is not being considered here). *To comprehend* is to understand a thing fully. A person who apprehends grasps the meaning of something; a person who comprehends knows that thing completely: "Sutton apprehends the meaning of what the expert says, but he cannot comprehend his detailed mathematical formulas." To apprehend is to bite into something; to comprehend, to digest it.

THREE CONS SERVING TIME

The adverbs *consistently* and *constantly* both suggest an ongoing situation. *Consistently* means "in a manner that is not contradictory." What is done consistently is done without change, without wavering: "The student consistently made excellent grades in his law courses." *Constantly* means "regularly," "persistently," "unceasingly." What occurs constantly occurs steadily: "McFarley complained that his desk was constantly piled high with miscellaneous papers." "His speech was constantly being interrupted by hecklers."

If the regularity of an action is interrupted at short intervals, by a ringing telephone, for example, a more appropriate word would be *continually*.

TO PUT IT RIGHT

There is a fine distinction between the verbs *to put* and *to place*. In fact, if the setting to rest is done sensitively, that should be a reminder of the distinction.

To place connotes carefulness and exactness; what is placed is done so with forethought. "The artist placed his picture on the easel"; "He placed a ring on his fiancée's finger"; "The crown was placed on the sovereign's head."

To put means "to bring to position in any way." It suggests an unconscious placement, a movement that may be automatic. A person puts his hands in his pockets, puts food in his mouth, puts the cat outside at night. There is less deliberateness to *putting* than there is to *placing*.

Idiom permits either *in* or *into* with *put:* "Dr. Hattler put the letter *in* (or *into*) a drawer," but "He placed the forceps *in* (not *into*) the patient's mouth."

ENTAILS END IT

Involve and *entail* bear some similarities in meaning, but differ in application.

Involve means "to enfold or envelop," as in "Undoubtedly Thomas has become involved in that scheme." It suggests circumstances that are entangling, possibly with attendant embarrassment.

Too frequently, however, *involve* is imprecisely substituted for such verbs as *cause, result in, mean, use,* or *imply.* In "The study involved a complete change in the schedule," *involved* could properly be replaced by *caused.* Other examples of misuse, with suggested corrections, are "The problem is closely *involved with* (should be *related to*) the kind of direction received" and "This treatment must *involve* (should be *contain* or *include*) convincing analysis to be taken seriously."

Entail implies involvement by necessity or consequence. It differs in one important sense from *involve* in that it suggests the imposition of a burden, as in "Completing this project on time will entail missing many nights with the family."

A distant cousin is the verb *implicate,* which means "to entwine or entangle." A person said to be implicated in a crime is considered guilty, at least to some extent. But a person who is *involved* in a crime, although certainly connected with it, may have become enmeshed involuntarily, an innocent victim.

A *wagging tail:* In a legal sense, *entail* means "to limit the succession of inherited property to the issue or to a particular class, instead of descending to all the heirs."

AN UNMARKED QUESTION

When does an interrogative sentence need no question mark? In such instances as the following: When a question (1) expects no reply—"May we all have the pleasure of seeing you and your family soon"; (2) makes a command—"Will you please leave now"; or (3) makes a request—"Would the Institute please send a copy of its catalog to our Florida office at the address listed below."

INTERROGATORY

Is it true that the spelling *councillor* is preferred to *councilor?*

Yes, but not by everyone. *Councillor* is a British spelling. In the United States, too, the weight is in favor of the double *l,* although *counselor,* an adviser, is spelled with one *l.*

VALUE IS NOT ALL MONETARY

Valuable implies either intrinsic or monetary worth, or usefulness: a valuable painting, a valuable property, a valuable service. *Valued* means "esteemed," something or someone held in high regard: a valued author, a valued edition, a valued membership. *Valued* has the further meaning of *appraised:* "The gems were valued at $50,000." And that which is priceless, of inestimable worth, is *invaluable:* invaluable benefits.

Of much value: The Restatement of the Law is both a valuable and a highly valued publication. A valued friend, however, is not "valuable," no matter how highly esteemed.

YOU MAY IF YOU CAN

Properly used, *can* means "to be able to or capable of"; *may* indicates permission. Neither in conversation nor in writing should those words be interchanged. Accepted usage is exemplified in these sentences: "Counsel may (has permission to) approach the bar, if he can" (is able to). Colloquially, it would be "Counsel can approach. . . ." *May*, in a simple sentence, has the further sense of possibility, a sense shared equally with its past tense *might:* "Counsel *may* (or *might*) decide to take a different tack." *May* is used with the present, present perfect, and future tenses, and *might* with the past and past perfect tenses. For example, "I tell you (have told you, shall tell you) the facts that you *may* analyze the matter." "I told you (had told you) the facts that you *might* analyze the matter." *Might* is also used in the main clause of a conditional sentence, even though the condition is only implied: "The President might run for reelection" (if he is so minded). "If the library acquires no more books, it might have to close" (the closing is conditioned on the failure to acquire more books).

Might expresses a supposition when used in the subjunctive: "The company has been acting as if it might merge." "The president spoke as though he might vote to sell."

Mighty good: When possibility is being considered, either *may* or *might* is acceptable, but *might* suggests a greater likelihood. To say that something *may* occur implies less assurance of its happening than if *might* were used.

DYING CAN BE TRYING

It may sound morbid, but reports of death rest easier if couched in grammatical terms.

When the meaning is "to cease living," *die* takes *of*. One dies of a disease, not from a disease: "The Colonel died *of* (not *from*) yellow fever." On the other hand, although a person can die from wounds, he cannot die from thirst. He dies of thirst. He may die *from* lack of care, or *from* fatigue, however, and his secrets may die *with* him. No rules—it's just a matter of idiom.

To *drown* is to die. A person does not die from drowning; he simply drowns. If lucky, he may have narrowly escaped death *by* drowning; if unlucky, he drowned, not "was drowned."

La Morte: A deadline today is not intended to kill anyone. But the word originally referred to a line drawn around a military prison beyond which a prisoner could not venture under penalty of being shot.

SHED SOME LIGHT

Possibly the confusion between *opaque* and *translucent* is attributable to publishers, who use these words in a similar vein. Publishers measure the ability of light to penetrate paper in terms of opacity and translucence. Sheets that are not translucent are opaque—impervious to light. An 89 to 92 per cent opacity is acceptable because type on the opposite side of a sheet is then not visible. But almost all paper stock is translucent, that is, according to definition, "permits the transmission of light, but so diffusely as not to permit perception of images."

Translucent and *transparent* are not synonyms; something transparent allows light to pass through, and images on the other side are visible. In fact, *transparent*, in an abstract sense, denotes "frank or open"; so much "light" penetrates that all is clear. When describing people, *opaque* suggests "obtuseness or stupidity." Nothing penetrates.

WHICH IS THIS?

The use of *this* and *which* to refer to a general or comprehensive idea expressed in a preceding phrase or clause is justified only when the reference is clear. Doubtful sentences should be recast.

Consider these ambiguous examples: "Horrocks realized that the witness was perjuring himself, but the other lawyers were unaware of *this.*" Does *this* refer to the witness's perjury or to the other lawyers' ignorance of Horrock's knowledge? In "The freshman spent his evenings in improving his accommodations, *which* the other students resented," was the resentment aimed at the freshman's improved accommodations or the time he spent in that pursuit?

Sometimes a noun that summarizes the previous idea will clarify the reference: "this fact," "this matter," "this mistake," "this assumption," "this" whatever. But sentences with a vague *which* are difficult to reform; the *which*'s are better omitted and the sentences recast. In "Roger Bernsee has only one case, which saddens him," the question is whether Bernsee is sad because he has only one case or whether the one case itself saddens him. If he is depressed because his files consist of only one matter, a direct statement without the *which* would be clearer: "Having only one case saddens Bernsee" or "Bernsee is saddened because he has only one case."

Sentences that begin with *this* or *that*, referring to an entire statement in a preceding sentence, require even more caution. But here again a supplementary noun indicating what idea was referred to would be helpful. Instead of "This no longer interests Mr. Prager," the thought might be amplified with "*this matter, those facts, that proposal,* or *these suppositions* no longer interest Mr. Prager."

Is the expression *a lapse of time* ever correct?

The objection is not that it is incorrect, but that it is wordy— *of time* is unnecessary in some contexts because one definition of *lapse* is "an interval of time": "The lapse between the filing of suit and its listing could not be explained." It is correct to say, however, *a lapse of two hours,* since here an exact amount of time is being mentioned.

TOO LITTLE SATISFACTION

A person can be both unsatisfied and dissatisfied at the same time. And that's a double unhappiness: "Murray was dissatisfied with the bill because the meal had left him unsatisfied."

A *dissatisfied* person is one who is displeased, offended, upset. He is discontent because something desired was not provided: "Pina was dissatisfied with his schedule." "Many people are dissatisfied with the programs to control inflation."

An *unsatisfied* person is discontent because his expectations—things he considers requisite—have not been met: "No matter how much he learned, his thirst for knowledge was unsatisfied." "Colado's excuse for being late left his supervisor unsatisfied."

LOOSE USAGE LACKS MEANING

The meanings of *claim, allege, assert,* and *maintain* are not bothersome; their loose usage is. These words should not be interchanged just for the sake of variety.

Claim, if used in the sense of to say or declare, raises a doubt about the strength or truth of the assertion. Statements such as the following may be viewed skeptically: "He claimed he had spent the money." "Ralston claimed he knew the Ambassador personally." Properly used, *claim* implies the right or title to a thing claimed, a demanding of one's due: "Foerster claimed he had a right to a refund."

Allege refers to a statement or assertion without adequate proof: "The district attorney alleged that the rape had been committed by Jason Cheever." *Assert* means "to declare in a positive fashion, that is, with assurance": "The defendant stoutly asserted his innocence." *Maintain* is to declare as true or being capable of proof: "The Senator *maintained* (not *claimed*) that the bill was beneficial."

Affirmed: Synonyms for *assert* are *declare, profess, affirm, aver,* and *warrant.*

BOOKS ARE UNAUTHORED

The word *author* should not be used as a transitive verb: "He authored the book we're discussing." Also incorrect is the feminine form "authoress."

An author is the "source of some form of intellectual work"—the author of the theory of gravity, the author of a beautiful mural. In literary usage, an author is a person who writes a book, an article, a play, and so forth. Although he composed the manuscript, it is incorrect to say he *authored* it. Careful writers avoid *author* as a verb, despite such a listing in some dictionaries. A properly worded statement requires expending a few more words: "He is the author of the book we're discussing." If the conciseness of a verb is needed, suitable replacements for "authored," in different fields of creativity, are *wrote, composed, originated, created, invented,* or *produced.*

If the author is a woman, she is nevertheless the author and should be so called, not *authoress.* The noun *author* may refer to either sex.

More neuters: A poet is one who writes poetry—male or female. The term *poetess* is archaic, as is *aviatrix, proprietress,* and all other words that needlessly distinguish the sexes.

VIE, VIDA, VITA

If it is agreed that simple words are preferred to the abstruse, then *viable,* derived from the French *vie,* "life," should be used sparingly. *Viable* means "capable of living" or "physically fit to live," but it is seldom used correctly. Rather, through extension, it is commonly used to mean "workable or practicable": "This system is more viable than Ulrich's." A proper use is in this sentence: "The viability of the program (its ability to survive under present conditions) is causing great concern."

NOLO CONTENDERE

Contend is a general term meaning "to maintain or assert by argument or to strive in opposition or rivalry." Because it is governed by so many idioms, *contend* is a difficult word to contend with. When it means "to maintain by assertions or arguments," *contend* takes *that* or *for:* "The plaintiff contended that the defendant was legally responsible." "Counsel contended for acquittal." When *to strive* is meant, usually *with,* but sometimes *on,* is required: "The lawyer had to contend with hostile witnesses." "The parties were contending on nearly equal terms." And then there is contend *against:* "Our fearless hero contended against all the obstacles he met."

No contest: Since *to contend* implies disagreement, it is inappropriately used as a synonym of *to say.* Aptness and variety can be gained by using *assert, declare, state, maintain,* or *aver.*

LITERARY SURGEONS USE MANY ERASURES

The striking of matter from written material can be described by several words, each with distinct connotations. *Erase,* the most common term, means "to remove something so that it no longer exists." Derived from the Latin *eradere*, "to scrape," *erase* suggests a scraping or rubbing out. In common usage, misspellings are erased, leaving a blank space in which to write the correct version. Memory, too, can be erased: "The years have erased from his memory many details of his youth."

Expunge, literally "to pick out with a sharp instrument," implies a complete erasure, as though a sponge had washed away what had been there. Originally *expunge* indicated setting pricks or dots above or below a word to be removed. Today *expunge* means "entire removal"; for example, "to expunge testimony from the record."

It is incorrect to equate *blot out* with *expunge;* but it may be equated with *obliterate*. *Blot out* and *obliterate* do not mean "to remove" but "to cover up"—with ink, chalk, paint—making the writing undecipherable.

It would be better, then, to expunge, not blot out, evil thoughts. Some "blotters" are ineffective.

INTERROGATORY

Some words of reference sound trite—and heavy. Would you list those that are best avoided?

The words in the following columns may be labeled "legalese" or "commercialese." They are easily replaced by more vigorous and less bookish terms.

aforementioned	said
aforesaid	same
herein	such
hereinafter	to wit
hereinabove	whatsoever
heretofore mentioned	whensoever
provided	wheresoever

HYPHENS END IT ALL

Hyphens indicate the separation of a word that is divided at the end of a line. Words are divided according to dictionary syllabication and other rules; these "other rules" are so numerous that the United States Government Printing Office has issued a 128-page supplement to its *Style Manual* devoted to the rules and suggested divisions of more than 12,500 words. The following editorial guidelines limit the indiscriminate use of dictionary syllabication.

1. Do not divide a single vowel from the remainder of the word:

   > eco nomic, not e conomic
   > above, not a bove
   > obese, not o bese

2. Do not divide a one- or two-letter syllable:

   > posi tively, not positive ly
   > homey, not home y
   > copy, not cop y

3. Do not divide monosyllables:

   > breadth, height, length

   or a word of only four letters:

   > also, into, over, only

4. Do not divide so that a single-vowel syllable within a word is carried over unless it precedes a final syllable of two letters:

   > readi ly, not read ily
   > rem edy, not reme dy, but
   > holi day, not hol iday
   > monu men tal, not mon umental

5. Do not divide the last syllable *able, ible,* or *uble:*

   > advis able, not advisa ble

293

revers ible, not reversi ble
vol uble, not volu ble

6. Divide compound words into their separate elements:
   any body, not anybo dy
   every one, not ever yone
   over taken, not overtak en

   This rule also applies to hyphenated compounds:
   self-interest, not self-int erest
   quasi-contract, not quasi-con tract

7. Do not divide syllables with a silent vowel:
   marched, tossed, faced

   but *-ing* endings may be separated:
   debat ing, climb ing, meet ing

   However, if the root ends in a silent vowel, the ending
   consonant sound is added to the *ing:*
   chuck ling, han dling, muf fling

For unusual end-of-line divisions, consult a dictionary
or style manual.

**Does a singular subject always take a singular verb? Does
a plural subject always take a plural verb?**

Ordinarily, yes. But these rules are not followed in every
construction. One exception is that even when a simple subject is singular, if the complete subject—which may include
a modifying *of* phrase—strongly conveys the idea of individuals, a plural verb is preferred. Examples are "An *average*
of five manuscripts *are* submitted each month (the emphasis
here is on individual items—the number five), versus "An
average of five manuscripts a month *is* not uncommon" (the
stress is on *average*). Sentences like these are subject to
interpretation.

ALMOST IS NOT GOOD ENOUGH

"The copy *almost* missed the publication deadline every day" means it never quite did. "The copy missed the publication deadline *almost* every day" means it did quite often. These examples point up the need for carefully placing the adverb *almost*. Unless positioned so that it modifies the intended word, misunderstanding may result.

Almost finished: Almost in the sense of "very nearly," rather than *most*, should be used in sentences like "*Almost* (not *Most*) anyone may attend the meeting." *Almost* takes no hyphen: "an almost perfect record," not "an almost-perfect record." Other adverbs needing careful placement are *also, at least, even, hardly, just, merely, not, only*, and *scarcely*.

IDIOMATIC IDIOMS

Idiomatic phrases lose their effect, if not their entire meaning, if they do not follow established constructions. Take the sometimes-heard expression *in light of*. Properly stated, it should be *in the light of*: "In the light of his explanation, we concur with his view." The idiom meaning "about or concerning" is *with respect to*: "A decision must be made with respect to payments." This idiom, however, as well as *in respect to* and *in respect of*, is wordy and therefore only mildly supported.

Both *in regard to* and *with regard to* are properly phrased—but not *in* or *with regards to*. The key word is *regard*. And *regarding* makes a concise variant. *On the contrary* introduces a new point of view—"On the contrary, we disagree with that principle"—whereas *to the contrary* acts as a modifier—"Whatever he asserts to the contrary, we disagree." The idiom that means "with the purpose of" is either *with the view of* (not *with the view to*) or *with a view to* (not *with a view of*). To keep the views straight, the *the* and *of* and the *a* and *to* should go together. Either *in the circumstances* or *under the circumstances* is acceptable.

REDUCE AND MINIMIZE

Minimize means "to reduce to the smallest possible amount, degree, size, or extent." It does not mean "to belittle, underrate, or diminish," although in popular usage it is frequently equated with those words. Ordinarily *minimize* is used for qualities or abstractions: "My efforts to minimize the danger were not appreciated." "The new system has helped minimize delays."

An absolute term, *minimize* comes from the Latin *minimus* and means "least." Since the word cannot properly be qualified, it may not be accompanied by *greatly, somewhat, considerably,* or other such adverbs. If a qualifier is wanted, sister words make good choices: further reduced, sharply diminished, but not *greatly minimized*.

To diminish is "to make smaller, less, or less important," which is not quite so reduced as *minimize* implies. The sense of *diminish* is subtraction and resultant loss, but not necessarily to the lowest point: "The funds were diminished by extravagant expenditures."

More to come: Minimize and *maximize* were coined by Jeremy Bentham, a theoretical jurist, in 1802. Although *minimize* has been widely accepted, the same cannot be said for *maximize*. This latter term is avoided by many writers, perhaps because of its harsh sound.

QUITE THE THING

The colloquial use of *quite* is quite common, as exemplified in this sentence. *Quite* means "completely, wholly, perfectly, positively," but is more frequently used in its colloquial sense of "considerably, rather, somewhat, and very": "It is quite warm today." "It is quite a long book." "The judge is quite ill."

Quite in some sentences could be construed in two ways. Consider "The present inventory controls are quite unsatisfactory." In its precise sense, *quite unsatisfactory* means "wholly or altogether unsatisfactory," but according to colloquial usage, it could mean either "very unsatisfactory" or "somewhat unsatisfactory."

Quite questionable: Many colloquial expressions are tied in with *quite*—"quite a few" or "quite a number" for *many;* "quite a little" for *more than a little* or *much;* and "quite a bit" for *a considerable amount.* Many of these *quite* expressions have become acceptable idioms. Quite so, my dear Holmes.

INTERROGATORY

"Nothing could be *farther* from the truth." Or is it *further?*

This question is particularly helpful because those words are often interchanged, a trend encouraged by some usage authorities. Nevertheless, even in general English, and certainly in formal writing, their distinctions should be maintained.

Farther refers to geographic distance; *further,* to degree of accomplishment: "Until the road is extended, we can proceed no farther." "Until the manuscript is completed, we can proceed no further." The *far* in *farther* gives a clue that distance is meant.

297

EXCUSEZ-MOI

When a person says "Excuse me" or "Pardon me," frequently both the intent and the occasion differ. *Excuse me* is a mild term used for small slips or requests, such as being allowed to pass in front of another person. *Pardon me* implies guilt, an awareness of transgressing a propriety. It also requests forgiveness. *Excuse me* expresses a mere hope that one is not annoyed. *Pardon me* looks for a favorable, understanding response.

In yesteryear, *pardon me* was the recommended form of apology for even a slight breach of etiquette. That is no longer the vogue. *Pardon me* sounds affected and is therefore too formal for today's more casual living. Except for serious trespasses—walking into the wrong bedroom, for example—*pardon me* is best replaced by *excuse me.*

A PROPOSAL YOU CAN'T REFUSE

A *proposal* is a plan, scheme, or offer. It presents something to be accepted or rejected somewhat quickly. Proposals ordinarily do not need prolonged deliberation: a proposal of marriage, a proposal to arbitrate, a proposal of settlement. A *proposition,* however, which also calls for consideration and determination, requires more study and evaluation than does a proposal and hence no reply is expected immediately. Propositions are usually written and detailed, with their terms described and their advantages emphasized.

The term *proposition* is often misused for *proposal, job, project, business undertaking, enterprise*—"It was not a paying proposition" (business undertaking). "That proposition (job) was too tough for him."

DO NOT UNDUE WHAT IS DUE

Undue means "unnecessary or unwarranted"—undue haste—or "not proper or fitting"—undue influence. The problem with *undue* is that it is often used redundantly. Take as an example "There was no need for undue fear." Since *no need* and *undue* say the same thing, the result is a double negative.

Probably, the addition of *undue* is simply an effort to emphasize a point; unfortunately, it deemphasizes. Consider these further examples: "The matter does not warrant undue concern" (which means that the matter does not warrant unwarranted concern) or "There is no reason for undue alarm" (which means that there is no reason for alarm for which there is no reason).

Still due: The adverb *unduly,* meaning "excessively," has its own problems. It is properly used in sentences with a standard of comparison, mentioned or implied. Otherwise, the word is meaningless. An example of correct use is "The book is unduly long considering its treatment of the subject."

ADMIT ONE ONLY

Although *admittance* and *admission* are interchangeable to some degree, each has acquired restricted areas of meaning. *Admittance* is limited to physical entry to a particular place or locality; it means "permitted entrance": *admittance* by invitation only; *no admittance* to the courtroom.

Admission, in contrast to *admittance,* refers to entrance for a particular purpose or the privilege, by virtue of qualification, to enter—*admission* to a society—and to figurative entry—*admission* of business records, *admission* of guilt.

IN-UN-DATED BY PREFIXES

The negative prefixes *in-* and *un-* are identical in meaning but not interchangeable in application, for convention has set their usage. Words prefixed by *in-* and *un-* have developed in no logical pattern; hence today only a dictionary can direct a person to the right prefix for a particular word. For instance, it is *inaudible* not *unaudible*, but *unacceptable* not *inacceptable; inexcusable* not *unexcusable*, but *undiscriminating* not *indiscriminating; insurmountable* not *unsurmountable*, but *unalterable* not *inalterable*. *Incapable* is now accepted, though years ago *uncapable* was in vogue.

To add further to the confusion, some words can begin with either *in-* or *un-: indecipherable, undecipherable; insubstantial, unsubstantial; incomprehensible, uncomprehensible*. The last word puts the finger on the whole mess.

PREDOMINANCE IS TOPS

The verb *predominate*, meaning "to have the chief power" or "to be most important or outstanding," is well established and problem-free. The adjective *predominant*, meaning "that which is of the greatest importance or most conspicuous," also arouses no concerns. What poses a question is the use of *predominate*, the verb form, as an interchangeable adjective with *predominant*—predominate or predominant characteristics.

Some dictionaries consider both these forms equally acceptable. Nonetheless, the adjective *predominant* should be preferred to *predominate*, as should the companion adverb *predominantly* to *predominately*. *Predominate* is best restricted to its verbal function.

Underside: Predominant implies the superlative degree and should therefore not be preceded by *more* or *most:* "The predominant (not the *more* or *most predominant*) objective was to fund the institution adequately."

WHAT'S YOUR CAPACITY?

There is no practical difference between "He has the ability to work hard" and "He has the capacity for hard work." Only the wording is different—*ability to* versus *capacity for.* When referring to intellectual power, however, the words are not synonymous.

Ability is defined as the power to do something physical, mental, financial, political, or legal: ability to dance, ability to study, ability to meet expenses, ability to assess property. A person with ability has acquired a level of attainment.

Capacity is the ability to hold or receive something. This power may be either intellectual or physical—the intellectual capacity of a scholar, the book capacity of a shelf, the lifting capacity of a crane. With reference to intellectual power, *ability* suggests the presence of a developed power; *capacity,* a power that is potential. A person with ability has the power to accomplish; a person with capacity has not necessarily arrived at that stage. Although ability can be improved through practice and experience, capacity cannot.

Capability: Ability takes an infinitive, not a gerund: "He has the ability to argue effectively," not "He has the ability of arguing effectively." But phrases with *ability* may be wordy. "He has the ability to negotiate well," for example, may be shortened to "He negotiates well."

SUBJECTS CAN COMPOUND PROBLEMS

An elementary rule of grammar is that a verb must agree with its subject in number. This means that a compound subject, one with two parts connected by *and*, requires a plural verb: "Tilton *and* Summerfield *are* serving as trustees."

This rule, however, has three exceptions. (1) A singular verb is permissible with certain compound subjects regarded as a unit: "Ham *and* eggs *is* first on the menu." "The sum *and* substance of his remarks *was* ignored." And Kipling's "The tumult *and* the shouting *dies*." (2) When two nouns refer to the same person, a singular verb is called for: "The secretary *and* treasurer *is* in his office." If two persons are meant, the sentence needs a plural verb and the article *the*: "The secretary *and the* treasurer *are* in their offices." (3) Multiple subjects modified by *each*, *every*, and *many a* take a singular verb: "Every lawyer *and* every judge *has* been notified." "Each document *and* each exhibit *is* to be handled with care." "Many a plaintiff *and* many a defendant *finds* himself paying more for a case than it's worth."

Are *fluctuate* and *vacillate* interchangeable?

In many instances. They both mean "to vary" cr "to move back and forth." A difference, however, is that *fluctuate* can apply to both persons and actions—"The defendant fluctuated between docility and defiance"; "The stock market fluctuates daily"—but *vacillate*, for the most part, applies to persons only—"The jurors vacillated between doubting and believing the witness's testimony."

THE CLAUSE THAT REFRESHES

Every sentence must have at least one clause, a group of words containing a subject and predicate, either stated or implied. A simple declarative sentence, for example, is a clause—"Robert checks his citations daily."

The clause forming a declarative sentence is called a principal or independent clause, since it can both stand alone and be separately punctuated. Such clauses are complete unto themselves: "*Secured Transactions* treats Article 9 in depth." Clauses that cannot stand alone are called subordinate or dependent. In the sentence "*Modern Defamation Law*, because it covers the field fully, is well recommended," the words enclosed in commas lean upon the principal clause for support to complete their meaning. They cannot stand by themselves. If those words, the dependent clause, were deleted, an independent clause would emerge: "*Modern Defamation Law* is well recommended."

Independent clauses can be joined by coordinating conjunctions (*and, or, but*, etc.)—"*Secured Transactions* is a fine book, but it is not a primer"—or by conjunctive adverbs (*however, therefore, nevertheless,* etc.)—"*Secured Transactions* is a fine book; however, it is not a primer."

Subordinate clauses are always introduced by subordinate conjunctions (*since, although, if, because, when, whereas*, etc.) or by relative pronouns—(*who, which, that*). These clauses function as single parts of speech—noun, adjective, or adverb. "*That he would recover a verdict* was doubtful" is a noun clause serving as the subject of *was*. Clauses introduced by relative pronouns normally function as adjectives. In "The courtroom *that* we *prefer* faces south," the relative clause modifies *courtroom*, and in "That man *who is wearing the thick glasses* is the district attorney," the subject *man* is described by the clause that follows. Clauses that begin with a subordinating conjunction normally serve adverbially: "The lawyer had just finished his cross-examination *when the defendant fainted.*" "*If he is going*, I will see him there."

RIGHT THIS WAY

One reason why it is easy to be right is that *right* serves as many parts of speech. With *right*, it is difficult to go wrong. For instance, *right* is a noun—"his right to vote"; a verb—"right the overturned chair"; an adjective—"the right door"; and an adverb—"do it right."

In its adverbial sense, there are two forms—*right* and *rightly*. Which one to use is a matter of idiom. *Right* means "straight or directly"—"The bailiff is walking right toward the bench"; *rightly* means "properly"—"The defendant rightly refuses to discuss his case with reporters."

The often-used expression "Write It Right," coined at the turn of the century, is as correct right now as it was then.

INTERROGATORY

What distinction, if any, is there between *the people* and *the public*?

Not much in most cases. The words are interchangeable. In the political sense of an electorate, however, *the people* is the proper choice. The *public* seems like an amorphous mass; some sense of individuals still clings to *people*.

304

ALL COLLECTIVES ARE NOT IN RUSSIA

Some words refer to more than one person or thing—
either, neither, everyone—but are nevertheless treated as
singulars: "Everyone *is* here." "Either *is* acceptable."
Conversely, some expressions, though preceded by a
singular modifier—"*A number of* students *are* arriving
early"—are treated as plurals. Other expressions that
seem plural in form—"Those 50 pounds was all he could
lift"—are singular in construction when the total amount
is being considered rather than individual units. This
last pertains to quantity, measure, and weight.

Nouns known as collective nouns may be either singular
or plural, depending upon whether the group is considered as a whole—in which case singulars are used—
or as individual members—in which case plurals are
used: "The family is the basis for societal life"; "That
family are always quarreling over money." "The faculty
is traveling in England" (the members are traveling in a
group); "The faculty are traveling to many parts of
Europe" (the members are traveling individually). "The
police has accomplished much in combatting juvenile
delinquency"; "The police are not always available when
you want them." "The committee is meeting now"; "The
committee are unable to agree on an agenda." Other
common collectives are *senate, army, group, assembly,
crowd, audience, herd, class, flock, jury, team.*

Once a choice is made on how to treat the collective
noun, the verbs and pronouns must agree: In "The Council *is* expected to send *their* representatives to the general
meeting," *their* should be changed to *its.* But "The
Council *have* selected *their* members to represent them
at the general meeting" says it right.

CAN A DEMOCRACY BE A REPUBLIC?

The United States is a republic. The United States is a democracy. Is it both? Yes, in a broad sense; no, in a narrow one.

The pledge of allegiance to the American flag says: "I pledge allegiance to the flag of the United States of America and to the *republic* for which it stands," thus acknowledging the kind of government that prevails. A *republic* is "a state in which the supreme power rests in the body of citizens entitled to vote and is exercised by representatives chosen directly by them."

A *democracy* is "a state in which the supreme power is vested in the people and exercised directly by them rather than by elected representatives," as in the ancient Greek city-states, called *demos*, or in New England town meetings. The United States is a representative democracy, a term that means a government in which power remains in the people but is exercised by their representatives.

As was aptly stated by James Madison: "In a democracy the people meet and exercise their government in person; in a republic, they assemble and administer it by their representatives and agents."

INTERROGATORY

Please criticize this sentence: "It was no use to talk to him because he was nothing like as smart as his brother."

The phrase *no use* needs the preposition *of* before it, since *use* is a noun, and *nothing like* is colloquial for "not nearly." Rephrased, the sentence should read: "It was *of* no use to talk to him because he was *not nearly so* smart as his brother."

SUCCESS IS HARD TO BEAT

In formal writing, *success* should not be used to mean the person or thing achieving success. Although it is proper to say "The seminar was successful," it is a colloquialism to say "The seminar was *a tremendous success.*" Likewise, "As a lawyer, Fleming is successful," but is not *a great success.*

The verb *to succeed* may replace *successful* in these instances. "As a lawyer, Fleming has succeeded." "Sandy always succeeds in convincing the manager," but not "Sandy is a success at convincing the manager."

No infinitum: An *-ing* form of a verb and not an infinitive should follow *succeed.* "Sutton succeeded in reaching the goals set for him" instead of "Sutton succeeded to reach. . . ."

NO USE COMPLAINING

The expression "I am used to doing it" is common; *used to* means "accustomed to." In this positive sense, no problem attaches. But that is not so when a past negative form of *used to* is called for, because there is no generally accepted negative form. Grammatically correct constructions sound strange—"Halston *used* not to mind checking citations all day" and "Butwick did not *use* to mind either"—but these are the ones nevertheless employed by careful writers.

When *use* appears with a negative in an interrogative sentence, the construction becomes even more contorted. Normally a question is worded, "Didn't Egnal *use* to attend seminars in Madison?" But to be correct in formal writing, the sentence should read *"Used* Egnal not to attend seminars in Madison?" Correct though it is, the sentence is gracelessly put. One solution is to substitute *formerly* or *once* for *used to:* "Didn't Egnal formerly attend seminars in Madison?" or "Didn't Egnal once attend. . .?"

Get used to it: (1) *Used* to, and not *use* to, is ordinarily required, especially in writing. With negative questions that contain the auxiliary *did*, as in the preceding example, *use* and not *used* is the correct form ("did he not use to"). (2) The heading of this article is technically incorrect; it should read, to satisfy purists, *no use in complaining* or *no use to complain* or *what's the use of complaining*. But the prepositions are regularly ignored, so *no use complaining*.

AVOID PRECIPITATE ACTION

The words *precipitate* and *precipitous*, though of common Latin origin, have dissimilar meanings. Not many other sound-alikes are as often confused as they are.

Precipitate means "headlong or rash," as in "Lawson is known for precipitate decisions" or "The termination of the contract was precipitate." The sense of *precipitate* is abrupt, hasty. In "Browning warned that precipitous action should not be taken at this time," *precipitate* should replace *precipitous*.

Precipitous means "steep." It suggests something with a precipice: "The precipitous mountain ledge was too dangerous to reach." The sense of *precipitous* is perpendicular and sheer.

Both words suggest abruptness, but *precipitous* usually applies to physical things. The final *s* in precipitous may be a reminder to equate the word with "steep."

MY COUNTRY 'TIS OF THEE

The article *the* should always precede the words *United States:* "*The* United States has (not *United States* has) more than 200 million inhabitants." Since *United States* has no adjective form, a sentence such as "They welcome cargo from United States ships" should be reworded "from American ships" or "from ships of *the* United States." Because of this lack of an adjective form, citizens of the United States refer to themselves as Americans, an inexactitude, since citizens of abutting countries are just as much Americans. But there is no word *United States-ian* as there is *Mexican* and *Canadian*. Citizens of the United States have no choice.

The name *United States* is a collective noun, representing the Federal Union. It therefore should be followed by a singular verb: "The United States is growing larger daily." Politicians, carried away by patriotic fervor, are not speaking of a national entity when they bellow "these United States." Although unintended, they are referring to individual states banded together. If that phrase were transcribed, it would be wrong to capitalize *united states.*

INTERROGATORY

Must a preposition associated with two or more verbs necessarily be repeated?

Not usually, unless the verbs are separated by a long parenthetical. In "Counsel refused to come or even speak to the defendant," for example, *to* is unnecessary after *come.* If different prepositions are called for, naturally each one is required: "Counsel refused to speak *to* or even look *at* the defendant."

WELL-DESIGNED SENTENCES

Sentences that follow the same word order can become monotonous. Most sentences begin with a subject, continue with a predicate, and end with a complement: "Thomas received the book." "Hansen was given a plaque." Sentence structures that are varied are bound to be less tiresome. The easiest way to avoid such monotony is to vary the length of sentences, interspersing among the long ones an occasional short sentence. Even a fragment.

Inverting sentence order adds emphasis and suspense to writing, but this method should be used sparingly. Contrast the normally ordered statement "The motto 'Be Prepared' is basic to the Boy Scout Code" with its inversion " 'Be Prepared,' the motto of the Boy Scouts, is basic to their Code." Ordinarily balanced sentences, those that employ grammatically equal structures, are most pleasing: "He came, he saw, he conquered"; "of the people, by the people, for the people." A trinity in this kind of structure is particularly attractive.

Beginning sentences with adverbs or adverbial clauses also avoids monotony: "Generally the courts are not open on Saturday." "Although occasionally the courts are open on Saturday, it is an uncommon practice." Sentences that begin with an infinitive, a prepositional or participial phrase, or a gerund afford a change in pattern, too: "To learn is what we want." "At this time we want to learn." "Graduating is our goal."

HOW RUDE CAN YOU BE?

At one time matters not germane to a subject were called *impertinent*. They are still so called, but less frequently. More often, irrelevancies are said to be *not pertinent*.

The generally accepted meaning of *impertinent* today is "inappropriate." *Impertinent* implies an unseemly, unwarranted intrusion into something that does not concern one or a display of rudeness or incivility:: "His bursting into the meeting was impertinent." "Impertinent questioning serves no useful purpose."

Like *impertinent, impudent* suggests rude and defiant boldness. It is defined as "shameless impertinence": an impudent child, an impudent reaction to a friendly gesture.

The highest degree of rudeness is *insolence*. That which is insolent is insulting, overbearing, openly contemptuous in speech or behavior: "His insolence warranted an action for contempt." In contrast to impertinence, which may be accidental, a result of ignorance, insolence is usually a planned, deliberate affront. No one stumbles into insolence.

INTERROGATORY

It was customary, years ago, to say "anyone's else." What rule has developed to change that possessive form?

None that I know. Many years ago, the expression was *anyone else's, anybody else's, everyone else's.* A vogue developed to make the pronoun possessive, changing it to *anyone's else,* and so forth. The vogue has passed, and the form has reverted to the original—*anyone else's.* A companion question concerns *each other's* and *one another's.* Although these expressions normally are followed by plural nouns—"The defendant and the jurors looked into one another's faces"—the possessives should not be plural (not *one anothers'*). And it is best, even in the possessive form, to use *each other's* to refer to two; *one another's* for more than two.

311

ETERNALLY HOPEFUL

The word *hopefully* is commonly used in general English to mean either "I hope"—"Hopefully, my son will pass the bar examination"—or "it is hoped"—"Arbitration is now in progress, hopefully for a substantial award." This usage stems from the lack of an appropriate word to express these simple thoughts.

Certainly in formal writing, *hopefully* should be employed only in accordance with its long-established meaning, "with hope or in a hopeful manner." It is properly used in the following examples: "He spoke hopefully about his prospects." "The lawyer looked hopefully at the judge for assistance."

WHAT A COUPLE! WHAT A PAIR!

A couple of things to bear in mind are that *couple* refers to two of a kind but may be treated as a singular or a plural noun depending on how it is used. When referring to a man and a woman together, *couple*, a collective noun, usually takes a plural verb—"The couple are involved in many social activities"—although this is a matter of choice. Whatever the choice, a following pronoun should be consistent in number: "The couple *are* most enchanting with *their* dance routine" or "*is* most enchanting with *its* dance routine."

When not referring to a man and woman, *couple* is best replaced by *two, a few,* or *several*. But if *couple* is used, and if it precedes a plural noun, *of* should connect them: "Peters spent a couple *of* hours there." "Peters spent a couple hours there" is substandard, even though a sister word, *dozen,* may properly be so used: "Peters bought a dozen (no *of*) gardenias."

A couple of thoughts: Pairs come in two's: a pair of shoes, a pair of earrings. To be useful, these things must be used together. *Couples* come in two's, too: an engaged couple, a couple of chain links. The implication is that these two things are united. When *couple* and a plural noun are divided by *less* or *more*, no *of* should follow *couple*: "A couple *of* pages" becomes "a couple *more* (no *of*) pages." The expression *couple together*, like *cooperate together*, *combine together*, and *attach together*, is redundant. *Together* should be omitted.

A DEFINITE AFFINITY

The sentence "Gerald Dalton has an affinity for baseball but not for studying" uses *affinity* in a typical way that should probably be avoided in formal writing. "Probably" is said because that usage is becoming accepted by some reputable writers.

The word stems from the Latin *affinitas*, "bordering on, related by marriage." It is defined as "a natural liking for, or attraction to, a person or thing." Purists have insisted, however, that the word, in denoting "a natural liking for," refers only to people and not to unfeeling objects or "a propensity for doing or being something." Hence it is improper to equate *affinity* with *aptitude*, *knack*, or *ability*. A person does not have an affinity, but rather a knack or talent for public speaking or sports or dancing. Suitable prepositions to use after *affinity* are *with* and *between*, as they point to a mutual relationship. *For* should not be used: "There is a special affinity between them—their scholarly interests."

Whether or not the strict sense of *affinity* will survive will only be known in time. It seems moribund, however.

COMPARING APPLES WITH ORANGES

Hasty writing may cause sentences like "Malone's stubbornness was as unyielding as a mule." Correctly stated, the example, in which noncomparable things are being compared, should read, "Malone's stubbornness was as unyielding as a *mule's* (stubbornness)" or "as unyielding as *that of* a mule."

Faulty comparisons may not be ambiguous—no one is confused by them—but they are absurd. Consider "Frankel negotiated better than any person in his office." Since Frankel himself is a member of the office staff, he could not negotiate better than *any* member of the staff, for that would include himself. He could, however, negotiate better than *any other* member.

Comparisons should be tested for balance to see whether the grammar tilts the scale.

CONTEMPORARY NEED NOT BE MODERN

What is contemporary is not necessarily occurring in the present; *contemporary* means "existing or occurring at the same time." Jefferson, for example, was a contemporary of Washington, for they belonged to the same period.

Since "contemporary thinking" can refer to the thoughts of any period, it is best to use the word guardedly, clarifying the period involved. Clarity can be achieved easily through such words as *now, then, at that time, in the past,* or *at the same time*. It would be ambiguous, for

314

instance, if a historian, after completing a lecture on the Revolutionary War, remarked, "When we consider contemporary points of view. . . ." An understandable reference is needed to clarify the period—now or then.

Naturally, if no past date has been mentioned and no date is inferable, *contemporary* does mean "now." *Contemporary* is then equated with *modern*, which refers to present or recent time. For example, contemporary architecture, in the absence of a time reference, is modern architecture. The statement "It is a Victorian house with contemporary furniture" is puzzling. Furniture contemporary with Queen Victoria? If Noguchi designed the furniture, the sentence should read, "It is a Victorian house with modern furniture."

Both new and old: Prefacing *contemporary* with the word *more* has always been unacceptable. The phrase *more modern*, however, is in current favor.

INTERROGATORY

Would you distinguish between describing someone as a *personality* and a *personage?*

Personality, in the sense noted, refers to a person of prominence or notoriety. It is a colloquialism for *celebrity* and suggests someone whose antics or public utterances make him newsworthy, a so-called public character. *Personage*, a formal term, denotes an important person, an individual of distinction: "The Prime Minister is a personage to be reckoned with." If a filing clerk is being referred to, *person* is the appropriate word, as it is for most people.

315

TAKE A LETTER, PLEASE

A certain amount of formality is inherent in business letter writing, but it need not be accompanied by brusqueness or dullness. Business letters, carefully planned and edited, act as personal messengers and should be presentable, tactful, and understandable.

More can be said about what not to say in business letters than what to say. First, letters should not begin with old-fashioned phrases—"This will acknowledge receipt of"; "In reply (or Replying) to your letter of"; "As per instructions in your letter of"; "I have before me your letter dated"; "We have your recent letter in which." Get to the point and refer to the date of the letter incidentally: "The book you requested in your letter of April 2 has been sent."

Good letter writers omit "elegant" words, unnecessary foreign phrases, and needless technical expressions. Simplicity is a watchword. Short sentences are always welcome, but too many may become monotonous, even staccatic.

Prefer the direct active voice to the indirect passive—expressions like "It has been decided that" or "Plans have been completed by the Advisory Committee" read better "You will be glad to hear" and "The Advisory Committee has completed plans."

Tact and good policy dictate that letters of rejection or disappointment should first state the reason for the disappointment so as to cushion the impact of the unfavorable news that follows. Letters with warm complimentary closings create more goodwill than those that end with the perfunctory "Very truly yours."

CUT IT OUT

To omit something is to purposely leave it unmentioned. Something omitted will never be seen. Another meaning of *omit*, not being considered here, is "to neglect through oversight."

To delete, from the Latin *delere*, "to wipe out or destroy," is to remove a word or larger part from a manuscript or proof, or simply to exclude it, as in "Censors delete objectionable material." Written words can be deleted or omitted. But a thought being considered for a speech, for example, may be omitted from it, but cannot be deleted unless incorporated into written form.

Printer's cant for *delete* is *dele*. A delete sign (✄) resembles a necktie with the ends flying.

APOSTROPHE—THE INVERTED COMMA

Possession, in the English language, is shown by the genitive case. An apostrophe and *s* is used with singular nouns—Albert's book, his son's watch—or with plural nouns not ending in *s*—men's, children's—and with indefinite pronouns—anyone's chances, everybody's business. An apostrophe alone is added to plural nouns ending in *s*—ladies', professors'.

Ordinarily the genitive case is not used with the names of inanimate objects; an *of* phrase is used instead—the legs of the chair, not the chair's legs. But it is idiomatic with nouns of time—two-week's vacation; of value—four dollars' worth; and of abstraction—for pity's sake.

The apostrophe is used in plurals of letters, words, and figures—two *d*'s, three *which*'s, the *1960*'s. This preferred style, however, is not followed by some respected writers. The omission of letters in contractions is indicated by an apostrophe—*don't, we'll, they're, it's.*

The plural of foreign words is not normally used in the genitive—the work of the alumni, not the alumni's work. The names of organizations and buildings are frequently written without an apostrophe because the plurals are regarded as nouns functioning as adjectives—teachers college—or because of the preference of the organization —Merchants Savings and Loan Company, American Bankers Association. An apostrophe should not be used with the following expressions, which are regularly formed plurals: pros and cons, ins and outs, yeas and nays. It should not be used in the genitive of personal pronouns—his, hers, its, ours, yours, theirs—or with shortened forms—phone, bus, squire, not 'phone, for instance.

An apostrophe and *s* are preferably used to form the plurals of lowercase letters—f.o.b.'s c.o.d.'s—but only an *s* with those that are capitalized—Nos., Drs., Esqs.

INTERROGATORY

When to capitalize directions, such as east or south (East or South?), is sometimes unclear. Can you state a formula or rule?

The names of the points of the compass—north, east, south, west—are lowercased unless they refer to a particular section of the United States. For example, Chicago is west of New York, but it is located in the Midwest. San Francisco is farther west; it is in the deep West. New York, compared with San Francisco, is in the far East—but not the Far East. That would put it in the Orient.

DENOTE IT TO UNDERSTAND IT

A guideline worth following in any writing is to pay attention to both the *denotation* and the *connotation* of words. In brief, a word *denotes* what it means and *connotes* what it suggests. "Meaning" alone does not convey the full message. Words must be understood in particular contexts.

What a word refers to, backtracking for a moment, is known as its referent. Usage over a long period has bestowed on the referent a core of meaning, its denotation. The denotation, the way the word is generally used, is recorded in dictionaries in defining or explanatory terms. For example, *Yorkshire pudding* is defined as a "pudding made of batter (unsweetened), baked under meat, so as to catch the drippings." This definition, of course, is not what *Yorkshire pudding* truly means. It does, however, direct attention to its referent. Hence the words *Yorkshire pudding* conjure up a picture that makes the pudding an understandable object as the reader recollects the word's referent.

To understand further how meanings are not in words themselves, but are acquired by reference, consider the word *plate*. A *plate* may be a shallow dish, a denture, a home base, a photographic sheet, or any thin, flat surface. Consider another—*set*. A *set* may be the way an object is positioned, a place where a film is made, the scenery for a play, a number of tennis games, the act of arranging hair, or any assembled group. When *plate* or *set* is used in a sentence, the reader understands what is meant regardless of the many definitions. The referent enables the reader to envision the "meaning" from the word's context.

319

GLEANINGS

The sentence "On the first go round three jurors voted to acquit, but the other nine voted to convict" should be recast "the nine *others* voted to convict." Saying *the other nine* implies a previous nine.

Preparatory to should be restricted to its meaning "in preparation for"—"He reviewed his notes preparatory to his scheduled address"—and not as a replacement of "before." It is pretentious in "He covered the bird cage preparatory to going to bed."

Reticent means "disinclined to speak, disposed to keep quiet." It therefore should not be used as in this statement: "The newly admitted lawyer was a little reticent to approach the bar." The word wanted is *reluctant*.

DON'T BE AFRAID

To be afraid is to be in a constant or habitual state of fear: "Russell is afraid of the dark." "Many people are afraid of flying." *Frightened* and *scared*, since they imply a sudden or temporary condition of alarm, an unnerving shock, are distinguishable from *afraid:* "The horse was *frightened* (or *scared*) by the screeching of the wheels."

In formal usage, *scared* and *frightened* should not be used intransitively. It is correct to say, "The mask frightens the child" or "The child is frightened by the mask," but it is incorrect to say, "The child frightens easily." A proper recast is "The child is frightened easily."

Using *of* with *frightened* or *scared* is colloquial for *afraid of:* "Butler is *afraid of* (not *scared of* or *frightened of*) snakes." *Frighten* and *scare* take *by:* "She was frightened by the prowler." The verb *frighten* is more dignified than *scared* and is preferred in formal usage.

320

SHIP AHOY!

With few exceptions, large vessels that travel the seas should be referred to as ships and not boats. At one time a boat was described only as a small open vessel moved by oars. Today many boats are motor driven, and some are not very small, for instance, a ferryboat. Ocean-going liners certainly should not be called boats; they are ships.

The seamen's lingo that points to directions aboard a ship is useful to the sea traveler. But since some of those phrases appear in general writing, keeping them straight is useful to the landlubber, too. A common expression is *fore* and *aft*. *Fore* refers to the bow or forward end. It can be remembered by thinking of *before*—what comes before is always ahead. The stern or rear of the ship is *aft*—it is after everything else. The *starboard* is the right side of the ship, looking forward, and the *port*, the left side. The *leeward* is the side farthest from the point from which the wind blows. Its opposite is the *windward* or *weather*.

Bon voyage: All *ship-* compounds are spelled as one word: *shipwreck, shipyard, shipowner*. Most *-boat* and *boat-* compounds are also written as one word: *lifeboat, rowboat, gunboat*—but *pilot boat; boatload, boathouse, boatbuilder*—but *boat train.*

INTERROGATORY

Is the word *nor* properly used in "He has no money nor morals"?

The use of *nor* is proper there because *money* and *morals* are not equivalents. If they were, as in "He has no gold or silver," then only *or* would be correct.

GRAB BAG

Unique means "one of its kind." It is not a synonym of *odd* or *unusual.*

The expression "He can't seem to learn French," is a colloquialism for "He seems unable to learn French."

Preferably, when *underhand* is sneaked in, it should be spelled that way, not *underhanded.*

The correct idiom is *no such,* not *no such a:* "There is no such bill in the hopper," not "no such a bill."

Although the word *process,* with its one *e,* is no spelling problem, *proceed,* with its two *e*'s, can confuse the spelling of its noun *procedure,* which has only one *e.*

FIXING THE PREFIX

Words that begin with the prefix *co-* might be spelled in three ways—cooperate, co-operate, coöperate; coordinate, co-ordinate, coördinate. The hyphened form is no longer in favor; the dieresis, which indicates the beginning of another syllable, occasionally appears in print; the solid word (cooperate, coordinate) is recommended.

Other short prefixes, for example, *de, pre, pro,* and *re,* should also be written solid; *deemphasize,* not *de-emphasize* or *deëmphasize.* Longer prefixes follow the same rule—*postscript, midyear, underflow, extracurricular, multicolor*—except when a vowel would be doubled or a consonant tripled. Then a hyphen is used: *anti-inflation, shell-like, semi-independent.*

A SERIOUS CASE OF MURDER

Matricide is the killing of a mother by a son or daughter; *patricide,* the killing of a father. Those words are derived from the Latin *mater* and *pater,* meaning "mother" and "father," and the Latin element *-cide,* meaning "kill." Other *-cide* words are *genocide,* the planned killing of a race, *homicide,* the killing of a human being, *regicide,* the killing of a king, *fratricide,* the killing of a brother, and *suicide,* the killing of one's self.

A broader term, one that denotes the killing of a mother, father, or other relative, is *parricide.* The word further encompasses the killing of a person whose relationship resembles that of a father, such as a ruler or a pope.

FINICKY CONSTRUCTIONS

No one can satisfactorily explain why it is that the gerund in "The delivery men object *to paying* their proportion of the increase" is sanctioned usage, whereas the infinitive in "The delivery men object *to pay* their proportion of the increase" is not. The development of these preferences by nouns, adjectives, and verbs for an infinitive or for a gerund with a preposition has been entirely arbitrary. And since no governing principles apply, a writer, wishing to be accurate, must rely on memory or a dictionary. In this instance, the example could countenance other verbs that idiomatically take infinitives, such as *refuse:* "The delivery men *refuse* to pay. . . ."

A long list could be compiled of words that take a gerund and words that take an infinitive. Some of the more common are *capable of drawing,* but *able to draw; prohibit from smoking,* but *forbid to smoke; dislike of dancing,* but *reluctance to dance; cannot help doing,* but *compelled to do;* the *habit of giving,* but the *tendency to give.*

But either gerunds or infinitives may be used comfortably with other common words: *the best way of expressing oneself* and *the best way to express oneself.*

CONFUTIOUS SAY

Thinking that the verb *refute* has the same meaning as *deny* is a misconception. And *refute* should not be equated with *contradict* or *dispute* either. To refute is "to destroy by argument."

A statement that is denied, for example, is disavowed, but it is not thus proved false or in error. If the statement is refuted, however, evidence has been advanced to disprove it. In "His immediate decision was to refute the charge," *refute* should be changed to *deny* or *repudiate.*

A stronger, but seldom-used word, is *confute.* It implies the demolishing of an opponent's argument by proving complete falsity in his position. To confute is to refute conclusively.

IS IT ANTI OR PRO-TAGONIST?

There are many words in the English language used to describe a person who opposes another person, like adversary, foe, contender, enemy, or antagonist—or a mere competitor or contestant.

A word loosely used to connote one who is the opposite of an antagonist is *protagonist.* But *protagonist* is not the antonym of *antagonist.* Though commonly employed to mean "proponent, leader, advocate, champion, or partisan," strictly speaking, it is none of these. A *protagonist,* derived from the Greek *protos,* meaning "first," and *agonistes,* "actor," is the leading character in a drama or other literary work and, at least in formal writing, should be used in just this sense.

Since there can be only one main character, expressions such as "chief protagonist" or "principal protagonist" are redundant. Also the plural form *protagonists*, when referring to a single work, is totally incorrect.

The extension of *protagonist* to mean a leading figure of a movement or cause or its spokesman is now so widespread, and has such a strong hold, that many careful writers and some respected dictionaries, too, accept it in that sense.

I SHALL—IF YOU WILL!

In both general conversation and everyday writing, the distinctions once made between *shall* and *will* have all but disappeared. *Will* in declarative sentences is used in all three persons; *shall*, for the most part, is confined to a first-person interrogative: "Shall we begin?"

Some writers, nonetheless, still observe established principles, "rules" that are certainly recommended for formal writing. According to these rules, *shall* when employed in the first person and *will* in the second and third persons express futurity, something that is expected to happen: "I shall be in New York next week." When the order is reversed, *will* in the first person and *shall* in the second and third persons express determination, command, intention, desire, or promise: "I will go next week."

Should and *would* are the past forms of *shall* and *will* and ordinarily follow the rules applicable to them. But *should* and *would* have developed some special meanings, too. *Should* is used in all three persons to express obligation or necessity: "We should leave now if we want to arrive on time." *Would* in all three persons is used to express customary action: "He would jog every day."

The prevailing tendency to disregard the "rules" governing the use of *shall* and *will* has permeated all levels. The following memorable statements by two World War II leaders are good cases in point—no one would want to change them: Winston Churchill's blood-tingling speech at Dunkirk, "We shall fight on the beaches, we shall fight on the landing grounds, . . . we shall never surrender"; and General Douglas MacArthur's vow upon leaving the Philippines, "I shall return." Both men spoke with utmost determination, yet neither used *will*.

May *sincerely* be used by itself as the closing of a letter?

The word *yours* should accompany it—"Sincerely yours" or "Yours sincerely." The closing "Sincerely" is not a reference to the manner of the writing, "in a sincere manner"; it is an adverb meant to modify *yours*, which therefore should be stated. The complimentary closing "Yours sincerely" expresses the intended thought, "I am sincerely yours."

INDEX

(Words and phrases dealt with specifically in the text have been italicized. The "I's" in brackets indicate Interrogatories.)

327

328

336

339

344

345

347